Cognitive Technologies

Editor-in-chief

Daniel Sonntag, DFKI, Saarbrücken, Saarland, Germany

The series Cognitive Technologies encompasses artificial intelligence and its subfields and related areas, such as natural-language processing and technologies, high-level computer vision, cognitive robotics, automated reasoning, multiagent systems, symbolic learning theories and practice, knowledge representation and the semantic web, and intelligent tutoring systems and AI and education. Cognitive science, including human and animal cognition and artificial life, is within the scope of this series, as is the integration of symbolic and subsymbolic computation. The series includes textbooks, monographs, coherent thematic state-of-the-art collections, and multiauthor anthologies.

More information about this series at http://www.springer.com/series/5216

Maria M. Hedblom

Image Schemas and Concept Invention

Cognitive, Logical, and Linguistic Investigations

 Springer

Maria M. Hedblom
Conceptual and Cognitive Modelling Research Group (CORE)
Free University of Bozen-Bolzano
Bolzano, Italy

ISSN 1611-2482   ISSN 2197-6635   (electronic)
Cognitive Technologies
ISBN 978-3-030-47331-0   ISBN 978-3-030-47329-7   (eBook)
https://doi.org/10.1007/978-3-030-47329-7

This Springer imprint is published by the registered company Springer Nature Switzerland AG
The registered company address is: Gewerbestrasse 11, 6330 Cham, Switzerland

To mom and dad.

Acknowledgements

This book is an edited version of my doctoral dissertation and as such it would not have been possible without the help of several influential mentors and contributors. I am grateful to everyone who took part in finalising this volume. Some deserve a special mention for their substantial contributions and assistance.

First, large parts of this volume are based on ideas, assistance and joint efforts from my scientific advisor Oliver Kutz.

Second, the invaluable help of Till Mossakowski is the reason that the development of ISL^{FOL}, the image schema logic, could be completed.

Third, many of the contributions of this volume are the direct result of the guidance of Fabian Neuhaus.

Fourth, the volume's eighth chapter is a co-authored result from the fruitful collaboration together with Dagmar Gromann.

Finally, Ronan Nugent, the editor of this volume, is the reason why the publication was made possible.

Contents

Part IV Image Schema Experiments

List of Figures

List of Tables

Part I
Introduction

Chapter 1
Creating Concepts: Considerations from Psychology and Artificial Intelligence

Abstract The symbol grounding problem is a prototypical problem in cognitive science and concerns how symbols gain their meaning. In this chapter, the symbol grounding problem is discussed in order to address the missing step for how artificial intelligence research can approach conceptual understanding and concept invention. A potential solution to the problem is offered through the theory of embodied cognition. However, Moravec's paradox states that high-level cognition such as calculation and memory require fairly little computer power, whereas low-level cognition in the form of sensorimotor processes require substantially more computer power. This means that any computationally embodied system faces challenges for knowledge representations. Additionally, the chapter introduces the state of the art in relevant research on creativity and concept invention from a cognitive perspective in order to lay the foundation for successive chapters. The chapter includes considerations on and discussion of:

- Artificial life
- Symbol grounding problem
- Embodied cognition
- Knowledge representation
- Creativity and concept invention
- Information transfer
- Conceptual blending

1.1 Setting the Scene

1.1.1 On Creating Artificial Life and Intelligence

It was on a dreary night of November that I beheld the accomplishment of my toils. With an anxiety that almost amounted to agony, I collected the instruments of life around me, that I might infuse a spark of being into the lifeless thing that lay at my feet.
- Mary Shelley, *Frankenstein*

© Springer Nature Switzerland AG 2020
M. M. Hedblom, *Image Schemas and Concept Invention*, Cognitive Technologies,
https://doi.org/10.1007/978-3-030-47329-7_1

The creation of life is a mystery that has kept the human mind busy since the dawn of cognitive thinking. In most religions there exists a creation story in which a divine spirit (or aliens) brings forth life on earth. In parallel, myths and legends speak of humans giving life to golems and homunculi and literature and pop-culture introduce monsters, living dead and robots that may not only take over the world, but become sentient with a will of their own. Perhaps the mystery of life, in particular the desire to create it, lay in the endeavour to build a *Tower of Babel* and to play God, perhaps it is to create a companion or to build a slave, perhaps it is simply to better understand what we are and where we come from. Regardless of reason, what once were the stuff of dreams and science-fiction is now something that modern science slowly is tapping into.

The introduction starts with a quote from Mary Shelley's *Frankenstein, or The Modern Prometheus*, in the scenario in which Dr Frankenstein is about to give life to a lifeless creature. While the likes of Dr Frankenstein might appear comical and ridiculous in a scientific context, biologists can manipulate DNA through CRISPR techniques (Cong et al., 2012), allowing the transfer of genetic properties from one species into another one. Research programs such as these can bypass natural evolution and generate 'new life' through innovative scientific methods. If we accept that biologists are concerned with the physical and biological aspects of generating new life, it can be argued that computer scientists have been responsible for constructing a mind.

In the early days of computer science, one goal was to simulate human cognition by generating artificial intelligence. Storing memory and performing calculations were some of the earliest signs of artificial intelligence to emerge through the computer sciences, and today there exist complex computer systems that successfully perform increasingly advanced tasks like face recognition, predicting outcomes in world politics, winning games of chess and Go, trading on the stock market, and recommender systems that introduce you to your next favourite film. Despite the remarkable progress seen in artificial intelligence research and that of computer systems, not least through the development of cognitive computing, one thing that neither biologists nor researchers of artificial intelligence have managed to simulate is the 'human soul.'

Regardless if you believe in the existence of an actual soul or not, there is one category of cognitive phenomena that still remains an issue for artificial intelligence research to simulate. Some phenomena belonging to this group are emotions, contextual appropriateness, natural language understanding and generation, and creativity, areas undoubtedly connected to personality and the human notion of a soul. Creativity is a particularly difficult field of research as it is an umbrella term for many cognitive processes that are still largely undefined. Naturally, if it is uncertain how human creativity works, it can be argued that the artificial simulation thereof is not any easier. An additional problem is that even the simplest of artificial systems, consisting of only a few lines of code, a few grammatical rules and a database of words, can randomly generate a poem, yet humans are often unwilling to ascribe to this kind of performance any creative ability (Colton and Wiggins, 2012). For creative ability, the presence of something more, something like a 'soul,' appears to be required for a human to acknowledge that a product is the result of a creative or innovative process.

Perhaps biased by his time's culture and religious views, Descartes proclaimed a classic view of the soul and spoke of the *Body-Mind Problem*. Still today this remains an open issue in philosophy and cognitive science as a whole, namely the relationship between the internal mind and the external body. The problem has been approached somewhat differently through the decades and, arguably, it was rephrased by Harnad (1990) into the *Symbol Grounding Problem*. This rephrasing allows the researcher to ignore all the problems that arise when trying to define something as abstract, loaded and elusive as a soul, or even a mind, by refocusing the problem to how symbols in the world (e.g. words, signs, pictures and behaviours) gain their meaning.

In the next section, this problem is introduced properly.

1.1.2 The Symbol Grounding Problem

One of the prototypical problems in cognitive science, linguistics, and artificial intelligence is the symbol grounding problem. Simply put it deals with the question of how symbols acquire meaning. More formally the problem can be summarised as Harnad (1990) describes it:

> How can the semantic interpretation of a formal symbol system be made intrinsic to the system, rather than just parasitic on the meanings in our heads? How can the meanings of the meaningless symbol tokens, manipulated solely on the basis of their (arbitrary) shapes, be grounded in anything but other meaningless symbols?

One of the most famous critiques of the development of (strong)[1] artificial intelligence that brought forth the symbol grounding problem, is the thought experiment *The Chinese Room* introduced by Searle (1980). In his seminal paper, Searle uses an analogy in which a person is isolated in a room in which different symbols enter the room from one direction. The person's purpose is to 'rewrite' these signs following a set of rules before returning them to the outside in another direction. What the person is unaware of is that the symbols actually are Chinese characters constructing meaningful sentences. Thus, by following the instruction rules the person ends up 'communicating' in Chinese. At this revelation, Searle proceeds to ask the reader: "Does the person in the room speak Chinese?" Most of us would probably intuitively take Searle's stance and argue that the person in the room does not speak Chinese because a fundamental part of cognition is missing. One suggestion of what is missing is *intentionality*[2]. In this setting, the Chinese characters lack meaning to

---

[1] Proclaimers of strong AI, or *Artificial General Intelligence* (AGI) as it also is called, defend the proposition that a system is a 'mind of its own' and can be claimed to understand and experience cognitive states. In opposition, weak AI supporters suppose that artificial systems can only 'illuminate' human behaviours.

[2] Intentionality is the power of minds to be about, to represent, or to stand for, things, properties and states of affairs (Jacob, 2014).

the translator. The general consensus to explain this intuition is that symbols do not acquire meaning solely in relation to other symbols.

In linguistics, the symbol grounding problem is often discussed in relation to *The Semiotic Triangle*, or the triangle of reference, see Figure 1.1 (Ogden and Richards, 1989). The semiotic triangle highlights the problem of how the real world *referent* relates to its symbolic *representation* and the mental *concept*. This differs from the symbol grounding problem as it does not abstract away from the mental representation, but include this neuro-cognitive domain as well.

The view of cognition has undergone many paradigm shifts through the years. The classic view *Computationalism* or 'cognition is computing' was introduced alongside the birth of computer science through the ideas of Newell and Simon (Gardner, 1985). While this provided excellent growing grounds for the initiation of artificial intelligence research, it proved to be difficult to explain not only the symbol grounding problem within this framework but also the human mind as a whole. It appears as though the human mind does not act in the logical way imposed by computationalism. One group of theories for cognition that has been growing in influence is that build on the *Embodied Mind Hypothesis* (Shapiro, 2011).

In the next section these two views of cognition with emphasis on the embodied mind hypothesis will be discussed as this provides an interesting stepping stone towards solving parts of the symbol grounding problem that was introduced in this section.

1.1.3 Computationalism vs. Embodied Cognition

In the cognitive sciences, the view of cognition has undergone several paradigm shifts during the last century. Initiating the birth of computer science, the traditional

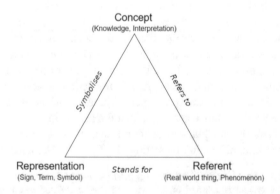

Fig. 1.1: The Semiotic Triangle: illustrating the relationship between the different aspects present in the conceptualisation of concepts.

view of cognition held the notion that 'cognition is computing.' The idea was that the brain worked as a direct storage facility for memories and mental representations and cognition was simply performing computations and calculations on these mental symbols. As computers were invented it was believed that human-level artificial intelligence (AGI or Strong AI) was just around the corner and would be integrated into our societies within a couple of decades (Gardner, 1985).

One of the reasons as to why the development of artificial intelligence has taken longer than initially expected is due to the complexity of building computer processing power that can match a human mind in speed and capacity as initially estimated by von Neumann (1958). However, despite the fact that some modern supercomputers exceed human brain power in many regards, we are still not able to speak of human-level artificial intelligence. For some reason, it appears as though computing power that corresponds to, or approximates, 'brain power' does not result in an artificial agent with the range of flexibility and adaptability that human intelligence display. As Moravec's (1988) paradox states, it has been demonstrated to be fairly straightforward to model high-level computation and reasoning that are difficult for human adults, but to model the low-level sensorimotor skills found in early infancy requires much more computational power. Another reason for this 'delay' is because the premise 'cognition is computing' appears to be if not straight out incorrect at least a grave simplification. The human mind does not seem to function in the binary, logical way that the pure reasoning behind computationalism presupposes.

Throughout the decades that followed Simon and Newell and the introduction of computer science, the view of cognition has gone through many stages; e.g. *Behaviourism*, *Connectionism*, and recently the research field has taken a liking to theories building from the concept of an *Embodied Mind*.

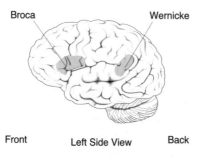

Fig. 1.2: Broca's and Wernicke's Areas

The embodied theories partly come from research findings in neuroscience in the last decades. Through case studies and modern neuroimaging (NI) techniques the roles of different brain regions and structures are slowly being deciphered. For example, the different neural structures found in the *Brodmann Areas* (BA) (Brodmann, 1909), and *Broca's* and *Wernicke's Areas* (roughly corresponding to BA 44-45 in the inferior frontal gyrus and BA 22 in the superior temporal gyrus, see

Figure 1.2.) have been identified to correspond to the cognitive functions behind language processing respectively language production. This means that obtaining information regarding human cognition is possible through more methods than traditional psychology and linguistic research. In particular, the development of NI allowed the emerging field of psycholinguistics to investigate the mental role of symbols' meanings. Research findings started to demonstrate neural activation in the sensorimotor cortex also when the body was at rest and only words were presented. For example, Tettamanti et al. (2005) found that listening to action-related words produces neural activation in the motor cortex. Further, investigations on patients suffering from *Motor Neuron Disease* demonstrate a clear connection to language dysfunction (Bak and Hodges, 2014).

From findings such as these theories of cognition emerged that emphasise sensorimotor processes as the source of cognitive development and concept formation (Lakoff and Johnson, 1999; Shapiro, 2011). The theory of embodied cognition is supported by independent findings from several disciplines including cognitive linguistics, psychology and neuroscience (e.g. Feldman and Narayanan (2004); Gallese and Lakoff (2005); Gibbs (2006); Louwerse and Jeuniaux (2010); Tettamanti et al. (2005); Wilson and Gibbs (2007)). However, despite the research support there are still conflicting views as to the degree to which cognition can be said to be embodied. For instance, Tomasino et al. (2014) found that while the motor cortex is activated upon processing action verbs, the activation could not be found when the same verbs were used in an abstract setting. This by necessity means the existence of a semantic distinction between words used in a concrete or an abstract sentence (see (Aziz-Zadeh and Damasio, 2008) for a more comprehensive overview on *Embodied Semantics*.). Additionally, it has been shown that extreme forms of embodied theories, in which meaning is directly connected to neural activation, are as incomplete as extreme forms of disembodied theories, in which no connection to the nervous system is implied (Meteyarda et al., 2012).

While this is a problem to be solved in the cognitive sciences, for knowledge representation in artificial intelligence this is no breaking point. Instead, the embodied mind hypothesis serves as a potential growing ground in which it may be possible to approach the symbol grounding problem. Arguably, if cognition comes as a direct consequence of the body's interactions with the environment, this means that there is a concrete method to interpret the connection between the real-world *referent*, the symbolic *representation* as well as the mental *concept*. In terms of artificial intelligence, this provides a practical foundation to approach simulations of different cognitive phenomena.

In the next section some elements of knowledge representation will be introduced on which this foundation can be artificially approached.

1.2 Knowledge Representation

1.2.1 Moravec's Paradox and the Persistence of Formal Logic

One of the major problems for artificial intelligence based on a cognitive foundation is how to formally represent cognitive phenomena. Classic artificial intelligence research builds on formal languages such as mathematics and logic. These languages are rigid and inflexible and with the rejection of computationalism as the primary view of cognition, more cognitively inspired computational methods have been developed. Simulating Hebbian learning (named after its discoverer (Hebb, 1949)) under the premise that 'cells that fire together, wire together,' are Neural Networks (NN) and more recently the statistical way the brain appears to function can be found in similar machine learning approaches. For instance, the work by Regier (1996) demonstrates how NNs can be used to model the early stages of human cognition. While it is tempting to exclusively turn to machine learning when formally approaching embodied cognition, it does have certain disadvantages.

In the 1980s Moravec pinpointed one of the biggest paradoxes in the advancement of artificial intelligence (Moravec, 1988). Namely, that for high-level cognition such as memory capacity and accuracy and speed of calculations which are difficult even for human adults, formal systems require fairly little computer power. Simultaneously, for modelling the low-level cognitive phenomena in the sensorimotor system that even infants quickly master, substantial computational efforts are required. In Section 1.4.1, two categories of processes involved in learning concepts will be discussed, distinguishing between perceptual and conceptual processes. Naturally, a neural network would be more suitable to simulate the perceptual, learning processes of concept emergence. However, it is not necessarily the same for the conceptual, more descriptive processes. When the perceptual processes are determined by repeated stimuli into generalisations, the connection between these generalisations to actual concepts might benefit from a more descriptive form of representations. The conceptual processes are built on generalisations from the perceptual processes, that can be approached through, for instance, deep learning methods. However, the semantics found in the conceptual processes would be better approached in a more classic logical fashion. Capturing the meaning of different concepts could be connected to particular sensorimotor patterns, the book's main topic - *image schemas*, and by formally representing them tapping into the connection between the embodied mind and the cognition resulting from it. This is beneficial when dealing with natural language understanding. Additionally, by representing them in accordance with previous research on concept invention they can more easily be integrated into the pre-existing body of work. Naturally, for a computational system to master both sets of processes a combination of classic knowledge representation and cognitive computing would be preferred (Besold et al., 2017)

Following the reasoning found in this chapter, it appears that it is not beneficial to completely reject the notion of symbolic representation in terms of classic logical representations. Embodied cognition, the symbol grounding problem and the semiotic triangle all illustrate that while mental representation may take the form of neural activation it is not unreasonable to describe this activation in a more concrete way than that possible with NN.

In order to deal with formal knowledge structures, one important task is how to build an appropriate *ontology*, a concept that will be introduced in the upcoming section.

1.2.2 Ontology

Originating from philosophy, ontology is the study of the nature of being and the relations between different categories of the world. It deals with concepts, their roles, and relationships that connect the different concepts present (Guarino et al., 2003). In the classic sense ontology concerns the nature and structure of reality. When learning concepts, categories are natural aspects of the nature of to describe and relate concepts. For cognitive phenomena there is no difference, as ontological structure also provides a more reliable description for involved concepts.

In AI ontologies provide a method to structure all the data a system has access to. To structure known objects, or concepts, their attributes and their relationships. The backbone of an ontology is the taxonomy, which deals with precisely this issue.

Ontologies come in different categories, upper-level or foundational ontologies aim to generate a general model for the world in which many scenarios fit. One example is the Descriptive Ontology for Linguistic and Cognitive Engineering (DOLCE) (Borgo and Masolo, 2010) which aims to be cognitively accurate in capturing the underlying categories found in natural language and commonsense.

Generalized Upper Model Knowledge Base (GUM) (Bateman et al., 1995) is another ontology that aims to assist natural language processing systems by accessing the categorical information presented.

1.2.3 The Reusability and Interoperability Problems

While the use of ontologies varies considerably, there are two recurring challenges: *reusability* and *interoperability*.

Reusability is an issue because the development of ontologies is typically done manually by experts and, thus, is an expensive process. Hence, it is desirable to be able to reuse existing ontologies during the development of new ontologies. This presupposes a framework that allows us to build *structured ontologies* by identifying modules and their relationships to each other. For example, it requires the ability to combine two existing ontologies in a way that handles the namespaces of the ontologies in an appropriate way. Further, the reuse of an existing ontology often requires that the ontology is adapted for its new purpose. For example, the adaption may require the extension of the ontology by new axioms, or the extraction of a subset of the ontology, or the change of its semantics from open world to closed world.

The interoperability challenge is closely related to the reusability challenge. Since the development of ontologies is not an exact science and is usually driven by project-specific requirements, two ontologies that have been developed independently will represent the same domain in different and, often, conflicting ways. Thus, in a situation where two independently developed ontologies are supposed to be reused as modules of a larger ontology, the differences between these ontologies will typically prevent them from working together properly. Overcoming this lack of interoperability may require an alignment or even an integration of these ontologies. This typically involves the identification of synonyms, homonyms, and the development of bridge axioms, which connect the two ontologies appropriately.

1.2.4 The Distributed Ontology, Model and Specification Language: DOL

Addressing the two challenges presented above, there is a diversity of notions providing design patterns for and interrelations among ontologies. The *Distributed Ontology, Model and Specification Language* (DOL) aims at providing a unified metalanguage for handling this diversity. In particular, DOL enjoys the following distinctive features:

- structuring constructs for building ontologies from existing ontologies, like imports, union, forgetting, interpolation, filtering, and open-world versus closed-world semantics;
- module extraction;
- mappings between ontologies, like interpretation of theories, conservative extensions etc.;
- alignments, interpretations, and networks of ontologies;
- combination of networks.

DOL is a metalanguage that allows the specification of (1) new ontologies based on existing ontologies, (2) relations between ontologies, and (3) networks of ontologies, including networks that specify blending diagrams[3]. These diagrams encode the relationships between the base ontology and the (two or more) input spaces. The blending diagrams can be executed by the *Heterogeneous Tool Set* (HETS), a proof management system. HETS is integrated into Ontohub[4], an ontology repository which allows users to manage and collaboratively work on ontologies. DOL, HETS, and Ontohub provide a powerful set of tools, which make it easy to specify and computationally execute conceptual blends, as seen for instance in the work

---

[3] Blending diagrams are built from the premise of the theory of Conceptual Blending which is introduced later in this chapter.

[4] http://www.ontohub.org

by Neuhaus et al. (2014). An extensive introduction to the features and the formal semantics of DOL can be found in Mossakowski et al. (2015).

DOL and its structuring language are designed as a multi-logic meta-language, already supporting all of the mainstream ontology languages in use today.

As symbol grounding is approached not only for the sake of concept *representation* but also for concept *generation*, the next section is intended to introduce concept invention in the umbrella setting of *Creativity*.

1.3 Creativity

Simplified, creativity is the cognitive mechanism to generate novel concepts, products and/or ideas. While there are a multitude of theories that aim to address the cognitive process behind creativity, the scientific investigation thereof encounters many problems. For instance, no complete understanding of what creativity is exists, nor an understanding of how it manifests. In fact, as of yet, there is no agreed on definition of creativity. Despite this, plenty of research is being conducted on this elusive topic, both from a cognitive perspective (e.g. Csikszentmihalyi (2014); Runco (2014); Sawyer (2011)) as well as a computational one (e.g. Besold et al. (2015); Boden (1998); Wiggins (2006)).

Creativity is found in many different domains: arts, music, dance, science, everyday problem-solving, etc., and naturally this requires not only different bodily skills but also different cognitive skills. Simultaneously, insight and novel discovery are as important as accessing existing knowledge and memory in the development of new theories and ideas (Jung et al., 2009). There is no question that creativity is a form of higher cognition as creative processes involve a collaboration of several cognitive functions (Runco and Chand, 1995). Also from a neuroscientific direction this is supported where research demonstrates activation of the pre-frontal cortex during creative tasks, an area which is known to orchestrate higher functions (Dietrich, 2004).

The study of creativity was initially pursued in much the same way as the study of intelligence. The desire was to evaluate human creativity by means of a *Creativity Quotient*, similar to the *Intelligence Quotient* (Andreasen, 2006). However, this was early deemed to be more difficult than expected due to the multidimensional character of creative capacity. While there are tests designed to measure creative capacity and thinking (e.g. Torrance et al.'s 2003 test for creative thinking) that, in particular situations, may be used to detect a person's capacity for creative and divergent thinking, the notion of a creativity quotient has been left to the history books. Instead, a large part of creativity research is investigating which cognitive components underlie creativity. Traditionally creativity was considered to be an associative process. Mednick (1962) introduced this under the *Associates Theory* and describes the creative process with the following words [p. 221]:

> ... we may proceed to define creative process as the forming of associative elements into new combinations which either meet specified requirements or are in some way useful.

However, it has been made increasingly clear that the creative process is a combination of divergent and convergent processes as creativity relies on both of these modes of thought (Guilford, 1967).

In *Divergent Thinking*, often referred to as 'associate thought,' associations are allowed to flow freely to find related concepts to the original problem or thought pattern. It is a process in which a problem is solved by defocusing from the actual problem and letting the mind flow and make associations, not rarely through analogies. The derived solution might be one of many possible ones and there is no one right answer. It deals with finding relationships and similarities between concepts and items where previously no connection existed (Gabora, 2010). Concrete examples of divergent thinking processes would be to 'brainstorm' or to draw 'mind maps' in which a person through association explores the conceptual space of a particular topic.

On the opposite side resides *Convergent Thinking*, or 'analytic thought.' It focuses thoughts on what is already known. Thoughts are focused at the problem at hand, for which there is only one correct solution. By analysing the problem through symbol manipulation and using deductive laws of cause and effect, the one correct, or optimal, solution will be arrived at (Gabora, 2010).

These two modes of thinking are thought to work in a recursive process where you zoom in and out from a particular problem or situation.

The classic explanation for the existence of creative thinking is that creativity is a form of problem-solving (Simon, 1988). It is in an encounter with a problem, when the routine behaviour no longer can be applied, that we display creative behaviour (Csikszentmihalyi, 1988; Smith et al., 1995). In artistic domains, this statement might feel misplaced as much of visual and auditory creativity appears to focus more on either spreading a message (or feeling) rather than solving a particular problem. However, for everyday creativity, it is clear that it is in unfamiliar situations that the most creative 'out of the box' solutions are presented.

Analogical thinking is an essential aspect of creativity. The core of analogy is to transfer knowledge to an unknown domain by using already existing knowledge. While this is considered a controlled method, it has been found that novices use far more creative solutions in analogical reasoning than those found by experts (Nagai, 2009). As analogy plays an important role in creative thinking it will be further discussed in later sections.

In the field of artificial intelligence, creativity has been designated to be 'the final frontier' (Colton and Wiggins, 2012). Yet despite the uncertainties found in research on creativity, *Computational Creativity* (CC) has become a research field in its own right. For CC the notion of 'creativity' is typically understood as a cognitive process defined and evaluated based on the *degree of novelty* and *usefulness* of the resulting artefact (Boden, 2009; Runco and Jaeger, 2012). Naturally, also the process by which creativity is expressed is relevant. However, since the cognitive mechanisms behind creativity remain a black box, CC has (out of necessity) primarily focused on the requirements of the product. CC has seen significant progress in the last decades. Using a variety of artificial intelligence techniques there are now a multitude of systems that paint, write poems and solve problems (see (Besold et al., 2015) for an overview). However, as the research field of computational creativity learnt the hard way: humans guard their creativity, both eagerly and jealously (Colton, 2008; Colton and Wiggins, 2012). Hence, much like how human-level artificial intelligence cannot be claimed to have been reached, neither has creative capacity.

Creativity is a large research field with many different topics and sub-disciplines. One of these disciplines is *Concept Invention*. It concerns the research question of how concepts can be learned from the environment and also invented in themselves. The next section is devoted to this research area.

1.4 Concept Invention

Research on concept formation is tightly connected with developmental psychology and cognitive linguistics, but has also seen an increased influence in artificial intelligence research through *Computational Concept Invention*. To understand concept invention, similar theories such as *Conceptual Metaphor Theory* and *Conceptual Blending* will be introduced in how they relate to creativity.

Within the field of creativity, concept invention is one of the most important aspects from a more linguistic point of view. As language skills starts to develop in early infancy children are remarkably creative in their word use and their ability to invent and adapt words to the context. Despite their limited skill set children are able to communicate what they want and what they mean. This captures the complexity of semantics in language referring back to the symbol grounding problem. Even among adults, concept invention is one of the highest forms of not only creative ability but also signs of intelligence. Slang, wordplay and jokes are perfect examples of concept invention and creative word use.

However, before diving into the formal difficulties of concept invention some key features of language development need to be established.

1.4.1 Learning and Inventing Concepts

Learning a language is obviously a process that involves a lot of linguistic input from the environment, in particular the parents. However, there are two major branches to how syntax is thought to be developed.

The first is the empiricist account, namely that listening to language is enough to learn grammar as well as names for objects. The second, introduced by Chomsky (1957), is the nativist view that proclaims an innate, universal grammar. According to Chomsky (2014), there is a particular part of the brain (Language Acquisition Device (LAD)) that is responsible for grammatical development. The idea that human thought has a preset linguistic structure has been debated over the years and with the success found in embodied theories of cognition the question remains: is this structured learned or innate? For the purposes of this volume, the answer to this question is disregarded in favour of looking at the benefits such structures offer to concept invention and language development, in particular in the computational domain.

Even in computational domains it is common to speak of concept formation, or computational concept formation, as a creative ability, but not exclusively so. Concept formation is not solely the ability to generate novel concepts, it also includes a whole range of cognitive abilities that stretches from perceiving the world, abstracting relevant information and through language or other means of expression providing titles and names to perceived concepts and experiences.

Developmental psychologist Mandler (2004) investigates cognitive development and concept formation in the 'sensorimotor period' (as introduced by Piaget (1952)) during early infancy. In the paper series *How to build a baby I, II,* and *III* (Mandler, 1988, 1992, 2005), Mandler studies the interconnected relationship between perception and concept invention. One important point Mandler (2005) makes is that perceptive characteristics such as shapes may be important for categorisation but they do not appear in themselves to be part of concepts and their meaning. For example, a particular shape or a colour might be a typical but not an essential property of an exemplary. For instance, while bananas typically are bent and yellow, there exist plenty of bananas that are both green and straight. It would be strange to argue that bananas such as these are anything but bananas as well. In order to describe this discrepancy between rules for perception and the semantic conceptualisation, Mandler (2009) distinguishes between two categories of cognitive processes that take place during concept formation: perceptual and conceptual processes. These two categories contain vital distinctions and will be further discussed below.

1.4.1.1 The Perceptual Process

The first, the *Perceptual Process*, is seen to be responsible for *object categorisation* based on similarity. Here the shape of objects plays a central role. For example, infants can at an early stage distinguish between animals such as dogs and birds, but it takes much longer before they consistently and correctly categorise and distinguish between animals that exhibit greater similarity such as cats and dogs (Mareschal and Quinn, 2001).

Cognitive science has developed several theories that all aim to explain the perceptual mechanisms behind concept formation. Some share similar characteristics and while it is probable that the human mind works on an intersection of these theories, they are interesting in themselves. Below some of these theories are briefly introduced.

Prototype Theory:

Prototype theory is based on the hypothesis that all object categories are built from prototypes derived from experience (Rosch and Mervis, 1975). Perceptions are categorised into a particular group if they sufficiently resemble the prototype. An example is 'dog.' There are many dog breeds that often greatly differ visually from each other. Still, (in most cases) people can intuitively relate instances they encounter to the generalised version of their 'prototypical dog.'

Recognition-by-components Theory:

The theory aims to identify visual components that are abstracted from the prototype[5] (Biederman, 1987). It is built on the idea that objects are constructed by a limited number of 2D or 3D geometric shapes called *geons* (see Figure 1.3 for a few examples). When these geons are combined with one another a more holistic shape comes to be and this is the foundation for object recognition. The number of geons has been debated but was originally introduced as 32 distinct shapes.

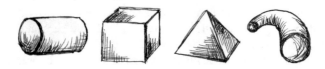

Fig. 1.3: Examples of Geons. From the left: Cylinder, Cube, Pyramid and Expanded Handle.

An example of how recognition-by-components theory works is to break down a coffee cup into two geons. Similarly to how a prototypical banana is a yellow curved cylinder, a coffee cup can be described as a hollow *cylinder* with *handle* on one side (see Figure 1.4). This can be extended to more complex objects. E.g. the 'prototypical dog' from above might be a particular construction of a *cylinder* for a torso, four *expanding cones* representing legs, an *expanding handle* for a tail and an *ellipsoid* for a head. Each of these parts can be divided to capture more details, e.g. *cones* for ears, creating a more detailed spatial description and/or ontology based on geons.

However, a visual description does not, as Mandler (2005) points out, in itself carry the nature of the object. To ascertain the usage and roles of an object, such as a coffee cup, where the capability to *contain* liquids is paramount, a different approach is required.

---

[5] There are also a significant amount of non-visual attributes that are included in the prototype. These will be addressed later on.

Fig. 1.4: The geons cylinder and handle correspond to a Coffee cup.

1.4.1.2 The Conceptual Process

The second category of components of Mandler's (2009) notion of concept formation is the *conceptual process*, during which an object's purpose and usage are
established. Here, the role of shape and visual characteristics is less clear and instead how and what the object is used for play the central role. Below two central
theories for this are introduced.

Affordance Theory:

The theory of Affordances proposes that all object meaning is defined not by the
visual characteristics found in recognition-by-components and similar ideas, but
rather meaning lies in the 'usages' and the 'purposes' of objects (Gibson, 1977).
Gibson calls these aspects 'affordances'. For a coffee cup the essential property is
that it can *contain* liquid (in this case specifically coffee), and for a vehicle, the most
paramount characteristic is that it needs to be able to offer transportation. If these
affordances are absent, the conceptualisation would need to be revised.

While this is a fairly straightforward idea the theory needs to be grounded not
only in reason but also in empirical results. Affordance theory is therefore often
combined with theory of image schemas, originally stemming from research on
cognitive linguistics.

Image Schemas:

Image schemas are described as conceptual building blocks learned from the body's
sensorimotor experiences. Similarly to the way geons capture visually perceived geometric shapes, image schemas capture spatiotemporal relationships[6] that can cap-

---

[6] Whether image schemas consistently are defined as spatiotemporal relationships is a contro-
versial topic. For the current purposes, it is sufficient to limit image schemas to spatiotemporal
relationships despite there maybe being more to the story.

ture the affordances of an object. For example, above it was established that an essential property of the coffee cup is that it can 'contain' liquid. This corresponds to the image schema of CONTAINMENT, which can be described as the interrelationship between an inside, an outside and a border (Lakoff, 1987).

As image schemas are the book's main focus, a more extensive introduction follows in Chapter 2, after the theoretical foundation has been sketched out.

To conclude on the nature of concept formation: visual characteristics play a significant role in identification and categorisation of objects and concepts. However, for the conceptual processes the primary components appear to be conceptual building blocks such as affordances and image schemas.

One important note on both concept formation and creativity as a whole is that it is not only the identification and the categorisation of existing objects in the world that are relevant, but also how new concepts are generated. There are many theories that attempt to explain this pheonomenon of generating novel concepts. Some of these theories forcus on the idea that creativity is the combination of already existing knowledge. For instance, Mednick's (1962) definition mentioned previously argued that creativity is the process of forming associative elements into new 'combinations.' Another influential theory is Conceptual Blending (CB) in which conceptual spaces are merged together. However, before CB is introduced further, a few relevant aspects of information transfer will be introduced.

1.5 Information Transfer

The transfer of information is an essential part of concept invention. This section explores information transfer in several different domains by looking more closely at analogy and *Conceptual Metaphor Theory*.

1.5.1 Analogy

Analogy is arguably one of the most important cognitive methods to transfer knowledge from one domain to another (Veale, 2012). By comparing two objects with different attributes to one another, knowledge previously not known about one of the objects can be gained simply by inferring a similarity between the relationship of the respective attributes. It is suggested that it is easier to learn and understand complicated phenomena through analogies rather than without. In everyday situations, analogies often take the form of similes: e.g. 'cute as a kitten,' 'brave as a lion;' or metaphors such as: 'the elephant in the room' or to 'to kick the bucket.' However, analogy is not in itself a linguistic phenomenon, it exists in all stages of cognition. Hofstadter (1995) even went as far as to claim that analogy is at the core of human cognition.

The underlying mechanism of analogical thinking is how information is transferred from a rich source domain onto an information-poor target domain through identifying similar structures. Simply put, an analogy comes in the following structure $a : b :: c : d$, meaning that c relates to d, in the same way as a relates to b.

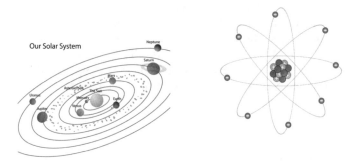

Fig. 1.5: The Rutherford Atom Model: In which the relationship between the constituents of the atom is described using the relationship between the sun and the planets in the solar system, following the structure: Sun:Nucleus::Planet:Electron.

A classic example of an influential analogy is the *Rutherford Atom Model* analogy (see Figure 1.5). When introducing his theory of the atomic structure Rutherford used the solar system as a model to explain the relationship between the nucleus and the electrons by comparing the nucleus to the sun, and the electrons to the planets. On a shallow level, the analogy does its job. It translate the information that the electrons are through attraction kept moving in a circular motion around the nucleus. Looking at it from the physics point of view, the wrong inference is made. In the case of the atom, it is electromagnetism that ensures that the electrons keep a particular distance to the nucleus, whereas in the solar system it is gravity.

In the creative process, an analogy may provide an explanation of how a problem might be solved, by inferring the properties of a similar relation between conceptual spaces. The classic example aims to explain the atomic structure by using the solar system as an analogical model. To explain the different layers of electrons and the electromagnetic pull therein, the properties and the gravitation from the sun and the planets are used.

Nagai (2009) talks about the difference between how experts and novices use analogies. Novices, considered to apply more creativity to problem-solving, are demonstratively more free in their analogy usage, whereas experts use more conventional analogies. Given that experts more often adapt to routine, it is not a strange conclusion to arrive at that novices can apply analogies more creatively. This thesis is also supported by neurolinguistic studies that demonstrate disjoint neural activation in conventional metaphors and novel metaphors. For instance, the work by

Schmidt et al. (2007) provides support for the idea that conventional metaphors have become part of everyday language rather than active analogical thinking.

One of the most important aspects of being able to perform and ultimately computationally calculate analogies is the successful identification of similar structures in both domains. For analogies in which the domains are vastly different it is not clear what information is intended to be transferred. For instance, in the simile "this cake is like a bird," it is unclear what is intended as cakes and birds does not have much in common. In comparison, it is easier to find similarities in the simile "this cake is like a cloud" where the fluffy texture of clouds can be transposed onto our conceptualisation of a cake. As demonstrated, identifying the underlying structure of analogies is a non-trivial problem to solve in the field of computational creativity and concept invention. As this is an important part of the presented research, this will be discussed in the next section.

1.5.2 The Search for Structure

As mentioned, an essential part of analogy is the search for common structure in the two domains. Returning to the previous example with the Rutherford atom model analogy can help demonstrate some of the aligned key concepts. For instance:

$$revolves\_around(planet, sun) :: revolves\_around(electron, nucleus)$$

$$greater\_than(sun, planet) :: greater\_than(nucleus, electron)$$

In analogies where the underlying structure is more or less obvious, this alignment is done automatically by humans. For the Rutherford atom model the first alignment is based on a SCALE relationship. Namely, that the sun is larger than the planets and, therefore, the nucleus must be larger than the electrons. Similarly, the circular movement is transferred from how the planets REVOLVE_AROUND the sun to how the electrons are thought to REVOLVE_AROUND the nucleus.

For an artificial system, the mapping of information between the entities in the analogy is not obvious, nor does any human 'commonsense' factor play a role in determining which information transfers are more or less likely[7]. In the artificial intelligence domain, analogy engines have been introduced with the intention to automatically find and transfer the common structure found in analogies. Two examples of such engines are the Structure Mapping Engine (SME) (Gentner, 1983) and Heuristic-Driven Theory-Projection (HDPT) (Schmidt et al., 2014), which will be discussed further in Chapter 6.

---

[7] Unless the system has been provided with such a tool.

1.5.3 Conceptual Metaphor

Conceptual metaphors, also called cognitive metaphors, are a specialised form of analogies in which a conceptual domain is used to explain the concepts of another (Lakoff and Johnson, 1980). Conceptual metaphors are an important part of human language and thinking, and therefore a vital part of natural language processing, machine translation and opinion mining among many other application scenarios (Shutova et al., 2013).

Cognitive metaphors arise out of an interconceptual mapping, that is, the association of two seemingly unrelated, distinct concepts. For instance, the conceptual metaphor ARGUMENT IS WAR is the underlying structure found in expressions such as 'he *shot down* all of my arguments' and 'the criticism was *right on target*.' In this example, the source domain WAR allows for an analogical transfer of war-related notions such as 'shooting' and 'target' onto the expression in the target domain of ARGUMENT. The verb 'shoot' indicates that 'people,' or animated agents, shoot inanimate 'objects.' In the conceptual metaphor this is violated as ARGUMENTS pose as both the implied 'bullet' and the target, as well as being abstract things. This violation is called *Selectional Restriction Violation* and has repeatedly been used to detect conceptual metaphors in text (Wilks, 1978).

Another important component of conceptual metaphors is *The Invariance Principle* which states that the underlying structure of the source domain needs to be the structure also of the target domain (Turner, 1992). In the previously mentioned example with the similes "this cake is like a bird" and "this cake is like a cloud," the second simile is cognitively relevant as a cake may have a texture resembling the fluffiness of clouds, but there exist few, if any, similar information structures between cakes and birds. Veale and Keane (1992) investigated this principle as 'conceptual scaffolding' with a focus on how this structure could be constituted by spatial and conceptual attributes that were then 'fleshed out' to give a metaphor meaning.

Conceptual metaphor theory and the search for the underlying conceptual structure is also present in creative generation of concepts. Conceptualisation is an important feature of the creative process. By sorting concepts in conceptual spaces through relationships or associations, the emergence of new concepts is hypothesised to be created through merging conceptual spaces (Grady, 2001). One recent theory that has had influence on how concepts are thought to be generated and invented is *Conceptual Blending* which builds on the cognitive mechanisms behind analogical reasoning (Fauconnier and Turner, 1998). The idea to use image schemas as a conceptual scaffold for information transfer in conceptual blending will be further discussed in Chapter 2 and further formally developed in Chapter 6.

1.6 Conceptual Blending

Fauconnier and Turner (1998) introduced a theory for concept invention built on the notion that creativity is a process of combining already existing knowledge into a new domain, see Figure 1.6. The theory was introduced under the name 'conceptual integration' but has become famous as 'conceptual blending.' It has found support and encouragement for further studies from both artificial and psychological directions (e.g. Gibbs (2000); Grady (2001); Yang et al. (2013)). The theory builds on the principles of analogical reasoning, in which one domain carries information over to another domain. The difference here is that information is mapped between two input spaces that are then merged into a novel space.

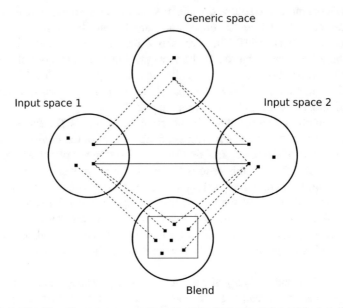

Fig. 1.6: The blending process as described by Fauconnier and Turner (1998).

Combinational creativity is thought to occur when mental spaces, or conceptual spaces, merge into new spaces called 'blends'[8]. These newly blended spaces inherit some of the attributes of the input spaces, yet possess emergent properties to develop their own characteristics. Following the lines of Fauconnier and Turner (1998), Veale (2012) explains the purpose of conceptual blending as follows:

> ... conceptual blending combines the smoothness of metaphor with the structural complexity and organizing power of analogy. We can think of blending as a cognitive operation in which conceptual ingredients do not flow in a single direction, but are thoroughly stirred together, to create a new structure with its own emergent meanings.

---

[8] In formal domains these are often called blendoids. Conceptually the terms are interchangeable, but the term blends is here used exclusively to avoid confusion.

The idea is that both literal and metaphoric expressions are based on multiple mental models and the internal mappings between the internal concepts therein in both target and source domains. Yang et al. (2013) use the following expression to explain the hypothesis: "That stone we saw in the natural history museum is a gem," here it is necessary to establish a mapping between the stone in the natural history museum and the gem. In a metaphoric expression such as: 'He knows power is an intoxicant,' the target domain 'power,' gain attributes from the source domain of 'intoxicant.' In order to understand blending theory, the concept of mental space needs to be understood. Boden (2004) describes them as conceptual spaces in which different conceptual groupings would have internal relations and associations to other conceptual spaces. This correlates with the blending theory's idea of mental spaces where Fauconnier and Turner (1998) define mental spaces as "...small conceptual packets constructed as we think and talk, for purposes of local understanding and action." They are considered to be partial assemblies of elements constructed by frames and cognitive models. The vast variety of mental spaces are interconnected to each other by relations of different strength and character and both the mental spaces in themselves as well as their interrelations are modified as thought and context unfold.

Abstract as it may be on a psychological level, after all it is still uncertain as to how knowledge is stored in the brain, it is easier to picture this phenomenon in AI. As mentioned, in AI ontologies are structured in taxonomies in which all relevant information for that particular conceptual space is included through classic knowledge representation, including the concepts, the relationships and the roles that are part of the ontology.

1.6.1 The Mechanics of Conceptual Blending

Following the methods behind analogical thinking, one of the central aspects of blending is the way in which 'common structure' between the input concepts is understood to steer the creation of the new concept. The 'merging' of the input spaces is moderated by this common structure, represented as the generic space, or as it is called in formal approaches, the base ontology[9]. The common structure of the input spaces is understood to play a vital role in rendering the newly constructed concept meaningful, as it ensures that the blended space also contains the structure found in the generic space.

However, despite this influential research, within computational creativity and AI in general, relatively little effort has been devoted to fully formalise these ideas and to make them amenable to computational techniques, but look to (Kutz et al., 2014; Schorlemmer et al., 2014) for overviews.

---

[9] In the limit case, the shared structure might be trivial, and a concept such as 'red pencil' might be understood as a blend too, by simply imposing properties from one input space onto another.

Unlike other combination techniques, *blending* aims at creatively generating (new) concepts on the basis of input theories whose domains are thematically distinct but whose specifications share some features.

For the cognitive machinery behind conceptual blending, it is important to understand that the model for conceptual integration takes two, or possibly more, input spaces that have some kind of analogical relation to one other, see Figure 1.6. Between these two input spaces, there is a partial cross-space mapping in which different elements in each space are connected. The generic space maps onto both of the inputs, and constitutes what the input layers have in common. The blended space, the 'blend,' is the resulting combination given the two inputs. What is needed to understand the problem will be fused from the input layers and what needs to be excluded will simply not take part in the blend. One important feature here is that the information that is being projected into the blend is selective, meaning that unnecessary, or counterproductive, elements are left out since they do not help solve the problem. The emergent structure of these conceptual blends also needs to be attended to. Due to the fact that conceptual spaces are mixed, new *relationships* and *compositions* can emerge and evolve. *Completion* is another of these emergent properties that bring additional structure to the blend: what might have been insufficient in one of the input spaces has more information in the blended space which might complete concepts and their interrelationship. Lastly, the emergent structure of elaboration develops the blend through imaginative mental stimulation given the current logics and principles.

This might go on indefinitely with new completion structures, as well as with new logics and principles that emerge through the continuation of elaborative processes (Fauconnier and Turner, 1998). It is suggested that this view of cognition is compatible with both human psychological and computation approaches to creative associations and will, therefore, be viewed as the foundation for the cognitive machinery in the creative process in the remainder of this volume.

1.6.2 The Gryphon: A Blending Example

Turner (2014) argues that human creativity came about as a blending process. One of the earliest examples of how one input space is merged with another is the estimated 35,000 year old ivory sculpture 'the lion man'[10]. It is a conceptual blend where a human figure has been given the head of a lion. Described as a figurative piece of art, Turner argues that it encompasses not only physical features of both input spaces but is intended to also embody the characteristics associated with them.

In this section, a similar and entirely fictive example is used to explain the creative capacity of blending. By being a non-existing entity in the world it captures the strength of human imagination. Many mythological creatures, or 'monsters,' build

---

[10] The sculpture is on display at Ulm Museum, Germany.

on the same principles behind the 'lion man,' while there are many examples of such blended creatures: for now, consider a gryphon.

A gryphon is a fictive creature with the body and the tail of a lion and with the head and the wings of an eagle, see Figure 1.7. The blend of the two creatures does not only involve the physical attributes of the animals, but also the characteristics associated with them. The lion provides attributes such as strength and power, and the eagle attributes such as precision and capacity for flight. Hence, such a blended creature has the skills to master both land and sky.

The gryphon exemplifies one particular blend of the two input spaces 'lion' and 'eagle.' There are other possibilities to blend a monster based on these two concepts. For example, one could consider an 'inverted gryphon,' which has the head of the lion and the body of the eagle but no wings. A third possible monster is a creature which has the shape and strength of a lion but cannot use its strength due to fragile bird-like bone structure. The last example shows that not all blends are equally successful. One criterion for a blend to be considered creative is that it needs to be 'useful' (Boden, 2009). Given the task of blending a monster, a successful blend is required to produce a dangerous creature – a lion with brittle bones does not meet this requirement as well as a gryphon.

Fig. 1.7: The mythological creature gryphon: a conceptual blend between a lion and an eagle.

The blended space preserves the information from the generic space. However, only some selected features of the input spaces are usually retained. In the gryphon example, the generic space contains the head, the body, and two limbs of a vertebrate. In the blend, the head in the generic space is mapped to the head of the lion and the head of the eagle, respectively. The same holds for the body. In contrast, the two limbs are mapped to the forelimbs of the lion and the hindlimbs (legs) of the eagle. For this reason, the gryphon has six limbs, namely two wings of the eagle, two hindlegs from the lion and two forelegs, which are inherited from both input spaces. Since the shape and features of lion legs and eagle legs are mutually exclusive (e.g. one has hair and the other has feathers), the forelegs of the gryphon cannot inherit all properties from both input spaces. Thus, a gryphon's forelegs are usually conceptualised as exemplifying either only the features of one animal or as inheriting a consistent subset of features from both input spaces.

For humans conceptual blending is effortless. We are able to create new blends spontaneously and have no difficulty to understand new conceptual blends when we encounter them. This includes the selection of suitable input spaces, the identification of a relevant generic space, the identification of irrelevant features of the input spaces, the performance of the blend, and the evaluation of the usefulness of the blend. In contrast, for an automated system, each of these steps provides a significant challenge. This is demonstrated in the work by Neuhaus et al. (2014), who aim to formally model the conceptual blending of monsters, inspired by mythological creatures such as a gryphon[11].

1.7 Chapter Conclusion

This chapter introduced the foundation of this volume. Here the symbol grounding problem was introduced together with cognitive and computational issues of conceptual understanding and grounding, as well as some issues found in research on creativity and concept invention. One of the major theories presented was the role of sensorimotor processes in conceptual development and the theory of embodied cognition. Additionally, creativity research was introduced as it provides one of the necessary stepping stones towards concept invention and computational concept generation. With this in mind, conceptual blending, built on the notion of analogical reasoning, was introduced as a theoretical mechanism behind concept generation through the combination of conceptual spaces.

In the next chapter, the embodied mind theory will be further discussed more specifically in relation to the theory of image schemas as it provides a potential theoretical starting point for conceptual grounding.

References

N. C. Andreasen. *The Creative Brain: The Science of Genius.* Plume, New York/Washington, D.C., 2006.

L. Aziz-Zadeh and A. Damasio. Embodied semantics for actions: Findings from functional brain imaging. *Journal of Physiology Paris*, 102(1-3):35–39, 2008.

T. H. Bak and J. R. Hodges. The effects of motor neurone disease on language: Further evidence. *Brain and Language*, 89:354–361, 2014.

---

[11] Visit `https://github.com/ConceptualBlending/conceptual_blending_project` for a tool that visualises these monster blends.

J. A. Bateman, B. Magnini, and G. Fabris. The generalized upper model knowledge base: Organization and use. *Towards very large knowledge bases*, pages 60–72, 1995.

T. R. Besold, M. Schorlemmer, and A. Smaill, editors. *Computational Creativity Research: Towards Creative Machines*, volume 7 of *Atlantis Thinking Machines*. Atlantis Press, 2015.

T. R. Besold, A. d'Avila Garcez, S. Bader, H. Bowman, P. Domingos, P. Hitzler, K.-U. Kühnberger, L. C. Lamb, D. Lowd, P. M. V. Lima, L. de Penning, G. Pinkas, H. Poon, and G. Zaverucha. Neural-symbolic learning and reasoning: A survey and interpretation. arXiv:1711.03902, 2017. Work in Progress.

I. Biederman. Recognition by components: A theory of human image understanding. *Psychological Review*, 94(2):115–117, 1987.

M. A. Boden. Creativity and artificial intelligence. *Artificial Intelligence*, 103(1): 347–356, 1998.

M. A. Boden. *The Creative Mind; Myths and Mechanisms*. Routledge, London, 2004.

M. A. Boden. Computer models of creativity. *AI Magazine*, Fall 2009.

S. Borgo and C. Masolo. Foundational Choices in DOLCE. In *Handbook on Ontologies*. Springer, 2010.

K. Brodmann. *Vergleichende Lokalisationslehre der Grosshirnrinde in ihren Prinzipien dargestellt auf Grund des Zellenbaues*. Verlag von Johann Ambrosius Barth, 1909.

N. Chomsky. *Syntactic structures*. Institute of Cognitive Science, The Hague: Mouton, 1957.

N. Chomsky. *Aspects of the Theory of Syntax*, volume 11. MIT Press, 2014.

S. Colton. Creativity versus the perception of creativity in computational systems. In *AAAI spring symposium: creative intelligent systems*, volume 8, 2008.

S. Colton and G. A. Wiggins. Computational creativity: The final frontier? *Frontiers in Artificial Intelligence and Applications*, 242:21–26, 2012.

L. Cong, F. A. Ran, D. Cox, S. Lin, R. Barretto, N. Habib, P. D. Hsu, X. Wu, W. Jiang, L. A. Marraffini, and F. Zhang. Multiplex Genome Engineering Using CRISPR/Cas Systems. *Science*, 339:819–823, 2012.

M. Csikszentmihalyi. The flow experience and its significance for human psychology. In M. Csikszentmihalyi and I. S. Csikszentmihalyi, editors, *Optimal experience: Psychological studies of flow in consciousness*, pages 15–35. Cambridge University Press, 1988.

M. Csikszentmihalyi. Society, culture, and person: A systems view of creativity. In *The Systems Model of Creativity*, pages 47–61. Springer, 2014.

A. Dietrich. The cognitive neuroscience of creativity. *Psychonomic bulletin & review*, 11(6):1011–26, 12 2004.

G. Fauconnier and M. Turner. Conceptual integration networks. *Cognitive Science*, 22(2):133—187, 1998.

J. Feldman and S. Narayanan. Embodied meaning in a neural theory of language. *Brain and Language*, 89(2):385–392, 2004.

L. Gabora. Revenge of the "neurds": Characterizing creative thought in terms of the structure and dynamics of memory. *Creativity Research Journal*, 22(1):1–13, 2010.

V. Gallese and G. Lakoff. The brain's concepts: the role of the sensory-motor system in conceptual knowledge. *Cognitive neuropsychology*, 22(3):455–79, 2005.

H. Gardner. *The Mind's New Science: A History of the Cognitive Revolution*. Basic Books, New York, 1985.

D. Gentner. Structure mapping: A theoretical framework for analogy. *Cognitive Science*, 7(2):155–170, 1983.

R. W. Gibbs. Making good psychology out of blending theory. *Cognitive Linguistics*, 11(3–4):347–358, 2000.

R. W. Gibbs. Metaphor interpretation as embodied simulation. *Mind & Language*, 21(3):434–458, 2006.

J. J. Gibson. The theory of affordances. In R. Shaw and J. Bransford, editors, *Perceiving, Acting, and Knowing: Toward an Ecological Psychology*, pages 67–82. NJ: Lawrence Erlbaum, Hillsdale, 1977.

J. E. Grady. Cognitive mechanisms of conceptual integration. *Cognitive Linguistics*, 11(3-4):335–345, 2001.

N. Guarino, D. Oberle, and S. Staab. What Is an Ontology. In S. Staab and R. Studer, editors, *Handbook on Ontologies*, pages 1–17. Springer Berlin Heidelberg, 2003.

J. P. Guilford. *The nature of human intelligence*. McGraw-Hill series in psychology. McGraw-Hill, 1967.

S. Harnad. The symbol grounding problem. *Physica D*, 42:335–346, 1990.

D. O. Hebb. *Organization of behavior: A Neuropsychological Theory*. Wiley & Sons, 1949.

D. Hofstadter. *Fluid Concepts and Creative Analogies*. Basic Books, 1995.

P. Jacob. Intentionality. In E. N. Zalta, editor, *The Stanford Encyclopedia of Philosophy*. Metaphysics Research Lab, Stanford University, winter 2014 edition, 2014.

R. E. Jung, C. Gasparovic, R. S. Chavez, R. Flores, S. M. Smith, A. Caprihan, and R. Yeo. Biochemical support for the "threshold" theory of creativity: a magnetic resonance spectroscopy study. *The Journal of neuroscience*, 29(16):19–25, 2009.

O. Kutz, J. A. Bateman, F. Neuhaus, T. Mossakowski, and M. Bhatt. E pluribus unum: Formalisation, Use-Cases, and Computational Support for Conceptual Blending. In T. R. Besold, M. Schorlemmer, and A. Smaill, editors, *Computational Creativity Research: Towards Creative Machines*, Thinking Machines. Atlantis, 2014.

G. Lakoff. *Women, Fire, and Dangerous Things. What Categories Reveal about the Mind*. University of Chicago Press, 1987.

G. Lakoff and M. Johnson. *Metaphors We Live By*. University of Chicago Press, 1980.

G. Lakoff and M. Johnson. *Philosophy in the Flesh*. Basic Books, 1999.

M. M. Louwerse and P. Jeuniaux. The linguistic and embodied nature of conceptual processing. *Cognition*, 114(1):96–104, 2010.

J. M. Mandler. How to build a baby: On the development of an accessible representational system. *Cognitive Development*, 3(2):113–136, 1988.

J. M. Mandler. How to build a baby: II. Conceptual primitives. *Psychological review*, 99(4):587–604, 1992.

J. M. Mandler. *The Foundations of Mind: Origins of Conceptual Thought: Origins of Conceptual Though*. Oxford University Press, New York, 2004.

J. M. Mandler. How to build a baby: III. Image schemas and the transition to verbal thought. *From Perception to Meaning: Image Schemas in Cognitive Linguistics*, (January):137–163, 2005.

J. M. Mandler. Perceptual and Conceptual Processes in Infancy. *Journal of Cognition and Development*, 1(1):3–36, 2009.

D. Mareschal and P. C. Quinn. Categorization in infancy. *Trends in Cognitive Sciences*, 5(10):443–450, 2001.

S. A. Mednick. The associative basis of the creative process. *Psychological review*, 69(3):220–32, 5 1962.

L. Meteyarda, S. R. Cuadradob, B. Bahramic, and G. Viglioccoa. Coming of age: a review of embodiment and the neuroscience of semantics. *Cortex*, 48:788–804, 2012.

H. Moravec. *Mind children: The future of robot and human intelligence*. Harvard University Press, 1988.

T. Mossakowski, M. Codescu, F. Neuhaus, and O. Kutz. *The Road to Universal Logic–Festschrift for 50th birthday of Jean-Yves Beziau, Volume II*, chapter The distributed ontology, modelling and specification language - DOL. Studies in Universal Logic. Birkhäuser, 2015.

Y. Nagai. Concept blending and dissimilarity: factors for creative concept generation process. *Design Studies*, 30:648–675, 2009.

F. Neuhaus, O. Kutz, M. Codescu, and T. Mossakowski. Fabricating Monsters is Hard - Towards the Automation of Conceptual Blending. In *Proceedings of Computational Creativity, Concept Invention, and General Intelligence (C3GI-14)*, volume 1-2014, pages 2–5, Prague, 2014. Publications of the Institute of Cognitive Science, Osnabrück.

C. K. Ogden and I. A. Richards. International library of psychology, philosophy and scientific method. Harcourt Brace Jovanovich, 8 edition, 1989.

J. Piaget. *The origins of intelligence in children*. NY: International University Press, New York, 1952. Translated by Margaret Cook.

T. Regier. *The Human Semantic Potential: Spatial Language and Constrained Connectionism*. MIT Press, 1996.

E. Rosch and C. B. Mervis. Family resemblances: Studies in the internal structure of categories. *Cognitive Psychology*, 7(4):573–605, 1975.

M. A. Runco. *Creativity: Theories and themes: Research, development, and practice*. Elsevier, 2014.

M. A. Runco and I. Chand. Cognition and creativity. *Educational Psychology review*, 7(3):243–267, 1995.

M. A. Runco and G. J. Jaeger. The standard definition of creativity. *Creativity Research Journal*, 24(1):92–96, 2012.

R. K. Sawyer. *Explaining creativity: The science of human innovation.* Oxford University Press, 2011.

G. L. Schmidt, C. J. DeBuse, and C. A. Seger. Right hemisphere metaphor processing? Characterizing the lateralization of semantic processes. *Brain Langauge,* 100(2):127–141, 2007.

M. Schmidt, U. Krumnack, H. Gust, and K.-U. Kühnberger. Heuristic-Driven Theory Projection: An Overview. In H. Prade and G. Richard, editors, *Computational Approaches to Analogical Reasoning: Current Trends,* volume 548 of *Computational Intelligence,* pages 163–194. Springer, 2014.

M. Schorlemmer, A. Smaill, K.-U. Kühnberger, O. Kutz, S. Colton, E. Cambouropoulos, and A. Pease. COINVENT: Towards a Computational Concept Invention Theory. In *Proceedings of the 5th International Conference on Computational Creativity,* Ljubljana, Slovenia, June 10–13 2014.

J. R. Searle. Minds, brains, and programs. *Behavioral and Brain Sciences,* 3(03): 417–457, 1980.

L. Shapiro. *Embodied Cognition.* New problems of philosophy. Routledge, London and New York, 2011.

E. Shutova, S. Teufel, and A. Korhonen. Statistical metaphor processing. *Computational Linguistics,* 39(2):301–353, 2013.

H. A. Simon. Creativity and motivation: A response to Csikszentmihalyi. *New Ideas in Psychology,* 6(2):177–181, 1 1988.

S. M. Smith, T. B. Ward, and R. A. Finke. *The creative cognition approach.* MIT Press, 1995.

M. Tettamanti, G. Buccino, M. C. Saccuman, V. Gallese, M. Danna, P. Scifo, F. Fazio, G. Rizzolatti, and D. Perani. Listening to action-related sentences activates fronto-parietal motor circuits. *Journal of Cognitive Neuroscience,* pages 273–281, 2005.

B. Tomasino, F. Fabbro, and P. Brambilla. How do conceptual representations interact with processing demands: An fMRI study on action- and abstract-related words. *Brain research,* 1591C:38–52, 2014.

E. P. Torrance, O. E. Ball, and H. T. Safter. *Torrance tests of creative thinking.* Scholastic Testing Service, 2003.

M. Turner. Language is a Virus. *Poetics Today,* 13(4):725–736, 1992.

M. Turner. *The Origin of Ideas: Blending, Creativity, and the Human Spark.* Oxford University Press, 2014.

T. Veale. From Conceptual Mash-ups to "Bad-Ass" Blends: A Robust Computational Model of Conceptual Blending. In *Proceedings of the 2012 International Conference on Computational Creativity,* pages 1–8, Dublin, Ireland, 2012.

T. Veale and M. T. Keane. Conceptual Scaffolding: a Spatially Founded Meaning Representation for Metaphor Comprehension. *Computational Intelligence,* 8(3): 494–519, 1992.

J. von Neumann. *The Computer and the Brain.* Yale University Press, New Haven, CT, USA, 1958.

G. A. Wiggins. Searching for computational creativity. *New Generation Computing,* 24(3):209–222, 2006.

Y. Wilks. Making preferences more active. *Artificial Intelligence*, 11(3):197–223, 1978.

N. L. Wilson and R. W. Gibbs. Real and imagined body movement primes metaphor comprehension. *Cognitive science*, 31(4):721–731, 2007.

F.-P. G. Yang, K. Bradley, M. Huq, D.-L. Wu, and D. C. Krawczyk. Contextual effects on conceptual blending in metaphors: An event-related potential study. *Journal of Neurolinguistics*, 26(2):312–326, 2013.

Chapter 2
Image Schemas: State of the Art in Spatiotemporal Conceptualisation

Abstract The previous chapter introduced this volume's research foundation and some core problems. Briefly introduced was the term 'image schema,' described as mental generalisations learned from the body's sensorimotor experiences. As the formal work on image schemas represents this volume's core contribution, this chapter provides a more thorough introduction. This includes investigating image schemas from their background in cognitive linguistics as well as presenting some empirical support that has been offered by research in developmental psychology. As image schemas are approached in the light of solving the symbol grounding problem for artificial intelligence and computational concept invention, the chapter will focus on introducing some of the requirements and problems that will be dealt with in the upcoming chapters. The chapter includes:

- History of image schemas
- Defining image schemas
- Image schemas in psychology and linguistics
- Structuring image schemas
- Image schemas in narratives

2.1 Image Schemas

2.1.1 Embodied Cognition and Image Schemas

Embodied cognition offers a concrete method on how to theoretically view the symbol grounding problem. The direct link between embodied experiences and representations in the mind is appealing not only from a cognitive perspective but from an artificial intelligence perspective as well.

However, embodied cognition in itself does not offer any solutions to how embodied experiences are mentally represented. Instead, both classic mental representations, as well as meaning being stored in the neural activation of the senso-

© Springer Nature Switzerland AG 2020   33
M. M. Hedblom, *Image Schemas and Concept Invention*, Cognitive Technologies,
https://doi.org/10.1007/978-3-030-47329-7_2

rimotor cortex, are offered as possibilities for how conceptual information is preserved (Shapiro, 2011). One theory that aims to bridge this gap of information of
how the embodied experience mentally manifests is the theory of image schemas
(Fernández, 2019).

The term Image schema[1] was simultaneously, but disjointly, introduced by
Lakoff (1987) and Johnson (1987) in the late 1980s. However, the philosophy behind the theory dates back (if not earlier) to the German philosopher Kant (1781)
who termed the notion of 'schema:' a non-empirical concept formed from sensorimotor experiences.

Since its introduction, the theory has become influential in theories of how to
ground higher cognitive phenomena, such as language and reasoning, in the low-
level sensations acquired from embodied experiences.

Image schemas are said to be the conceptual building blocks that are learned from
the embodied experience in early infancy (Mandler, 2004). They are preverbal and
while language and reasoning build from them, they are not in themselves learned
from language. While there are discussions on which concepts should be included
in the term image schema, a common restriction is to describe them as the generic
spatiotemporal relationships[2] learned from repeated interaction with and perception
of the environment and the objects therein. The first pertinent distinction is that
image schemas can be both static and dynamic (Tseng, 2007).

While there is currently no consensus on the number of existing image schemas
or which notions are image-schematic to begin with, some common examples are
CONTAINMENT, SUPPORT and LINK (see Figure 2.1). Despite working on the
topic of introducing novel image-schematic concepts and how to structure them,
no concrete stand on which image schemas should be included in a canon of image
schemas is made. Instead, conventions from the literature are used where already
introduced image schemas and their primitives are written with small caps, while
spatial and conceptual primitives that are still up for general agreement are written
in simple lower case. The only exception where novel image schemas are written
with small caps are those that can be provided with empirical support.

2.1.2 A Brief History of Image Schemas

As mentioned, the theory was introduced in its current form by Lakoff (1987) and
Johnson (1987) but the ideas date back in history.

Most prominent in the history of philosophy and epistemology is how Kant introduced the notion of a 'schema.' It denotes a mental construct, or a concept, that while
non-empirical in itself is based on sensational experiences. The Kantian schema laid

---

[1] In plural: image schemas or image schemata after the Greek plural form of 'schema.'

[2] Image schemas are by definition multimodal, extracted from all sensorimotor inputs, and it might
be limiting to speak of them as spatiotemporal relationships. However, for the current purposes,
this restriction will be proven useful in more applied scenarios.

the foundation for theories in which embodied experience was related to mental constructs.

Fig. 2.1: Image Schema Examples. From the left: CONTAINMENT, SUPPORT and LINK.

However, the Kantian 'schema' only takes half of the image schemas into account. The second part, 'image,' has led to image schemas often being mistaken for abstract visual representations, partly due to the (somewhat unfortunate) terminology and partly due to the proportionally high representation of vision in our perception. However, as Oakley (2010) points out "...image schemas are neither images nor schemas in the familiar sense of each term as used in philosophy, cognitive psychology or anthropology." Instead, in the same way that embodied experiences are multimodal, so are image schemas. For instance, auditory experiences appear more abstract and have, therefore, a distinct logic and different expressions than the ones found solely in vision and more concrete situations. As an example, a piece of music may be 'shared' between an audience in a completely different way than a piece of cake can be. The way we abstract away from auditory experiences might, thus, differ greatly from the corresponding process for visually perceived experiences, and similarly for other sensory modalities and/or combinations thereof. Hence, it is important to make the distinction that image schemas are not simply abstract visual representations but are of a completely different nature and quality. Image schemas are instead mental patterns capturing the most general abstraction of experience and are consequently not 'images' as such. Instead, the term 'image' was introduced due to inspiration from cognitive linguistics, more precisely the work by Talmy (1988).

Talmy (1983) made observations that spatial relations seem to have different meanings in language. His research highlights how spatial relations can be decomposed into conceptual primitives ('images') that recur across languages. Some of these images were CONTAINMENT and SOURCE_PATH_GOAL. He specifically pointed out that these spatial images came in three different categories: *orientational* (e.g. ABOVE), *topological* (e.g. CONTACT), and *force-dynamic* (e.g. SUPPORT) (Lakoff and Núñez, 2000; Talmy, 1988). Static image schemas are naturally more straightforward to define than dynamic image schemas. However, image schemas are spatio*temporal*, meaning that their dynamic aspects also need to be taken into account. For instance, consider how the image schema CONTAINMENT can describe the situation in which a cup already contains coffee, but also the situation in which the coffee is poured from a source: a kettle, to a goal: a cup, defined as an IN and OUT schema.

Inspired by the research of Kant (1781) and Talmy (1983, 1988), Lakoff (1987) introduced the term 'image schemas' to express the spatial relationships found in language based on embodied experiences.

While Talmy (2000) was the one to introduce these spatial concepts, other researchers have focused on conceptual primes and semantic primitives (e.g. Mandler (1992); Wierzbicka (1996)).

While Lakoff (1987) and Johnson (1987) were working more or less simultaneously on the introduction of image schemas, Johnson was the one to focus on the embodied properties of image schemas.

As the progression of cognitive science took a more concrete nature through the increased influence of neuroscience and the growing knowledge of the specialisation of the brain, the view of connectionism also started to influence the view of image schema research.

One of the most influential research contributions on neural networks and connectionism in terms of semantic primes is the work by Regier (1996), who developed a substantial network to model the brain and cognitive phenomena such as image schemas. This work was supported by neuroscientific research in which, for instance, Feldman and Narayanan (2004) continued to build neural models of image schemas.

In the last few decades, the image schema research has taken a different direction as the prime research goal is no longer exclusively to model human cognition, but also to simulate it in a formal domain. Geographical information science (GI-Science)[3], artificial intelligence, computational creativity and a range of other computational areas has taken a liking to the idea of using image schemas as a form of design patterns when constructing models of narratives and ontologies[4].

2.2 Defining 'Image Schema'

The interdisciplinary history of image schema research hints at one of the major obstacles for further research, namely that as of yet there exists no agreed upon terminology. The term 'image schema' is poorly defined with definitions that vary between research disciplines, individual scientists as well as methodologies.

Today image schemas are studied in several fields of research including, amongst others, neuroscience (e.g. Rohrer (2005)), developmental psychology (e.g. Mandler (1992); Watters (1996)), cognitive linguistics (e.g. Hampe and Grady (2005); Tseng (2007)) and formal knowledge representation and artificial intelligence (e.g. Bennett and Cialone (2014); Frank and Raubal (1999); Kuhn (2007); St. Amant et al. (2006)). With different disciplines come different focus and different scientific backgrounds. Therefore, it follows as no surprise that the terminology on image schemas

---

[3] GIScience is the scientific discipline investigating representations of geographic concepts and relations (Kresse and Danko, 2012).

[4] As in design ontology patterns (Gangemi and Presutti, 2009).

has been left somewhat unclear. An additional reason for this problem is the disputed relationship between socio-cultural aspects and the neurobiology of embodied cognition (Hampe, 2005), which has further complicated the attempts to make a concrete definition of image schemas.

When Johnson (1987) introduced image schemas he described them using the following words:

> An image schema is a recurring, dynamic pattern of our perceptual interactions and motor programs that gives coherence and structure to our experience.

The linguist Oakley (2010) instead defines an image schema as:

> ...a condensed re-description of perceptual experience for the purpose of mapping spatial structure onto conceptual structure.

Another definition, paraphrased from Hampe (2005), is that image schemas are "...directly meaningful ("experiential"/"embodied"), pre-conceptual structures, which arise from or are grounded in human recurrent bodily movements through space, perceptual interactions and ways of manipulating objects." Further, she points out that it follows that they are highly schematic *Gestalts*[5] that capture the structural contours of sensory-motor experience, integrating information from multiple modalities, and exist as continuous and analogue patterns beneath conscious awareness, prior to and independently of other concepts; and are both internally structured and highly flexible.

While research in cognitive linguistics has several interpretations of what it means to have linguistic primitives, the formal domain of image schema research has taken a slightly more straightforward view. As a representative of this research group, Kuhn (2007) defines image schemas as "...the pre-linguistic structures of object relations in time and space." This is a common focus in more formal image schema research to further define image schemas as spatiotemporal relationships, as research on *Qualitative Spatial Reasoning* (QSR)[6] and Geographic Information Science research can then provide a good research foundation.

One problem with agreeing on a definition of image schemas is that the current definitions do not provide an individuation criterion between image schemas. This in turn, leads to two other problems. The first, here called *The Structure Problem*, captures that it is hard to evaluate which spatiotemporal constructs qualify to be described as image schemas as many similar conceptual structures are spoken of interchangeably under one image schema. The second problem, here called *The Categorisation Problem*, captures that it is difficult to determine which image schema a particular construct belongs to. As image schemas are abstract concepts it is likely that in the human brain, the nature and borders between different schemas may be flexible and up for the context to define. However, for computer science, these two problems are essential to solve before any formal representation of image schemas can be either successful or useful. Both of these two problems will be discussed

---

[5] Gestalts in the sense of Gestalt theory and Gestalt laws.

[6] QSR is an area of AI that studies spatiotemporal reasoning that approximates human commonsense understanding of space (Ligozat, 2011).

further in the two upcoming sections, and Chapter 3 and Chapter 5 will present suggestions on how these two problems can be overcome in formal settings.

2.2.1 The Structure Problem

Regarding spatiotemporal constructions, it is not certain when they qualify as image schemas or not. One of the criteria for a mental construct to be considered an image schema is that it needs to follow the general rules of *Gestalt Theory*[7] (Lakoff and Núñez, 2000). For example, it is not possible to remove the 'border' from the CON-TAINMENT image schema, nor is it possible to speak of solely 'an inside' without at least implicitly considering 'a border' and 'an outside' as well. However, even with this strict definition Bennett and Cialone (2014) could identify no fewer than eight different kinds of static CONTAINMENT through a corpus study. This was done exclusively for static forms of CONTAINMENT, and if transformations and movement IN and OUT are included then the 'number' of CONTAINMENT schemas would increase even further. This indicates that each image schema cannot be described as an isolated theory that can easily be defined, but that they are complex webs of associated notions and transformations. Other support for image schema networks stems from the idea to structure image schemas as conceptual clusters (Santibáñez, 2002).

However, these image schema clusters can be shown to vary in complexity as well, ranging from conceptual primitives to image schemas and increasingly complex mental manifestations. This is supported by how, as a child accumulates experience with its environment, the image schemas become increasingly fine-tuned and more specialised for the context (Rohrer, 2005).

These conceptual components are a research field on their own, but they are often included under image schema research as well. Here, spatial or temporal components construct more complex image schemas. Some influences are Mandler's (1992) spatial primitives, Talmy's (2005) conceptual primitives and Wierzbicka's (1996) semantic primes.

One way to solve this problem is to divide the image-schematic components into a hierarchy based on how specific and/or complex they are. Mandler and Cánovas (2014) divide image schemas into three levels:

1. *Spatial primitives:* The first building blocks that allow us to understand what we perceive: PATH, CONTAINMENT, THING, CONTACT, etc.
2. *Image schemas:* Representations of simple spatial events using the primitives: PATH OF THING, THING INTO CONTAINER, etc.
3. *Schematic integrations:* The first conceptual representations to include non-spatial elements, by projecting feelings or non-spatial perceptions onto blends structured by image schemas.

---

[7] Gestalt psychology aims to understand the laws behind the ability to make sense and acquire meaningful perceptions in a seemingly chaotic world. The main hypothesis proposes that the mind has the capacity to 'self-organise' its perceptions (Koffka, 1935).

This means that the literature on image schemas mentions a plenitude of different conceptual structures on different levels of specificity that still are referred to as belonging to one particular image schema. This is a problem not only for formal investigations of image schemas, but also for linguistic and psychological investigation. The structural problem will be addressed in the upcoming chapter.

2.2.2 The Categorisation Problem

Image schemas are not only hard to categorise and structure within their own 'image schema,' but also difficult as more complex image schemas often appear as combinations of simpler image schemas (Oakley, 2010). As image schemas often share conceptual primitives and have similar characteristics it is difficult to determine which image schema a particular structure belongs to. This problem is here introduced as the categorisation problem.

For example, it is clear that apples can be SUPPORTed by plates, likewise, they can be placed 'inside' (CONTAINMENT) bowls. But in the case of an overflowing fruit bowl, in which the apple, by perception, is 'outside' of the bowl it is still possible to say that the apple is *in* the fruit bowl.

This problem is amplified further by the heterogeneous way image schemas seem to manifest. For instance, image schemas by their nature undergo spatiotemporal transformations (Oakley, 2010). This means that the image schema itself is not an isolated notion but instead a dynamic one. From a formal point of view it might be beneficial (i.e. simpler) to focus on static image schemas alone. However, this comprises a major simplification and is not cognitively adequate, as image schemas also essentially model change over time. The notion of CONTAINMENT is, in its most basic form, defined as the relationship of an inside, an outside, and a border (Johnson, 1987). Yet, looking at cognitive development, it is not this relationship that the understanding of CONTAINMENT seems to stem from. Instead, it appears as though the most important grounds for image schema development lie in the change over time, here the movement IN and OUT of a container (Mandler and Cánovas, 2014). Many scenarios involving movement, most commonly associated with the image schema SOURCE_PATH_GOAL, can be combined with other image schemas. The movement into a container (above THING INTO CONTAINER), or the IN schema, could be described as the combination of both SOURCE_PATH_GOAL and CONTAINMENT.

The categorisation problem concerns how to determine which image schema a particular image-schematic concept belongs to. This problem will be addressed in Chapter 3 and Chapter 5.

2.3 Common Image Schemas and Their Definitions

Despite the current lack of a clear-cut image schema repository, the present research
will use of a set of commonly investigated image schemas and will mention, in relation to previous work or the work conducted, a full range of other image-schematic
components. This section will present and describe those relevant image schemas.
This list is by no means exclusive nor exhaustive in regards to the full range of
discussed or possible image schemas.

CONTAINMENT: One of the most studied image schemas. It denotes the relationship between an inside and an outside and the border in between. From a dynamic
  aspect, it also contains image-schematic components such as IN and OUT.
SOURCE_PATH_GOAL: Concerns movement from a source to a goal. It contains
  spatial primitives such as a path and a trajectory.
CYCLE: The returning pattern, such as the daily cycle.
CONTACT: Physical (or sometimes abstract) contact between two objects.
SUPPORT: Denotes a relationship between two objects in which one object offers
  physical (or abstract) support to the other.
LINK: An enforced connection between objects or regions, where transitivity en-
  sures that the linked object reacts to the stimuli of the other object.
VERTICALITY: Relative position such as High/Low and Above/Below are part of
  the image schema, likewise vertical orientation, also dynamical movement UP-
  DOWN is part of the image schema.
SCALING: Deals with how object size ranges from small to large, as well as the
  dynamic transformation of Growing/Shrinking.
NEAR_FAR: The concept of distance. Associated to SCALING as children are believed to learn the concept from how objects grow visually larger when they move
  closer and vice versa.
BLOCKAGE: A complex image schema capturing the understanding that movement can be hindered.
CAUSED_MOVEMENT: A complex image schema in which movement of one object is transferred to another.
SELF_MOVEMENT: A complex image schema in which movement can start without external stimuli. The image schema is tightly connected to the notion of
  agency.
ATTRACTION: The force relationship that ensures that one object is drawn to another.
SELF_MOVEMENT: A complex image schema in which objects initiate movement by themselves. It is also often characterised by irrational movement patterns
  and is thought to be an early stage of identifying animated life.

2.4 Reasoning with Image Schemas

Cognitive support for image schemas comes from how they offer infants conceptual grounds to make predictions about their surroundings (Gibbs and Colston, 1995; Mandler, 2004). Indeed, work in linguistics (e.g. Dodge and Lakoff (2005)) and psychology (e.g. Mandler and Cánovas (2014)) reveals image-schematic involvement in reasoning and language development. In developmental psychology, the image schema demonstrates how key concepts are transferred through analogical reasoning and conceptual metaphors (Kövecses, 2010).

For instance, if the image schema CONTAINMENT has been learned by exposure to everyday events such as 'embraces,' 'entering/exiting' houses, and 'eating,' the understanding that 'objects can be within other objects' can be transferred to other situations. Provided the infant has sufficient knowledge about the involved objects/domain elements, it can use CONTAINMENT to predict that water will remain in a glass when it is poured therein, that people can be inside cars, and so on. Likewise, if an infant has been exposed to enough set dining tables, it might have understood that 'tables SUPPORT plates.' In combination with experiences such as 'laying on the ground' and 'sitting on a swing' the child learns to generalise these experiences under the image schema SUPPORT. This generalisation can consequently be transferred to other situations in which the object relation is similar to that it has already observed and categorised. Thus, through analogical reasoning the infant can infer that 'desks will SUPPORT books.' The corresponding knowledge transfer becomes an essential part of cognition and can, as the cognitive development reaches increasingly more abstract understanding in early adolescence (Piaget, 1952), provide a foundation for abstract thought as well.

One important distinction, made by Lakoff and Núñez (2000), is between 'expected movement' and 'actual movement.' For example, if an infant has learned the image schema of SUPPORT it may still not comprehend that a water surface follows a different set of physical laws than the wooden surface of a dining table. This is believed to be the foundation to how new image-schematic alterations and structures are acquired. While a rubber duck will float on the water surface, a stone will not. The surprise of the unfulfilled expectations allows the child to restructure its expectations for future scenarios.

2.4.1 Image Schemas as Information Skeletons in Conceptual Metaphors

This analogical transfer of information is proposed to be present also as language is developed, in particular where abstract concepts are concerned. In the previous chapter, conceptual metaphor theory was discussed in how metaphors often are based on underlying conceptual structures such as UP is GOOD/DOWN is BAD. Stripping these structures down often results in a skeleton of image schemas (see

Figure 2.2). In the previous examples, VERTICALITY constructs this skeleton. This is demonstrated in how image schemas sometimes constitute the transferred information in conceptual metaphors (Kövecses, 2010). For example, we can 'offer SUPPORT to a friend in need' and '*put in* a good word for someone,' both expressions that offer some evidence. Pauwels (1995) even went so far to claim that any abstract use of the word 'put' requires the understanding of CONTAINMENT. CONTAINMENT is an important image schema in the conceptualisation of mental or emotional states: 'one can *get out of* a depression' and 'people *fall in* love.' Likewise, the VERTICALITY schema is often used to explain the emotional scale between 'happiness/sadness' as well as social status. For instance, consider the expressions 'To *fall* from grace,' 'to be *high* in spirit,' 'to feel *down*,' and '*to climb* the career ladder.'

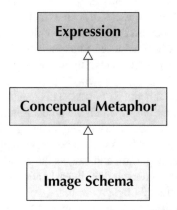

Fig. 2.2: The hierarchy of the conceptual structure in metaphors.

The involved verb/preposition apply the idea of VERTICALITY to abstract domains which follow the common metaphoric pattern that 'up' is good and 'down' is bad. Abstract examples of the PATH-following schema are 'the flow of money,' 'life is a journey' and 'to walk the line.'

These examples of how image schemas are used in language to explain abstract notions are still rooted in the direct expression associated with image schemas. Here, CONTAINMENT is associated with verbs/prepositions, such as in, out, through, enclosed etc., and PATH-following is associated with words such as movement, process, going, to-from etc. (this phenomenon is used in Chapter 8 to automatically identify image schemas in natural language).

This spatiotemporal information transfer can also be found in non-linguistic domains, such as the abstract concepts in the arts and music (e.g. Antović (2009); Antović et al. (2013); Dancygier and Vandelanotte (2017), development of mathematical understanding (e.g. Lakoff and Núñez (2000); Vandervert (2017)), and time conceptualisation (e.g. Boroditsky (2000)). Time is particularly interesting as it often is viewed as a spatial PATH or region on which events are perceived as 'physical' OBJECTS (Lambalgen and Hamm, 2005). For example, expressions such as 'we meet *on* Thursday,' map information from a concrete situation such as 'a book on a table' to the abstract process and time period.

There exists one more possible level of skeletal information abstraction by using image schemas. Namely, how image schemas can be seen as direct 'building blocks' for the conceptualisation of concepts. While some words and concepts cannot (entirely) be described using only image schemas, as other characteristics and object properties might be equally important, some concepts can be. A cup can be described as a container (CONTAINMENT), or a chair as an object providing SUPPORT, building on the idea of affordances. More abstract concepts such as 'Transportation' can also be broken down into image schemas. Transportation being a combination of PATH and either SUPPORT or CONTAINMENT (this use of image schemas is empirically investigated in Chapter 7). This kind of combination is parallel in its constellation, but there are also combinations of image schemas that alter the nature of the image schema. For example, a common conceptualisation of the concept 'marriage' implies a LINKED_PATH (image schema combinations are investigated further in Chapter 5). Here the components of the image schemas are merged rather than sequentially added. This illustrates the Gestalt structure of image schemas, meaning that no component can be removed or added without changing the internal logics of the image schemas (Lakoff and Núñez, 2000).

2.4.2 Combining Image Schemas

It has been demonstrated to be an important aspect of image schemas that they can be combined with one another (Kuhn, 2007; Mandler and Cánovas, 2014; Oakley, 2010; Walton and Worboys, 2009). There are at least three fundamentally different ways this can be done (these will be further discussed and formally approached in Chapter 5). First, the image schemas can *merge* with one another to alter the characteristics of the image schemas involved. For instance, the image schema PATH can easily merge with the image schema LINK, leading to the more complex image-schematic concept LINKED_PATH. As PATH illustrates a movement through space, and LINK illustrates the causal relationship between two (or more) objects, a LINKED_PATH represents joint movement on two paths; e.g. a truck and trailer moving along a highway, or the joint movement of two separate magnets. An example is the conceptualisation of the concept 'marriage,' where two individuals go through life together (Mandler, 2004). Alternatively, marriage may also be conceptualised as CONTAINMENT. This is reflected by metaphors like 'marriage is a prison,' 'marriage is a safe harbour,' and 'open marriage.' Depending on whether one chooses CONTAINMENT or LINKED_PATH as a base for the conceptualisation of marriage, a different vocabulary and different metaphors are supported.

Second, as mentioned, PATH can be combined with SUPPORT (or CONTAINMENT) and result in the concept 'transportation' (Kuhn, 2007). This is a combination that behaves as a *collection* as each image-schematic structure remains conceptually intact.

Finally, image schemas can be *structurally* combined to form more complex image-schematic notions. A metaphorical example is the idiom 'to hit the wall.' In most contexts, this does not mean to physically crash into a wall, but instead implies a mental breakdown often caused by long-term stress. This idiom captures the image schema of BLOCKAGE. It is clear that BLOCKAGE is not an atomic image schema but rather a sequential combination of several ones. Breaking it down, there are two OBJECTs, one SOURCE_PATH_GOAL and at least one time point when the two objects are in CONTACT. Connecting it to the idiom it is possible to see how a physical PATH is mapped to the time and processes that precede the moment of the 'crash.' This line of reasoning is properly dealt with in Chapter 5.

2.4.3 Image Schema Profiles

Taking one step further to discuss how image schemas and their combinations are used in conceptualisations can be demonstrated in how children already early during cognitive development can reason and conceptualise simple events (Sobel and Kirkham, 2006).

Oakley (2010) describes how *Image Schema Profiles* are a collection of image schemas that together describe the conceptualisation of particular events and concepts. For instance, in complex conceptualisations involving many aspects such as 'going to the library,' the scenario can be described using a series of image schemas, in this particular case:

- SOURCE_PATH_GOAL
- CONTAINMENT
- COLLECTION
- PART_WHOLE
- TRANSFER
- ITERATION

Through conceptualisation of events over time, these image schemas go through 'image schema transformations.' These are the dynamic notions of particular sensorimotor experiences that translate into the complex layers of image schemas. For instance, an infant learns that objects SCALE from small to large, and vice versa, as objects move closer/further away. This means that from the perspective of image-schematic transformations the NEAR_FAR image schema has conceptual overlap with the SCALE image schema.

Image schema profiles are the 'event' parallel to how image schemas can be seen as building blocks for concepts. Chapter 5 will be looking at how image schemas also construct the conceptual skeleton for larger scale conceptualisations and more complex image schemas.

2.5 Image Schemas in Language and Conceptualisations

Image schemas were originally introduced as a means to explain linguistic phenomena from the perspective of the embodied mind. This section aims to introduce some of the relevant work performed in the cognitive linguistics of image-schematic structures.

2.5.1 Cross-Lingual Investigations

One of the more common methods to study image schemas is by comparing their manifestation in different languages. As image schemas stem from the body's sensorimotor experiences it should follow that they are language independent. However, as language expression is a socio-cultural product, certain fine-tuning might be required. This is supported by research that shows that the conceptual system underlying image schemas may change in individual languages, but the fundamental conceptual notions vary marginally cross-linguistically (Mandler and Cánovas, 2014). One example is how different degrees of specificity of CONTAINMENT can be expressed in different languages. For instance, Korean differentiates between tight or loose CONTAINMENT, a distinction not present in English (McDonough et al., 2003). Likewise, regarding SOURCE_PATH_GOAL and the linguistic identification of motion information, Papafragou et al. (2006) found that native English speakers are more likely to linguistically encode manner of motion information than Greek speakers. This was generalised to cross-linguistic asymmetries and the authors could differentiate between *Manner languages* (e.g. German, Russian, Chinese) from PATH *languages* (e.g. French, Spanish, Turkish). Since the SOURCE_PATH_GOAL schema is not only spatial but also temporal, time as a concept has frequently been considered as an important aspect. Regarding image-schematic conceptualisation of time, the classic western view is that of a PATH. However, Fuhrman et al. (2011) found that in Chinese a vertical representation of time is preferred over the English horizontal one. Additionally, Núñez and Sweetser (2006) found that the spatial construal of time can vary in the sense of whether the future is depicted as in front of or behind the speaker.

In the experiment by Lakusta and Landau (2005) participants were asked to verbalise visualisations, such as change of possessions necessitating a transaction between agents. The purpose was to identify the linguistic encoding of different specialisations of PATHs in English-speaking children and adults. Their findings showed an asymmetrically higher frequency of PATH_GOALs over SOURCE_PATHs, heavily implying that the SOURCE_PATH_GOAL schema has multiple members of different levels of detail and information.

Also looking at the different components of SOURCE_PATH_GOAL is the work by Watters (1996) who looked at *Tepehua*, an eastern Mexican language, where suffixes and prefixes alter the image-schematic character of verbs. For instance,

by these additions, spatial primitives such as a GOAL would be added to the
SOURCE_PATH_GOAL schema.

2.5.2 Particular Image Schema Investigations

Ekberg (1995) performed a study aiming to identify the different usages of the image
schema VERTICALITY by looking at both English and Swedish expressions. Her
work showed that in language, VERTICALITY and its connecting prepositions are
used in five different scenarios that do not always include the vertical axis. Instead,
VERTICALITY is also used to express things like horizontality (as in 'walking up
the corridor') and goals (as in 'reach up to the counter'). She makes a strong claim
that image schema characteristics pervade the meaning structure even in the most
commonplace grammatical items.

Also investigating the relationship between VERTICALITY and horizontality is
the work by Serra-Borneto (1996). By looking at conceptually perceptual and non-
perceptual occurrences of the words 'liegen' and 'stehen'[8] he could motivate the
idea that image schema theory provides a cognitive explanation for the subtle meaning shifts. Gibbs et al. (1994) also looked at the word 'stand' by focusing on polysemy and found empirical support for the notion that image schemas organise experience and as such organise semantic structure.

A study performed on the concept of 'straight' was done by Cienki (1998). While
'straight' had not been introduced as an image schema in its own right, Cienki
demonstrated by comparison to the VERTICALITY schema how 'straight' could be
detected as a recurrent pattern of action, perception and conceptualisation. In natural language 'straight' is often used when talking about morals and ethics as in
expression such as "give it to me *straight*." It could be argued that straight should be
described as a visual characteristic rather than an image-schematic one (much like
colours are used to explain emotional states 'to see *red*' as a description of anger, 'to
have the *blues*' when feeling sad or 'to be *green* with envy'). However, the 'straight'
is not solely a phenomenon in Indo-European discourse, but can also be seen to have
similar conceptual implications in the domain of ethics in other languages such as
Hungarian and Japanese.

Rhee (2002) looked at the word 'against' to distinguish four processes for semantic change: metaphor, generalisation, subjectification, frame-to-focus variation. His
main argument is that semantic change involves image schemas and their transformation, as although meaning may change during these transformations, the image-
schematic structure does not. The same claim was made by Verspoor (1995). However, this was argued against by Matsumoto (1995), as Japanese does display a
change in image-schematic structures as well.

---

[8] German for 'to lie' and 'to stand.'

2.5.3 Multimodal Image Schemas and Synaesthesia

Wagner et al. (1981) performed an experiment on synaesthesia[9] where they paired perceptual events that share no physical features, e.g. visual drawings and sound sequences. For example, they had children look at dotted lines together with either pulsing sound or consistent sound and found that the image-schematic structure was an important aspect for connecting the different aspects.

Antović (2009) tested the conceptual metaphor theory mentioned in Chapter 1, by empirically investigating the conceptualisation of basic musical relations. Their results indicated that children to a large extent conceptualised music by using metaphors based on image schemas such as VERTICALITY or SCALING to explain for instance pitches. In a second study, Antović et al. (2013) addressed the perceptual basis for developing abstract concepts. The study further supported the preference for visuospatial descriptions for music conceptualisations.

2.6 Chapter Conclusion

This chapter gave a thorough introduction to the theory of image schemas. The theory originates from cognitive linguistics as a means to explain the extent of spatial language in conceptual metaphors and abstract language. Here image schemas were discussed as the conceptual building blocks generalised from sensorimotor experiences in early infancy. This means that they provide a theoretical stepping stone between embodied experiences and mental representations. In this role, they provide an information skeleton that can be used to structure conceptual information and be used for information transfer in analogical reasoning and conceptual blending.

Due to the interdisciplinary research topic, image schemas are hard to define and two major problems exist concerning building a repository of image schemas: the structure problem, which deals with identifying the borders for what conceptual structures should be considered image-schematic and how they can be organised; and the categorisation problem, which deals with the difficulty to determine which image-schematic structure belongs to which image schema. This is the major topic for the upcoming Chapter 3, in which it is suggested that image schemas be ordered in a hierarchy based on family resemblance.

Additionally, the problem of how image schemas can be combined with one another to generate image schema profiles, and the underlying conceptualisation of concepts and events was discussed. This is the primary topic for Chapter 5 and the ideas that structure Chapter 7.

In the following chapters, the work on image schemas will be transposed into a formal domain with the intention of using the conceptual information present in

---

[9] Synaesthesia is the perceptual phenomenon in which one sensory stimulus elicits involuntary reactions in another sensory or cognitive pathway.

image schemas as a cognitive inspiration for natural language understanding and concept invention in artificial intelligence.

References

M. Antović. Musical Metaphors in Serbian and Romani Children: An Empirical Study. *Metaphor and Symbol*, 24(3):184–202, 2009.

M. Antović, A. Bennett, and M. Turner. Running in circles or moving along lines: Conceptualization of musical elements in sighted and blind children. *Musicae Scientiae*, 17(2):229–245, 2013.

B. Bennett and C. Cialone. Corpus Guided Sense Cluster Analysis: a methodology for ontology development (with examples from the spatial domain). In P. Garbacz and O. Kutz, editors, *8th International Conference on Formal Ontology in Information Systems (FOIS)*, volume 267 of *Frontiers in Artificial Intelligence and Applications*, pages 213–226. IOS Press, 2014.

L. Boroditsky. Metaphoric structuring: Understanding time through spatial metaphors. *Cognition*, 75(1):1–28, 2000.

A. Cienki. STRAIGHT : An Image Schema and its metaphorical extensions. (9): 107–149, 1998.

B. Dancygier and L. Vandelanotte. Image-schematic scaffolding in textual and visual artefacts. *Journal of Pragmatics*, 122:91–106, 2017.

E. Dodge and G. Lakoff. Image schemas: From linguistic analysis to neural grounding. In B. Hampe and J. E. Grady, editors, *From perception to meaning: Image schemas in cognitive linguistics*, pages 57–91. Mouton de Gruyter, Berlin, New York, 2005.

L. Ekberg. Lexical and Syntactical Constructions and the Construction of Meaning: Proceedings of the bi-annual ICLA meeting in Albuquerque, July 1995. pages 69–88, Amsterdam, 1995. John Benjamins Publishing Company.

J. Feldman and S. Narayanan. Embodied meaning in a neural theory of language. *Brain and Language*, 89(2):385–392, 2004.

M. A. F. Fernández. Cognitive meaning: Review of the concepts of imagination, image schema and mental image and consequences on the conceptualization of emotions. In *Complexity Applications in Language and Communication Sciences*, pages 313–323. Springer, 2019.

A. U. Frank and M. Raubal. Formal specification of image schemata – a step towards interoperability in geographic information systems. *Spatial Cognition and Computation*, 1(1):67–101, 1999.

O. Fuhrman, K. McCormick, E. Chen, H. Jiang, D. Shu, S. Mao, and L. Boroditsky. How linguistic and cultural forces shape conceptions of time: English and Mandarin time in 3D. *Cognitive science*, 35(7):1305–1328, 2011.

A. Gangemi and V. Presutti. Ontology design patterns. In *Handbook on ontologies*, pages 221–243. Springer, 2009.

R. W. Gibbs and H. L. Colston. The cognitive psychological reality of image schemas and their transformation. *Cognitive Linguistics*, 6:347–378, 1995.

R. W. Gibbs, D. A. Beitel, M. Harrington, and P. E. Sanders. Taking a Stand on the Meanings of Stand: Bodily Experience as Motivation for Polysemy. *Journal of Semantics*, 11(4):231–251, 1994.

B. Hampe. Image schemas in cognitive linguistics: Introduction. In B. Hampe and J. E. Grady, editors, *From perception to meaning: Image schemas in cognitive linguistics*, pages 1–14. Walter de Gruyter, 2005.

B. Hampe and J. E. Grady. *From perception to meaning: Image schemas in cognitive linguistics*, volume 29 of *Cognitive Linguistics Research*. Walter de Gruyter, Berlin, 2005.

M. Johnson. *The Body in the Mind: The Bodily Basis of Meaning, Imagination, and Reason*. University of Chicago Press, 1987.

I. Kant. *Critique of Pure Reason*. Oeuvre. Cambridge University Press, 1781.

K. Koffka. *Principles of gestalt psychology*. International library of psychology, philosophy, and scientific method. Harcourt, Brace and Company, 1935.

Z. Kövecses. *Metaphor: A Practical Introduction*. Oxford University Press, New York, USA, 2010.

W. Kresse and D. M. Danko. *Springer handbook of geographic information*. Springer Science & Business Media, 2012.

W. Kuhn. An Image-Schematic Account of Spatial Categories. In S. Winter, M. Duckham, L. Kulik, and B. Kuipers, editors, *Spatial Information Theory*, volume 4736 of *Lecture Notes in Computer Science*, pages 152–168. Springer, 2007.

G. Lakoff. *Women, Fire, and Dangerous Things. What Categories Reveal about the Mind*. University of Chicago Press, 1987.

G. Lakoff and R. Núñez. *Where Mathematics Comes From: How the Embodied Mind Brings Mathematics into Being*. Basic Books, New York, 2000.

L. Lakusta and B. Landau. Starting at the end: The importance of goals in spatial language. *Cognition*, 96(1):1–33, 2005.

M. V. Lambalgen and F. Hamm. *The Proper Treatment of Events*. Explorations in Semantics. Wiley, 2005.

G. Ligozat. *Qualitative Spatial and Temporal Reasoning*. Wiley, 2011.

J. M. Mandler. How to build a baby: II. Conceptual primitives. *Psychological review*, 99(4):587–604, 1992.

J. M. Mandler. *The Foundations of Mind: Origins of Conceptual Thought: Origins of Conceptual Though*. Oxford University Press, New York, 2004.

J. M. Mandler and C. P. Cánovas. On defining image schemas. *Language and Cognition*, 6(4):510–532, May 2014.

Y. Matsumoto. Lexical and Syntactical Constructions and the Construction of Meaning: Proceedings of the bi-annual ICLA meeting in Albuquerque, July 1995. pages 287–307, Amsterdam, 1995. John Benjamins Publishing Company.

L. McDonough, S. Choi, and J. M. Mandler. Understanding spatial relations: Flexible infants, lexical adults. *Cognitive Psychology*, 46(3):229–259, 5 2003.

R. E. Núñez and E. Sweetser. With the future behind them: Convergent evidence from Aymara language and gesture in the crosslinguistic comparison of spatial construals of time. *Cognitive science*, 30(3):401–450, 2006.

T. Oakley. Image schema. In D. Geeraerts and H. Cuyckens, editors, *The Oxford Handbook of Cognitive Linguistics*, pages 214–235. Oxford University Press, Oxford, 2010.

A. Papafragou, C. Massey, and L. Gleitman. When English proposes what Greek presupposes: The cross-linguistic encoding of motion events. *Cognition*, 98(3): B75–B87, 2006.

P. Pauwels. Levels of metaphorization: The case of put. In L. Goossens, editor, *By Word of Mouth: Metaphor, metonymy and linguistic action in a cognitive perspective*, pages 125–158. John Benjamins Publishing Company, Amsterdam, 1995.

J. Piaget. *The origins of intelligence in children*. NY: International University Press, New York, 1952. Translated by Margaret Cook.

T. Regier. *The Human Semantic Potential: Spatial Language and Constrained Connectionism*. MIT Press, 1996.

S. Rhee. Semantic Changes of English Preposition against A Grammaticalization Perspective. *Language Research*, 38(2):563–583, 2002.

T. Rohrer. Image schemata in the brain. In B. Hampe and J. E. Grady, editors, *From perception to meaning: Image schemas in cognitive linguistics*, volume 29 of *Cognitive Linguistics Research*, pages 165–196. Walter de Gruyter, 2005.

F. Santibáñez. The object image-schema and other dependent schemas. *Atlantis*, 24 (2):183–201, 2002.

C. Serra-Borneto. *Cognitive linguistics in the Redwoods: The expansion of a new paradigm in linguistics*, chapter 'Liegen' and 'stehen' in German: a study in horizontality and verticality, pages 459–505. Cognitive Linguistics Research. Mouton de Gruyter, Berlin, 1996.

L. Shapiro. *Embodied Cognition*. New problems of philosophy. Routledge, London and New York, 2011.

D. Sobel and N. Kirkham. Blickets and babies: the development of causal reasoning in toddlers and infants. *Developmental Psychology*, 42(6):1103–1115, 2006.

R. St. Amant, C. T. Morrison, Y.-H. Chang, P. R. Cohen, and C. Beal. An image schema language. In *International Conference on Cognitive Modeling (ICCM)*, pages 292–297, 2006.

L. Talmy. How language structures space. In *Spatial orientation*, pages 225–282. Springer, 1983.

L. Talmy. Force dynamics in language and cognition. *Cognitive science*, 12(1): 49–100, 1988.

L. Talmy. *Toward a cognitive semantics*, volume 2. MIT press, Cambridge, UK, 2000.

L. Talmy. The fundamental system of spatial schemas in language. In B. Hampe and J. E. Grady, editors, *From perception to meaning: Image schemas in cognitive linguistics*, volume 29 of *Cognitive Linguistics Research*, pages 199–234. Walter de Gruyter, 2005.

M.-Y. Tseng. Exploring image schemas as a critical concept: Toward a critical-cognitive linguistic account of image-schematic interactions. *Journal of literary semantics*, 36:135–157, 2007.

L. Vandervert. The Origin of Mathematics and Number Sense in the Cerebellum: with Implications for Finger Counting and Dyscalculia. *Cerebellum & Ataxias*, 4 (12), 2017.

M. Verspoor. Lexical and Syntactical Constructions and the Construction of Meaning: Proceedings of the bi-annual ICLA meeting in Albuquerque, July 1995. pages 433–449, Amsterdam, 1995. John Benjamins Publishing Company.

S. Wagner, E. Winner, D. Cicchetti, and H. Gardner. "Metaphorical" Mapping in Human Infants. *Child Development*, 52(2):728–731, 1981.

L. Walton and M. Worboys. An algebraic approach to image schemas for geographic space. In *Proceedings of the 9th International Conference on Spatial Information Theory (COSIT)*, pages 357–370, France, 2009.

J. K. Watters. *Cognitive linguistics in the Redwoods: The expansion of a new paradigm in linguistics*, chapter Frames and the semantics of applicatives in Tepehua, pages 971–996. Cognitive Linguistics Research. Mouton de Gruyter, Berlin, 1996.

A. Wierzbicka. *Semantics: Primes and Universals*. Oxford University Press, UK, 1996.

Part II
Formal Framework for Image Schemas

Chapter 3
Formal Structure: Image Schemas as Families of Theories

Abstract The previous chapters introduced some core problems for computational concept invention as well as for the theory of image schemas. Here the structure problem and the categorisation problem were mentioned. The problems capture the problems of determining which conceptual structures are image-schematic respectively which structures belong to which image schema. This chapter addresses these problems by introducing a formal method to structure image-schematic notions. The categorisation problem is approached by allowing notions of similar structure to be part of an image-schematic family that groups together similar concepts rather than having strict definitions of a particular image schema. Simultaneously, the structure problem is approached by ordering this family into a hierarchy where simpler concepts are made increasingly complex through the addition of conceptual and spatial primitives. These methods solve, to some degree, the issues regarding defining and classifying image-schematic notions for artificial intelligence research while simultaneously providing a formal method for how to structure them. As a proof of concept two image schema families are introduced: the Two-Object family and the PATH family. The first deals with spatial relationships between two objects and the latter with dynamic movement of one object. Formally these families will be represented using theory graphs. The chapter includes:

- The Two-Object Family
- Linguistic and psychological motivation behind SOURCE_PATH_GOAL
- The PATH Family
- Formal aspects of image schema families

3.1 Family Connections

In Chapter 2 two problems for image schema research were highlighted: The categorisation problem and the structure problem. These problems arise as it is (seemingly) clear that one particular image schema is fine-tuned during cognitive develop-

© Springer Nature Switzerland AG 2020

M. M. Hedblom, *Image Schemas and Concept Invention*, Cognitive Technologies,
https://doi.org/10.1007/978-3-030-47329-7_3

ment (Rohrer, 2005), and from an empirical point of view appear in many different forms later on (Bennett and Cialone, 2014; Gromann and Hedblom, 2016).

These problems might remain in research fields such as psychology and linguistics until a better understanding of the human mind has been acquired. However, in order to be able to utilise image schemas in formal approaches to concept invention, these problems needr to be addressed. Whether or not the formal modelling of these issues becomes entirely cognitively accurate is for now deemed less important than a functional solution. Despite the utilised practical approach to image schemas where applicability has higher priority than cognitive accuracy, the suggested approach is motivated and inspired by findings in developmental psychology and cognitive linguistics.

The main claim in this chapter is that image schemas should be sorted based on resemblance into members of tightly connected image schema families. In particular, each of the image schemas covers a particular conceptual-cognitive scenario within the scope of the schema family. An image schema family may be formally represented as a set (i.e. a *family*) of interlinked theories. This means that the structure problem is approached by clustering similar image-schematic structures together, disregarding any potential borders. Likewise, the categorisation problem is approached by hierarchically ordering the image-schematic structures based on their internal complexity. An essential part of this method of structuring is that for each level in the family hierarchy additional image-schematic elements from either the same or other image schemas are added. This accounts also for the conceptual overlap between different image schema concepts, adding additional substance on how to address the categorisation problem while simultaneously providing an important point that the literature on image schemas previously has only touched upon.

As proof of concept, two families of image schemas will be introduced. First, the 'Two-Object' family which captures (some of)[1] the static relationships between two objects. The Two-Object family encompasses the image schemas CONTACT, SUPPORT and LINK. This is done by inheriting certain conceptual properties from the other image schemas VERTICALITY and ATTRACTION. It will be demonstrated why this is of importance later in the chapter.

The second family is the 'PATH' family, which captures (some of) the dynamic members of the SOURCE_PATH_GOAL image schema concerning the movement of an object. The PATH family ranges from the spatial primitive of basic movement, to more complex image schema notions such as SOURCE_PATH and PATH_GOAL. Higher levels of the family include MOVEMENT_IN_LOOPS, in which movement-related aspects of the image schema CYCLE are inherited, and in which the start and end in the SOURCE_PATH_GOAL schema are interpreted to be identical.

Overlapping image schemas that are combinations of the PATH family and another image schema family are, for example, BLOCKAGE, LINKED_PATH and REVOLVING_MOVEMENT. While the chapter touches on the topic of image schema combinations, this will be properly discussed in the upcoming Chapter 5.

---

[1] It is likely that there exist relationships that are not included here.

The selection of these two families captures the essence of image schemas being both spatial and temporal object relations and as such provide a good foundation to build a proof of concept for further research.

3.2 The Two-Object Family

Consistently, image schemas have been defined as spatiotemporal relationships between objects and their environment. This means that for any formal representation of image schemas, an important aspect is to formally model relationships between objects. In a natural scenario several objects may play a role, however, at this stage it is superfluous to include more than two objects. Additionally, the formal representation of relationships between two objects can easily be extended to include additional objects should it be deemed necessary in order to model a particular scenario. With this in mind, the family is for the time being restricted to relationships existing between two objects. The image-schematic relationships between two objects that will be considered are CONTACT, SUPPORT and LINK. As mentioned, the family graphs are ordered by their internal complexity based on the image-schematic components introduced by Mandler and Cánovas (2014): *Spatial Primitives, Image Schemas* and *Conceptual Integrations* (see Section 2.2.1 for details). In order to successfully construct the Two-Object family, components from additional image schemas will need to be 'borrowed.' Therefore, the section starts by introducing two other image schemas, namely VERTICALITY and ATTRACTION.

3.2.1 Components from VERTICALITY *and* ATTRACTION

While both VERTICALITY and ATTRACTION are image schemas that belong to their own families, it is possible to isolate their components by identifying some core characteristics. Below, each image schema will be motivated and the relevant components for the Two-Object family will be extracted.

VERTICALITY:

VERTICALITY is believed to be one of the earliest image schemas to be learned based on the human body's vertical axis and the perceived effect gravity has on objects (Johnson, 1987). In its static form, VERTICALITY represents orientation and relational notions such as above and below. It is common in natural language and often features as the backbone of conceptual metaphors, for instance, in the expressions 'to stand on higher ground' and 'to feel down.' From a dynamic perspective, VERTICALITY encompasses vertical movement in terms of UP-DOWN. In language, metaphoric expressions such as 'the rise to power' and 'falling from grace' encompass, like the static examples, the conceptual metaphors that UP is GOOD/DOWN is BAD while building on the conceptual scaffolding of VERTICALITY (Kövecses, 2010).

Image schemas come in different characters (orientational, topological and force-dynamical). VERTICALITY encompasses vertical orientation and it can be argued that it plays a central role in many other image schemas. Later it will be illustrated how VERTICALITY is involved in distinguishing members of the Two-Object family, such as CONTACT and SUPPORT. For the current version of the Two-Object family, the only component used from VERTICALITY is the notion of being 'above.'

ATTRACTION:

Just like with VERTICALITY, an image schema such as ATTRACTION which encompasses conceptual aspects of force (or using Mandler's (2010) words "the feeling of umph") is experienced and conceptualised in the first six months of a child's life. Objects fall to the ground, not because of VERTICALITY in itself, but because of the 'ATTRACTION objects have to the ground.'[2] Metaphorically speaking, ATTRACTION can be found in language expressions such 'I'm drawn to you' or 'they gravitated towards each other straight away.' ATTRACTION is part of the force group of image schemas (Johnson, 1987) and while it is more complicated than simple 'force towards/from,' it can be ascertained that for the purpose of representing simple force relations, ATTRACTION provides the required primitives. For the current purpose, the only conceptual primitive borrowed from the ATTRACTION image schema will be 'force' as in: x puts force on y.

Below, conceptual primitives of VERTICALITY and ATTRACTION will be included in other image schemas to describe how increasingly complex concepts come about.

3.2.2 The Two-Object Family: CONTACT, SUPPORT and LINK

The family hierarchy builds on the idea that for each advancing member of the family, additional image-schematic components are added. Working on object relations, this means that at the top of the graph is OBJECT, see Figure 3.1. Note here that OBJECT is represented twice to account for the two merging image-schematic families associated with CONTACT/SUPPORT and the one associated with LINK. While OBJECT in itself is not part of a Two-Object family, it is a prerequisite to being able to build object relations between more than one object. Here it is important to note that the branching from each and every member of the graph is in no means intended to be exclusive and exhaustive. The branching from OBJECT to CONTACT could also contain the branching towards multiple objects in general, in which there exist no

---

[2] Children naturally do not understand gravity, yet they learn to predict that objects are 'forced' downwards.

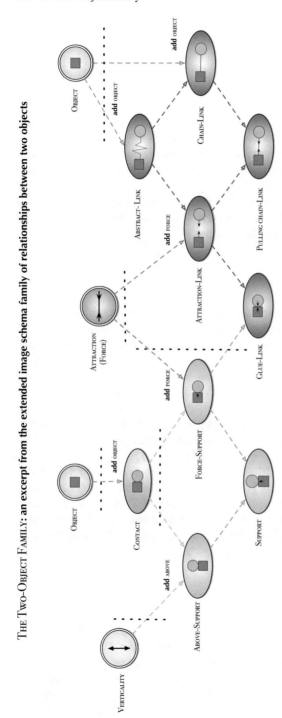

Fig. 3.1: How the Two-Object family morphs from CONTACT to SUPPORT and LINK through the addition of image-schematic components and integration of VERTICALITY (above) and ATTRACTION (force).

CONTACT relations. This noted, the graph still demonstrates important aspects of relationships between two objects.

CONTACT:

CONTACT is one of the more primitive image schemas involving two objects. In its most general form it represents the object relation in which two (or more) objects are physically touching each other. Figure 3.1 illustrates how image schemas can be conceptually extended by adding specifications from the above-mentioned VERTICALITY and ATTRACTION.

After CONTACT has been constructed by ensuring contact between two objects, the graph can branch in different directions. One of the most obvious, and presented here, is how CONTACT can advance into SUPPORT.

SUPPORT:

It is unlikely that infants understand the forces behind an image schema like SUPPORT. Therefore, in many scenarios it might be sufficient to speak of SUPPORT in terms of CONTACT with 'above' orientation. By merging the image schema CONTACT with the static form of VERTICALITY (as in 'above') you get an above-SUPPORT image schema. For instance, in sentences such as 'the book is on the table' and even the more abstract support 'a shoulder to cry on,' what is demonstrated is the orientational relation in which there is CONTACT and 'above'-ness.

If instead of VERTICALITY, force is added to CONTACT, force-SUPPORT can be distinguished. Here the important aspect is that the supporting object offers physical support, which does not have to be vertical. For instance, a plank that 'leans against a wall' also captures a form of SUPPORT. Abstract expressions such as 'offering support to a friend in need' require some abstract form of force, but not really any VERTICALITY. The most accurate and traditional form of SUPPORT is constructed when both above-SUPPORT and force-SUPPORT are combined and a CONTACT relation is built that has both the traditional 'above'-ness as well as offering the 'physical force' support.

LINK:

The idea that addition of spatial primitives, or image-schematic components, further distinguishes the image schemas can also be demonstrated in how LINK can be formally constructed to be a small family of different levels of LINKage. After branching out from, arguably the most generic form of LINK, namely abstract-LINK, the image schema becomes more specific with additions from the notion of force as seen above with how CONTACT turns into force-SUPPORT, or it can go through a third object, a sort of 'chain,' generating a chain-LINK.

When LINK inherits properties from ATTRACTION another abstract LINK develops in which there is no physical CONTACT but instead simply ATTRACTION. It can be described simply using an abstract connection, such as in 'magnetism' (pushing the relationship closer to the conceptualisation of the image schema ATTRACTION) or even in a concept such as 'agreement,' but it can also be described using a 'PATH' that connects the two objects. A PATH is in itself not an OBJECT, but a spatial primitive found in the SOURCE_PATH_GOAL schema capturing the abstract road that connects the SOURCE with the GOAL (Lakoff and Núñez, 2000).

Just like the more complete version of SUPPORT, a more complex LINK can be created by combing attraction-LINK with chain-LINK into a concept in which the chain pulls on the connected objects.

Figure 3.1 also demonstrates how two families can overlap. For glue-LINK, attraction-LINK is merged with the properties of the force-SUPPORT to generate a LINK that behaves like 'glue.' For example, the expression 'to be stuck together' demonstrates an abstract form of (involuntary) LINKage.[3]

In Chapter 4, this family will be formalised by introducing a logic language with which image schemas can be formally represented. Below, the SOURCE_PATH_GOAL image schema is properly introduced by restructuring it into a PATH-following family.

3.3 The PATH Family

The dynamic aspects of image schemas are more complex to model than the static aspects. In order to address this, the build-up to motivate a PATH family will go into more depth on both linguistic and psychological research to motivate its members.

3.3.1 From SOURCE_PATH_GOAL to a PATH Family

3.3.1.1 The Classic View of SOURCE_PATH_GOAL

From the cognitive linguistics point of view, Lakoff and Núñez (2000) present a well worked out perspective of the SOURCE_PATH_GOAL schema, see Figure 3.2. Their work follows linguistic convention (Talmy, 2005) where the moving, active object is called the 'trajector' and the goal, or the end destination, is called the 'landmark.' In SOURCE_PATH_GOAL, both a direction and a 'purpose' are implied to take part in the image schema, which changes the conceptual nature of the movement. One of the important aspects is what Lakoff and Núñez (2000) call 'elements,' or roles, which alter the image schema character, listed in Table 3.1. One of the most important points is the clear distinction between end location and goal, as they distin-

---

[3] The author acknowledges that additional LINKs may exist that were not here considered.

guish between 'path,' the actual trajectory of a movement, and 'route,' the expected movement. This means that in the classic view of SOURCE_PATH_GOAL there is a distinction between END_PATH and GOAL respectively START_PATH and SOURCE. These components are another example of how image schemas are constellations of simpler conceptual blocks that can be added to alter the characteristics of the image schemas.

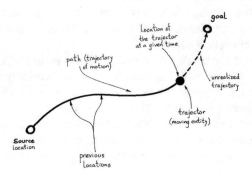

Fig. 3.2: The SOURCE_PATH_GOAL schema as illustrated by Lakoff and Núñez (2000).

Table 3.1: Elements of SOURCE_PATH_GOAL according to Lakoff and Núñez (2000).

Element	Description
trajector	The object
source	The initial location
goal	The intended end location
route	A pre-realised route from source to goal
path	The trajectory of motion
position	The position of the trajector at a given time
direction	The direction of the trajector at a given time
end location	End location, may not correspond to the goal location

3.3.1.2 Cognitive Build-up to SOURCE_PATH_GOAL

By looking at SOURCE_PATH_GOAL from the developmental psychology direction it is possible to distinguish the different stages of how the conceptualisation of the image schema is learned.

From a neurological perspective, the processing of objects in motion has higher priority than the processing of static objects. In most scenarios, this follows as an obvious consequence for our immediate well-being, in other words, to avoid dangerous situations or to interact with potential mates and peers, etc. Thus, it follows that the image schemas concerning the understanding of movement are some of the first to be learned in early infancy (Rohrer, 2005). As presented above the SOURCE_PATH_GOAL image schema implies more than solely movement of objects, as also Lakoff and Núñez (2000) speak of different elements of the image schema. In order to understand how SOURCE_PATH_GOAL is fine-tuned and in 'more completion' internally structured, experiments with children have provided some insights on how the different members of a PATH family may develop.

Mandler (2004) and Mandler and Cánovas (2014) study the SOURCE_PATH_GOAL schema from a developmental psychological direction. It is clear that already at an early age children pay more attention to moving objects than resting objects. Trivial as it may seem, this requires children to detect the spatial primitive OBJECT (or THING) and the temporal schema MOVEMENT_OF_OBJECT. OBJECT is understood here in a wide sense that includes not only objects of solid materials, but entities like waves on a pond and shadows. Additionally, Mandler and Cánovas (2014) discuss MOVE as a spatial primitive of its own. However, as both MOVE and OBJECT are primitives present in all[4] kinds of movement, these two primitives are consistently implied.

The first member of a PATH family is the joint relation between MOVE and OBJECT, namely MOVEMENT_OF_OBJECT. It is here to be considered as a temporally dependent image schema since movement by necessity involves a temporal dimension. It is not perceived as a full-fledged 'conceptual primitive,' as it always involves at least one spatial primitive , i.e. an object that moves. Another important observation is that children tend to remember movement PATHs better than objects themselves. This follows the reasoning by Lakoff and Núñez (2000), further indicating that a PATH[5] is a spatial primitive, a conceptual primitive disjoint from both MOVE and from OBJECT.

Keeping things simple, Mandler and Cánovas (2014) point out that, although difficult to conceptualise for adults, it is possible for PATHs to be non-continuous and there is no need for a goal-directed trajectory. In short, the PATH schema could be described as random movement such as in Brownian motion. As image schemas stretch over all senses, a non-visual analogy would be the difference between a sequence of arbitrary noises and a melody and/or a musical scale. The first demonstrates random movement, whereas the latter follows a predictable trajectory.

In addition to these two basic spatial primitives: OBJECT and MOVE, and as the child becomes more and more familiar with PATH-following, image schemas that contain more spatial information are learned. This means that in more advanced stages, image schemas may include beyond MOVEMENT_OF_OBJECT and the spa-

---

[4] There might be movement scenarios in which MOVE and/or OBJECT are not present, but for the current purposes these scenarios will be omitted.

[5] This spatial primitive PATH is not to be confused with the collective name for the image schema family PATH-following.

tial PATH itself also the spatial primitive END_PATH, and later also a START_PATH (Mandler and Cánovas, 2014). Already at five months, infants can distinguish PATH-following that has an END_PATH (in the PATH family introduced as the image schema PATH_GOAL) from the initial PATH, while the START_PATH is less interesting until the end of the first year of life. This is further supported by linguistic analyses in which an END_PATH is initially more interesting than a START_PATH (Johanson and Papafragou, 2014).

Table 3.2 summarises the spatial primitives that may be involved in image schemas belonging to the PATH-following family. While the content is based on the research of Mandler and Cánovas (2014) minor alterations have been made to better match the terminology in Table 3.1.

Table 3.2: Spatial primitives of the PATH-following family according to Mandler and Cánovas (2014).

Spatial primitive	Description
OBJECT	An object
MOVE	Indication of movement
PATH	The path the object moves along
START_PATH	The initial location
END_PATH	The final location

The distinction, made by Lakoff and Núñez, between the *expected* movement and the *actual* movement is primarily interesting for a description of how image schemas relate to actual events and how new image schemas are learned. Consider, for example, a situation where a child observes the movement of a billiard ball and is surprised that the ball stops because it is blocked by another billiard ball (formally explored by Kutz et al. (2017)). In this case, a given instance of the MOVE-MENT_ALONG_PATH schema formed the expectations of the child, which were disappointed by the actual physical movement, because the expected END_PATH (the goal) does not correspond to the actual END_PATH (end location). Given a repeated exposure to similar events, the child may develop the new image schema, here BLOCKAGE. After learning BLOCKAGE, the child will no longer be surprised by blocked movement since the expected END_PATH (the goal) will correspond to the actual END_PATH (end location)[6]. While the terminological distinction between *expected trajectory* and *actual trajectory* is useful, these do not necessarily need to constitute two different spatial primitives. Indeed, spatial primitives are parts of image schemas and, thus, always parts of conceptualisations, and not parts of actual events.

While the notions of PATH-following presented by Lakoff and Núñez (2000) and Mandler and Cánovas (2014) coincide widely, there are differences in terminology and definitions. In order to adhere to consistent terminology, the present research

---

[6] The stages found in BLOCKAGE are formally approached in Chapter 5

primarily follows the terminology introduced by the latter (Mandler and Cánovas, 2014).

In language, these patterns can be similarly observed, strengthening the hypothesis that image schemas are not isolated notions, but should be seen as interconnected families of theories or concepts. The next section aims to demonstrate this phenomenon.

3.3.2 Linguistic Support for PATH-following

This section considers a few examples of concepts which involve members of the PATH-following family, for an overview see Table 3.3.

The most straightforward examples of concepts that involve PATH-following are concepts that are about the spatial relationship of movement between different points. Prepositions such as *from, to, across* and *through* all indicate a kind of PATH-following[7]. This also includes key verbs that describe movement, e.g. *coming* and *going*. Another example, here for the image schema SOURCE_PATH_GOAL, is 'going from Berlin to Prague.' Note that many cases do not provide information about START_PATH and END_PATH of a movement; e.g. 'leaving Berlin' and 'travelling to Berlin' are examples of the image schemas SOURCE_PATH and PATH_GOAL, respectively. 'Meandering' is an example of a concept that realises MOVEMENT_ALONG_PATH, which involves a PATH but no START_PATH or END_PATH. In contrast, no discernible PATH is involved in 'roaming the city,' which is an example of MOVEMENT_OF_OBJECT. These examples illustrate that image schemas may be ordered hierarchically with respect to their content: SOURCE_PATH_GOAL contains more spatial primitives and more information than, for example, MOVEMENT_ALONG_PATH, which is the root of the PATH-following family, and MOVEMENT_ALONG_PATH is more specific than MOVEMENT_OF_OBJECT. Figure 3.3 depicts the members and their connections involved in the PATH family.

Beyond concepts that involve movement, PATH-following plays an important role in many abstract concepts and conceptual metaphors. For instance, the concept of 'going for a joy ride' realises the image schema SOURCE_PATH, since it has a START_PATH and a PATH but no END_PATH. Similarly, the expression 'running for president' describes the process of trying to get elected as president metaphorically as a PATH_GOAL. In this metaphor the PATH consists of the various stages of the process (e.g. announcing a candidacy and being nominated by a party) with the inauguration as END_PATH.

Another classic conceptual metaphor 'life is a journey,' studied by Ahrens and Say (1999), makes an analogical mapping between the passing of time in life, and the passing of spatial regions on a journey. This metaphor gains information

---

[7] Some prepositions include other image schemas at the same time. E.g. 'through' involves apart from PATH also some notion of CONTAINMENT. See Chapter 5 for more on image-schematic combinations and overlaps.

PATH: **Selected image schemas of movement along paths and in loops**

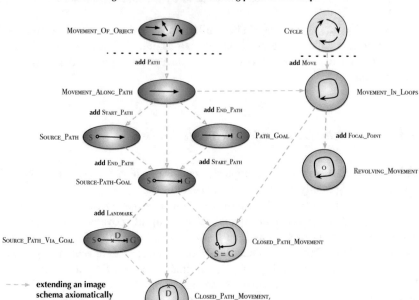

Fig. 3.3: Selected image schemas of path and cyclic movement as a graph. The coloured arrows described as "extending an image schema axiomatically" respectively "extending by new spatial primitives and axioms," illustrate by which means the PATH family is formally extended. This will be demonstrated in the upcoming chapter.

from the spatial primitives connected to the image schema SOURCE_PATH_GOAL. Here, the most important spatial primitives are START_PATH and END_PATH. In this metaphor, these concepts are mapped to the moments of birth and death, as well as the PATH itself, illustrating how 'life goes on' in a successive motion without 'temporal' branching.

A different perspective on life and death is expressed in the metaphorical expression 'the circle of life.' It implies that life leads to death, but as a cycle movement also that death gives rise to life, corresponding to the image schema MOVEMENT_IN_LOOPS. This image schema can be considered as a version of PATH-following, in which START_PATH and END_PATH coincide at the same 'location.'

In the next section, this linguistic reasoning will be ontologically represented as a family of movement image schemas.

Table 3.3: Summary of the mentioned expressions and their level in the PATH-following hierarchy.

	Expression	Level in hierarchy
Concrete:	Roaming the city	MOVEMENT_OF_OBJECT
	Meandering	MOVEMENT_ALONG_PATH
	Leaving Berlin	SOURCE_PATH
	Travelling to Berlin	PATH_GOAL
	Going from Prague to Berlin	SOURCE_PATH_GOAL
Abstract:	Going for a joy ride	SOURCE_PATH
	Running for president	PATH_GOAL
	Life is a journey	SOURCE_PATH_GOAL
	The circle of life	MOVEMENT_IN_LOOPS

3.3.3 From MOVEMENT_OF_OBJECT to CYCLE: The PATH Family

Based on the support presented in the previous sections, Figure 3.3 contains some of the first basic stages of the image schema family PATH-following. It ranges from Mandler's (2004) general definition presented above, of object movement in any trajectory, to increasingly more complex constructions. Below is a breakdown of some of the members.

The image schema family is organised primarily via adding new spatial primitives to the participating image schemas and/or by refining an image schema's properties (In Chapter 4, this will be done through extending the axiomatisation). In general, different sets of criteria may be used, depending, for example, on the context of usage, thereby putting particular image schemas (say, REVOLVE_AROUND) into a variety of families and thereby solving the categorisation problems as many image-schematic notions can be part of several families. Apart from a selection of spatial primitives, other dimensions might be deemed relevant for defining a particular family, such as their role in the developmental process.

MOVEMENT_OF_OBJECT:

The first level of a PATH ontology is MOVEMENT_OF_OBJECT. This is the instance of PATH-following that only contains the spatial primitives OBJECT and MOVE.

MOVEMENT_ALONG_PATH:

The second step in the theory graph in Figure 3.3 is MOVEMENT_ALONG_PATH. This member branches out from MOVEMENT_OF_OBJECT by adding the spatial primitive PATH, meaning that the conceptual difference is that the OBJECT follows a defined PATH.

In consequence, it is possible to further describe the relationship between the PATH and the OBJECT, as the OBJECT needs to pass through all the locations of the path in (a temporal) order.

SOURCE_PATH and PATH_GOAL:

SOURCE_PATH is the result of adding the spatial primitive START_PATH to MOVE-MENT_ALONG_PATH. The START_PATH is the first location on the PATH. What distinguishes SOURCE_PATH from other movements is that there is a distinct starting point in the location START_PATH.

Analogously PATH_GOAL can be defined but with and END_PATH instead of a START_PATH.

SOURCE_PATH_GOAL and CLOSED_PATH_MOVEMENT:

In the cognitive linguistic literature the SOURCE_PATH_GOAL schema is described as the classic instance of movement (Johnson, 1987; Lakoff and Núñez, 2000). In the PATH family, this member can be constructed by taking the union of the SOURCE_PATH and the PATH_GOAL schemas. This is analogous to the behaviour demonstrated in Section 3.2, where SUPPORT was described as the union of the force-SUPPORT and the attraction-SUPPORT.

CLOSED_PATH_MOVEMENT:

The SOURCE_PATH_GOAL image schema may be further specialised by equalising (the location of) the START_PATH and the END_PATH. In this case, the path is closed in the sense that any object which follows the path will end up at the location where it started its movement. The difference between a closed path and a looping path is that the closed path has a start and an end (e.g. a race on a circular track), while the looping path has neither (like an orbit). It is possible to further refine the schema by adding more designated points (i.e. 'landmarks') or other related spatial primitives.

SOURCE_PATH_VIA_GOAL:

Another member of the family is the SOURCE_PATH_VIA_GOAL. It is a refinement of the SOURCE_PATH_GOAL image schema but with an additional location on the path that the object by necessity must visit.

Following the reasoning presented above, CLOSED_PATH_MOVEMENT and SOURCE_PATH_VIA_GOAL can be combined in the obvious way. To follow a completely different branch of the family is to look more closely at MOVEMENT_IN_LOOPS.

MOVEMENT_IN_LOOPS and REVOLVING_MOVEMENT:

One way MOVEMENT_ALONG_PATH can be specialised is as the image schema of MOVEMENT_IN_LOOPS. Note that this change does not involve adding a new spatial primitive, but just an additional characteristic of the path by merging it with spatial primitives from the CYCLE image schema. The resulting image schema can be further refined by adding the spatial information of a *focal point*, which the path revolves around. This leads to the notion of *orbiting*, or, by continuously moving the orbiting path away from the focal point, creates the concept of *spirals*.

In Figure 3.4 the PATH family is represented as a theory graph made in HETS, available on the ontology repository[8], to demonstrate how these graphs look in the ontological scenario.

3.4 Formal Representation Using Theory Graphs

Formally, the idea of family structure can be represented as a graph[9] of theories in *The Distributed Ontology, Modeling and Specification Language* (DOL) (Mossakowski et al., 2015b).

Many of the image-schematic representations can be described using logical languages such as Description Logic (DL), First-order Logic (FOL) and the Image Schema Logic (ISL^{FOL})[10]. However, for image schema families to function as interconnected ontologies a language in which the bridges of the image-schematic structures are taken into account, is required. This is the purpose behind the use of theory graphs.

As mentioned in Chapter 1, DOL is a metalanguage that enables reuse, integration and alignment of existent logical theories, here OMS[11]. A library in DOL consists of basic OMS language modules, such as modules written in the Web Ontology Language (OWL) or Common Logic.

This choice is motivated primarily by two general features of DOL: (1) the heterogeneous approach, which allows for a variety of image-schematic formalisations without being limited to a single logic, and (2) the focus on linking and modularity. Therefore, DOL provides a rich toolkit to further formally develop the idea of *image schema families* in a variety of directions.

In more detail, DOL aims at providing a unified metalanguage for handling the diversity of ontology, modelling, and specification languages, for which it uses the umbrella term 'OMS.' In particular, DOL includes syntactic constructs for:

---

[8] www.ontohub.org

[9] These graphs are diagrams in the sense of category theory.

[10] That will be introduced in the upcoming Chapter 4.

[11] OMS stands for *Ontologies, Models and Specifications modules*, which are defined as logical theories.

1. 'as-is' use of OMS formulated (as a logical theory) in a specific ontology, modelling or specification language, and
2. defining new OMS by modifying and combining existing OMS (which are possibly written in different languages), and
3. mappings between OMS, resulting in networks of OMS.

DOL is equipped with an abstract model-theoretic semantics. The theoretical underpinnings of the DOL language have been described in detail by Kutz et al. (2010) and Mossakowski et al. (2012), whilst a full description of the language can be found in (Mossakowski et al., 2015a) or (in a more condensed form) in (Mossakowski et al., 2013).

Building on similar ideas to those underlying the first-order ontology repository COLORE[12] designed by Grüninger et al. (2012), it is here proposed to capture image schemas as interrelated families of (heterogeneous) theories. Similar ideas for structuring commonsense notions have also been applied to various notions of time (Allen and Hayes, 1985; Benthem, 1983). This general approach also covers the introduction of non-spatial elements such as 'force' as a basic ingredient of image schemas, argued for by, for instance, Gärdenfors (2007) and Mandler (2010), and constitutes the core of Mandler and Cánovas's (2014) *conceptual integrations* mentioned in Chapter 2.

3.5 Chapter Conclusion

This chapter concerned the notion of how to represent image schemas as families of theories. This is motivated by psychological research in which children can be found to develop and fine-tune their image schemas as they are repeatedly exposed to particular relationships (Mandler, 2008; Rohrer, 2005). Likewise, empirical support from linguistics demonstrated how different language constructions capture different levels of a particular image schema.

Formally these families are represented using theory graphs, in which the image schemas are hierarchically ordered from the most general and by extension through the addition of spatial and conceptual primitives from the same or other image schemas, develop into increasingly more complex constructions.

As a proof of concept, the chapter introduces two important families, the Two-Object family and the PATH family. While the members presented in these families are by no means to be considered exclusive and exhaustive, they capture some of the most essential static relationships between two objects (CONTACT, SUPPORT and LINK) respectively some of the dynamic, and temporal, object movements (e.g. MOVEMENT_OF_OBJECT, SOURCE_PATH_GOAL and REVOLVING_MOVEMENT).

In the upcoming chapter, these families will be addressed from a formal perspective through the introduction of the Image Schema Logic ISL^{FOL}, a spatiotemporal

---

[12] See http://stl.mie.utoronto.ca/colore/

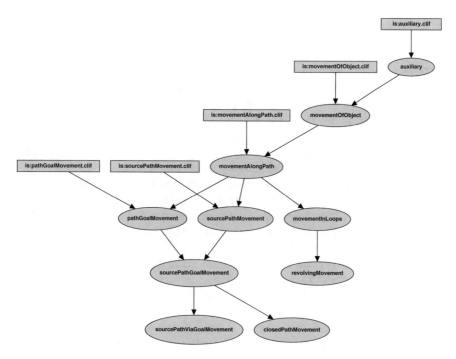

Fig. 3.4: Selected image schemas of path and cyclic movement as a theory graph made in HETS.

combination logic by which the individual image schema members can be formally represented.

References

K. Ahrens and A. L. Say. Mapping image schemas and translating metaphors. In *Proceedings of Pacific Asia Conference on Language, Information and Computation*, pages 1–8, February 1999.

J. F. Allen and P. J. Hayes. A Common-Sense Theory of Time. In *Proceedings of the 9th International Joint Conference on Artificial Intelligence (IJCAI-85)*, pages 528–531, Los Angeles, CA, USA, 1985.

B. Bennett and C. Cialone. Corpus Guided Sense Cluster Analysis: a methodology for ontology development (with examples from the spatial domain). In P. Garbacz and O. Kutz, editors, *8th International Conference on Formal Ontology in Information Systems (FOIS)*, volume 267 of *Frontiers in Artificial Intelligence and Applications*, pages 213–226. IOS Press, 2014.

J. V. Benthem. *The Logic of Time: A Model-Theoretic Investigation into the Varieties of Temporal Ontology and Temporal Discourse*. D. Reidel Publishing Company, Dordrecht, Holland, 1983.

P. Gärdenfors. *Embodiment in Cognition and Culture*, volume 71 of *Advances in Consciousness Research*, chapter Cognitive semantics and image schemas with embodied forces, pages 57–76. John Benjamins Publishing Company, 2007.

D. Gromann and M. M. Hedblom. Breaking Down Finance: A method for concept simplification by identifying movement structures from the image schema Path-following. In *Proceedings of the 2nd Joint Ontology Workshops (JOWO)*, volume 1660, Annecy, France, 2016. CEUR-WS online proceedings.

M. Grüninger, T. Hahmann, A. Hashemi, D. Ong, and A. Ozgovde. Modular First-Order Ontologies Via Repositories. *Applied Ontology*, 7(2):169–209, 2012.

M. Johanson and A. Papafragou. What does children's spatial language reveal about spatial concepts? Evidence from the use of containment expressions. *Cognitive Science*, 38(5):881–910, 2014.

M. Johnson. *The Body in the Mind: The Bodily Basis of Meaning, Imagination, and Reason*. University of Chicago Press, 1987.

Z. Kövecses. *Metaphor: A Practical Introduction*. Oxford University Press, New York, USA, 2010.

O. Kutz, T. Mossakowski, and D. Lücke. Carnap, Goguen, and the Hyperontologies: Logical Pluralism and Heterogeneous Structuring in Ontology Design. *Logica Universalis*, 4(2):255–333, 2010. Special Issue on 'Is Logic Universal?'.

O. Kutz, N. Troquard, S. Borgo, M. M. Hedblom, and D. Porello. The Mouse and the Ball: Towards a cognitively-based and ontologically-grounded logic of agency. In *Proceedings of COCO at SAC 2017*, Pau, France, 2017.

G. Lakoff and R. Núñez. *Where Mathematics Comes From: How the Embodied Mind Brings Mathematics into Being*. Basic Books, New York, 2000.

J. M. Mandler. *The Foundations of Mind: Origins of Conceptual Thought: Origins of Conceptual Though*. Oxford University Press, New York, 2004.

J. M. Mandler. On the Birth and Growth of Concepts. *Philosophical Psychology*, 21(2):207–230, 2008.

J. M. Mandler. The spatial foundations of the conceptual system. *Language and Cognition*, 2(1):21–44, 2010.

J. M. Mandler and C. P. Cánovas. On defining image schemas. *Language and Cognition*, 6(4):510–532, May 2014.

T. Mossakowski, C. Lange, and O. Kutz. Three Semantics for the Core of the Distributed Ontology Language. In M. Grüninger, editor, *7th International Conference on Formal Ontology in Information Systems (FOIS)*, Frontiers in Artificial Intelligence and Applications. IOS Press, 2012.

T. Mossakowski, O. Kutz, M. Codescu, and C. Lange. The Distributed Ontology, Modeling and Specification Language. In C. Del Vescovo, T. Hahmann, D. Pearce, and D. Walther, editors, *Proceedings of the 7th International Workshop on Modular Ontologies (WoMO-13)*, volume 1081. CEUR-WS, 2013.

T. Mossakowski, M. Codescu, F. Neuhaus, and O. Kutz. *The Road to Universal Logic–Festschrift for 50th birthday of Jean-Yves Beziau, Volume II*, chapter The distributed ontology, modelling and specification language - DOL. Studies in Universal Logic. Birkhäuser, 2015a.

T. Mossakowski, M. Codescu, F. Neuhaus, and O. Kutz. *The Distributed Ontology, Modeling and Specification Language – DOL*, pages 489–520. Springer International Publishing, Cham, 2015b.

T. Rohrer. Image schemata in the brain. In B. Hampe and J. E. Grady, editors, *From perception to meaning: Image schemas in cognitive linguistics*, volume 29 of *Cognitive Linguistics Research*, pages 165–196. Walter de Gruyter, 2005.

L. Talmy. The fundamental system of spatial schemas in language. In B. Hampe and J. E. Grady, editors, *From perception to meaning: Image schemas in cognitive linguistics*, volume 29 of *Cognitive Linguistics Research*, pages 199–234. Walter de Gruyter, 2005.

Chapter 4
Introducing ISL^{FOL}: A Logical Language for Image Schemas

Abstract In the previous chapter, image schemas were suggested to be formally represented as families of theories in which spatiotemporal relationships of similar character were structured hierarchically. This was motivated by findings from developmental psychology and empirical support from linguistic expressions. While the family structure is interesting from a cognitive perspective in itself, in order for image schemas to be integrated into computational concept understanding and invention, a more specific formal representation is required. As of yet, there exists no clear-cut and satisfactory method to logically approach image schemas. Aiming to rectify this problem, this chapter introduces the Image Schema Logic ISL^{FOL1}. The logic is based on previous formalisations of image schemas in which the Region Connection Calculus (RCC) has been demonstrated to efficiently model spatial relationships. Simultaneously, the Qualitative Trajectory Calculus (QTC) is used to model relative object movement between objects and Linear Temporal Logic (LTL) is used as a method to capture the sequential dimension of image-schematic events. The chapter includes considerations and discussions on:

- Problems with formalising image schemas
- Previous formalisation approaches
- Introducing ISL^{FOL}
- A formalisation of the Two-Object family
- A formalisation of the PATH-following family

4.1 Formally Dealing with Spatiotemporal Relationships

One of the core motivations behind formally representing image schemas in the first place is to use them as information skeletons for metaphor, analogies and conceptual blending. Formal systems dealing with analogical transfer, such as HDTP, rely on a mostly syntactic process that through anti-unification abstracts away from

---

[1] ISL^{FOL} is a modified version of the ISL^{M} that was introduced in (Hedblom et al., 2017).

© Springer Nature Switzerland AG 2020

M. M. Hedblom, *Image Schemas and Concept Invention*, Cognitive Technologies,
https://doi.org/10.1007/978-3-030-47329-7_4

predicates such as those in FOL. However, there is no actual information in the anti-unification process to determine which inferences from each space in the analogy belong to each other, often generating the wrong inference. Providing a formal representation method that diverges from this level of axiomatisation to a more semantically rich method would provide benefits to the automatic interpretation as well as making the formal language more readable to humans. Looking to the state of the art in geographical information science a novel logical language built on the existence of different calculi dealing with spatiotemporal relationships will be introduced. In the upcoming chapter, this formal language for image schemas will be introduced that aims to bridge these problems and better model the semantic content present in the image schemas.

Additionally, it could provide formalised patterns that could be used as ontology design patterns when providing large-scale axiomatisations such as seen in the work by Morgenstern (2001).

4.1.1 Problems with Formalising Image Schemas

One of the biggest problems in formal image schema research is to find an adequate method by which image schemas should be represented. While there have been several approaches to formalise image schemas (e.g. Bennett and Cialone (2014); Galton (2010); Kuhn (2002); St. Amant et al. (2006)), there exists as of yet no complete formal modelling method to properly represent image schemas. As image schemas are spatiotemporal object relations, few, if any, logical representation languages manage to tame all required properties found in image schemas alone.

As mentioned, two major problems for successfully formalising image schemas are, first, that they are by definition abstract cognitive patterns, something difficult to capture in formal languages. The second problem is that while it can be argued that it is fairly straightforward to capture their static relationships, the dynamic and temporal dimension provides for a complication in terms of formal representation.

Therefore, this chapter addresses this problem by introducing a novel logic for image schemas using the Eight Region Connection Calculus (RCC-8), Qualitative Trajectory Calculus (QTC) and Linear Temporal Logic (LTL). It is believed that this combination allows for a logic expressive enough to represent image schemas. This is built on the notions presented in Chapter 3, namely that image schemas can be formally represented as families of theories and by combining elements from different image schema structures increasingly complex concepts can be built (as will be demonstrated in Chapter 5).

After the syntax and the semantics of the logic have been introduced, the image schema graphs presented in the previous chapter will be formalised using this logic.

4.1.2 Previous Formalisations of Image Schemas

Despite image schemas' original status as being abstract, cognitive phenomena, work on developing a theory and corresponding formalisations has become an increasingly common sight in the context of cognitively inspired AI. This is mainly due to the prospect that image schemas could offer a systematic approach for conceptualisation and concept acquisition based on embodied theories. One major problem, however, is how to formally represent them in an adequate, but still computationally useful way.

Research in AI building on the processing of sensorimotor experiences includes connectionist models as, for instance, described by Regier (1996), which learn to classify visual stimuli into linguistic categories. Similar in approach, but with direct connection to the theory of image schemas, is the work by Nayak and Mukerjee (2012), who developed a system that, based on video input of OBJECTs moving IN and OUT of containers, learned the concept of CONTAINMENT. Another system is *Dev E-R* which models the sensorimotor stages in cognitive development and fine-tunes its knowledge based on the amount of visual stimuli (Aguilar and Pérez y Pérez, 2015).

More theoretical investigations of how image schemas are involved in formal domains have been reported by Lakoff and Núñez (2000). They illustrate how image schemas, through the experience of embodied conceptual metaphors, form the foundations for abstract concepts in mathematics. Using basic image-schematic structures such as the PATH-schema they suggest how, for instance, basic arithmetic or a notion of rational numbers can mentally be developed by the child and, taking into account further experiences and image schemas, evolve into increasingly abstract mathematical concepts.

While these and similar efforts demonstrate how the development of abstract concepts may be approached in a constructive way within the framework of cognitive science and image schemas, this does not in itself provide any answers on how to formally treat the problem.

Frank and Raubal (1999) presented a then up-to-date review of attempts to formalise image schemas. They discussed the prospects of representing them with calculi or as function representations, and also proposed a method on how to formally structure image schemas using a relational calculus both on a large scale as in GIS and small scale such as on a table surface.

Bennett and Cialone (2014) approached the problem from a linguistic and formal perspective. With the desire to map image-schematic language to a logic for ontology development, they searched for synonyms to the CONTAINMENT image schema (contain, surround, enclose, etc.) in a text corpus of a biology textbook. By relating to the well-known RCC-8 topological relations (Randell et al., 1992), they identified and formally represented eight different kinds of containers. Fuchs (2013) also uses the natural sciences as a domain to identify the role of image schemas. In his work, Fuchs outlines how image schemas are involved in narrative by looking more closely at the concept of force as frequently evoked in physics. Fuchs motivates his research not only by the question of how children learn these abstract concepts in infancy but also by how image schema narratives may aid education for adults.

The work by Kuhn (2007) looks at image schemas from a top-down perspective by using noun phrases in WordNet glosses and connects them with spatial abstractions that model image-schematic affordances. Particularly interesting is Kuhn's analysis of nesting and combining image schemas in natural language to represent more complex concepts, e.g. 'transportation' brings together SUPPORT and PATH. Also interested in the affordances found in image schema is the work by Galton (2010) who used the RCC-6 relations to investigate the affordances and requirements of the CONTAINMENT schema. This is related to the work by Steedman (2002) who looks at the affordances of going IN and OUT of rooms given that the doors are either opened or closed. These approaches are particularly interesting as they do not only take the image schema in its static environment into account, but also look at the dynamics of the image schemas in terms of combining CONTAINMENT with PATH.

Other work on formalising image schemas include the work by St. Amant et al. (2006), who combined image schemas using bigraphs to illustrate how different events can be described as series of image-schematic relationships.

The intrinsic difficulty of mapping the diversity of spatial and temporal formalisms to more commonsense understandings of time and space is well known (Bateman et al., 2010; Galton, 1992). The approach followed here is to focus the attention on the spatiotemporal modelling of image schemas, and how they give rise to affordances via a formal understanding of how they are understood to participate in/or co-determine possible actions in an environment.

The nature of the task of modelling image schemas clearly supports the logical pluralism positions defended in (Kutz et al., 2014), namely that no single formalism will be sufficient to cover the variety of representations that can be attempted across the array of image schemas and diverse modelling levels. A logical language that embraces logical modelling aspects from different calculi and languages would be better suited.

Cognitive Semantics, i.e., empirically supported formal semantics underlying the modelling of image schemas, affordances and their temporal-dynamic instantiations is seen to provide an interface between the cognitive perspective and logic-based KR approaches. A similar bridge is proposed in hybrid approaches such as that by Oltramari (2012), who seeks to bridge cognitive 'embodied' features with ontology development.

The *cognitive logics* that are initiated intend to develop a focus on understanding the interplay between the mostly spatial, image-schematic representations, and affordance-based narratives, temporal stories conflicting with the semantics of typical temporal logics.

4.2 Introducing ISL^{FOL}: The Image Schema Logic

In general, the rich models of time investigated in more cognitively driven studies on how humans understand time in poetry, everyday cognition, language in general, and communication can not be mapped easily to existing temporal logic approaches, as demonstrated by, for instance, Pagán Cánovas (2010) and Boroditsky (2000).

The limitations of off-the-shelf calculi also extend to the spatial domain. The well-known Region Connection Calculus (RCC) has been used extensively in qualitative spatial reasoning (Cohn et al., 1997). However, cognitive studies have supported the claim that humans do not typically make, or accept, some of the distinctions inherent in the RCC calculus (Knauff et al., 1997). A simpler calculus (usually called RCC-5), can be obtained by removing the distinction between e.g. 'proper part' and 'tangential proper part,' however by collapsing the logic to pure mereology (Lehmann and Cohn, 1994). At the other end of the spectrum is the work of Bennett and Cialone (2014), who attempted to model the image schema of CONTAINMENT from the linguistic perspective.

The different aspects of the suggested language are introduced under their respective responsibility: *the spatial dimension*, divided into topology of regions and cardinal directions, *the movement dimension*, divided into relative object movement and points of reference, and *the temporal dimension*.

4.2.1 The Spatial Dimension

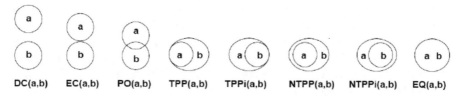

DC(a,b)   EC(a,b)   PO(a,b)   TPP(a,b)   TPPi(a,b)   NTPP(a,b)   NTPPi(a,b)   EQ(a,b)

Fig. 4.1: The eight RCC-8 relations.

4.2.1.1 Topology of Regions

Following the work that has been laid out by amongst other Galton (2010) and Bennett and Cialone (2014) the Region Connection Calculus (RCC) is used as a method to represent the spatial relationships that the image schemas constitute, more precisely the RCC-8 relations, see Figure 4.1 (Randell et al., 1992). The reason is that a mere mereology would not suffice for modelling image schemas as it is necessary to distinguish whether two objects touch each other (Externally Connected: EC) or do not touch each other (Disconnected: DC).

4.2.1.2 Cardinal Directions

Directions can be absolute or relative. Usually, left and right denote relative directions (Scivos and Nebel, 2004), which however are conceptually and computationally much more complicated than (absolute) cardinal directions (Ligozat, 1998) like North or West. Here a naive egocentric view (i.e. with a fixed observer that is not part of the model) is assumed, from which directions like left/right, front/behind and above/below can be recognised as cardinal directions. This leads to six binary predicates on objects: *Left*, *Right*, *FrontOf*, *Behind*, *Above* and *Below*. Note that these relations are unions of base relations in a three-dimensional cardinal direction calculus as in (Ligozat, 1998), and the latter can be recovered from these relations by taking suitable intersections and complements (for example, it is possible that none of the above six relations hold, which happens to be the case if two regions are equal or largely overlap).

4.2.1.3 Point of Reference

As a naive egocentric view based on that all scenarios is presumed to be described also contain a 'perceiver' outside of the model. This means that the perceiver himself, or a subset of his location, is providing a point of reference. In order to represent this formally, it is assumed that the perceiver is at a location that can be described as the constant point '*Me*'[2]. In 3D Euclidean space it is intended to take the position $Me = (0,0,0)$. This means that objects always move in relation not only to other objects but to an abstract representation of the 'perceiver.' In the case that a perceiver is moving along with an object, then the objects are not perceived to move. For instance, point *Me* moves together with an object such as a car, given that a person is inside a moving car. This follows the intuition that it is the outside of the car that moves rather than the car itself.

4.2.2 The Movement Dimension

In order to take the dynamic aspects of the image schemas into account the Qualitative Trajectory Calculus (QTC) (Weghe et al., 2006) is used to represent how two objects relate in terms of movement. In its variant QTC$_{B1D}$, the trajectories of objects are described in relation to one another. QTC works on relative movement

---

[2] The constant name *Me* is used to emphasise that this reference point is at the location of a perceiver.

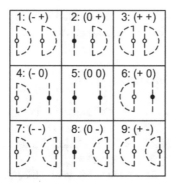

Fig. 4.2: The relationship between moving objects in QTC (Chavoshi et al., 2015).

between disjoint 'moving point objects.' While Weghe et al. (2006) use nine different relations[3], see Figure 4.2, these are composed of two independent parts, with
three possibilities for each part. The calculus is here simplified by only considering
these three possibilities:

- if object O_1 moves towards O_2's position, this is represented as:
  $O_1 \rightsquigarrow O_2$,
- if O_1 moves away from O_2's position, this is represented as:
  $O_1 \hookleftarrow O_2$
- while O_1 being at rest with respect to O_2's position is expressed as:
  $O_1 \mid\circ O_2$.

This way of writing the relative movement of two objects is intuitive and expressive.
Arguably, one could claim that if one object moves away from another object, both
could be perceived as moving away from the each other. But as a naive egocentric
view is presupposed, one object will remain in a fixed position in regards to the perceiver. The calculus of Weghe et al. (2006) can be recovered by taking intersections
of these relations, combining the description of the movement of O_1 with respect
to O_2's position with the description of the movement of O_2 with respect to O_1's
position. For example, $O_1 \rightsquigarrow O_2 \wedge O_2 \hookleftarrow O_1$ is denoted by O_1-+O_2 in (Weghe et al.,
2006).

Secondly, in the current scenario, where extended regions modelled in RCC are
considered as the spatial objects subjected to 'relative movement,' here an appropriate definition of the 'location' of an object is needed in order to meaningfully
measure the distance between two regions. Note that in the original QTC calculus spatial objects are abstracted to points in space, and therefore the problem does
not arise there. This is further discussed in Section 4.2.4.2, which is devoted to the
semantics of ISL^{FOL}.

---

[3] The reason for using nine relations is the wish to obtain a partition of the space of all relations
between two objects, as is usually done in qualitative spatial reasoning.

With QTC, it is possible to speak about relative movement for a given time point. What is missing is the ability to speak about the future.

4.2.2.1 The Movement Dimension – Paths

Note that QTC has been defined for DC objects only, and technically, all QTC relations between two objects imply that these are DC. This needs to be generalised to objects that are in any arbitrary RCC-8 relation. To do this the following adaption of the QTC semantics is required, see below.

Dependent on situation, the distance between objects can, and needs to be, calculated differently. For instance, the distance between two regions can be based on the usual Euclidean distance d:

$$d(Y,Z) = \inf\{d(y,z) \mid y \in Y, z \in Z\}$$

The distance can be calculated from the shortest possible distance between objects. This is the kind of distance needed when two objects are in contact with each other (EC). For instance, imagine a ball rolling off a table, the ball is in contact with the table until the minimal distance between the objects is greater than 0. Or it can be calculated based on the maximal distance. In the case that the objects are overlapping (Partial Overlap: PO) or become proper parts (Proper Part: PP), as would be the case in several forms of CONTAINMENT, a combination of these two points are needed. Imagine if you drop a ball into a basket. The ball will not stop its movement, until it hits the 'back of the basket' with the 'front' of the ball. This form of going INto a container, also implies blockage. However, for many forms of CONTAINMENT it is enough to describe how one object 'overlaps' the region of another object. For this it is possible to calculate distance based on the geometric centre, centroid C, of the object.

The centroid of a finite set of k points $x_1, x_2, \ldots, x_k$ in $\mathbb{R}^n$ is:

$$C = \frac{x_1 + x_2 + \cdots + x_k}{k}$$

For now ISL^{FOL} is limited to calculating the distance between objects based on the geometric centre, but for future extension different distance calculations will need to be accounted for.

4.2.3 The Temporal Dimension

For temporal representation, the simple linear temporal logic (LTL) over the reals is used (Kröger and Merz, 2008; Reynolds, 2010).

The syntax is as follows:

$$\varphi ::= p \mid \top \mid \neg \varphi \mid \varphi \wedge \varphi \mid \varphi \mathbf{U} \varphi \mid \exists x{:}s.\,\varphi$$

$\varphi \mathbf{U} \psi$ reads as "φ holds, until ψ holds." $\mathbf{U}$ associates to the right, that is, $\varphi \mathbf{U} \psi \mathbf{U} \chi$ is parsed as $\varphi \mathbf{U} (\psi \mathbf{U} \chi)$. Additionally, as is standard in temporal logic, the following derived operators can be defined and used when describing the image schemas and image-schematic scenarios:

- **F**φ (at some time in the future, φ) is defined as $\top \mathbf{U} \varphi$,
- **G**φ (at all times in the future, φ) is defined as $\neg \mathbf{F} \neg \varphi$.
- $\forall x{:}s.\,\varphi$ as $\neg \exists x{:}s.\,\neg \varphi$

Moreover, for material implication $\rightarrow$ is used and $\leftrightarrow$ is used for biimplication, while $\underline{\vee}$ is used for the exclusive or.

4.2.4 The Combined Logic ISL^{FOL}

4.2.4.1 Syntax of ISL^{FOL}

The syntax of ISL^{FOL} is defined over the combined languages of Region Connection Calculus (RCC-8), Qualitative Trajectory Calculus (QTC$_{B1D}$), Cardinal Directions (CD), First-Order Logic (FOL) and Linear Temporal Logic (LTL) over the reals, with 3D Euclidean space assumed for the spatial domain, see Figure 4.3. Note that LTL is needed over real time in order to interpret QTC relations as its semantics assume continuous time. ISL^{FOL} therefore stands for 'Image Schema Logic' and $M = \langle \text{RCC-8}, QTC_{B1D}, CD, LTL, \text{3D-Euclid} \rangle$. The combination of the spatial and temporal modalities follows the temporalisation strategy of Finger and Gabbay (1993).

Signatures, in the sense of vocabularies, are built over the fixed set of three sorts $S = \{Object, Region, Path\}$. A signature $\Sigma = (F_r, F_f, P_r, P_f)$ consists of a many-sorted (over sorts S) first-order signature (F_r, P_r) of rigid function and predicate symbols and one (F_f, P_f) of flexible function and predicate symbols. Here, each function symbol is typed with an arity $w \rightarrow s$ and each predicate symbol with an arity w, where $w \in S^*$ is the string of argument sorts and $s \in S$ is the result sort. Overloading is not allowed, that is, each symbol must have unique arity and rigidity. In the context of modelling image schemas, though not playing a central role in the present work, rigid symbols will be useful to handle the modelling of objects that do not change their position nor their extension during a period of time (like a house), while flexible symbols will be useful for modelling objects that essentially have to change (like a moving ball or a balloon being inflated).

Σ-**Sentences** are first-order LTL temporal formulas (see Section 4.2.3) built over (ground) atomic formulas taken from the union of RCC-8 statements (see Section 4.2.1), 3D cardinal directions (see Section 4.2.1.2), QTC$_{B1D}$ (see Section 4.2.2), and standard first-order application of predicates.

Let X be an S-sorted set of variables, that is, X is a triple of sets $(X_{Object}, X_{Region}, X_{Path})$. In parallel for all $s \in S$, the set $T_s(X)$ of terms of sort $s \in S$ is defined to be the least set such that:

- Me is a term $Me \in T_{Region}$,
- if $x \in X_s$, then $x \in T_s(X)$ (variables are terms),
- if $f : w \rightarrow s \in F_r \cup F_f$ and $t_1 \in T_{s_1}(X), \dots, t_n \in T_{s_n}(X)$, then $f(t_1, \dots, t_n) \in T_s(X)$ (terms are closed under application of function symbols),
- if $t \in T_{Object}(X)$, then $t \in T_{Region}(X)$ (objects can be implicitly coerced to the region they occupy),
- if $t \in T_{Path}(X)$, then $source(t), goal(t) \in T_{Region}(X)$ (the source and the target of a path are (one-point) regions).

The set of atomic formulas contains

- $t = u$ for $t, u \in T_s(X)$,
- $p(t_1, \dots, t_n)$ for $p : w \in P_r \cup P_f$ and $t_1 \in T_{s_1}(X), \dots, t_n \in T_{s_n}(X)$,
- $DC(t, u)$, $EC(t, u)$, $OV(t, u)$, $EQ(t, u)$, $TPP(t, u)$, $TPPi(t, u)$, $NTPP(t, u)$, $NTPPi(t, u)$, for terms $t, u \in T_{Region}(X) \cup T_{Path}(X)$,
- $Left(t, u)$, $Right(t, u)$, $FrontOf(t, u)$, $Behind(t, u)$, $Above(t, u)$, $Below(t, u)$, for terms $t, u \in T_{Region}(X) \cup T_{Path}(X)$,
- $t \rightsquigarrow u, t \leftarrowtail u, t \mid\circ u$, for terms $t \in T_{Object}, u \in T_{Region}(X)$.

ISL^{FOL}-fomulas are first-order LTL formulas (See Section 4.2.3) over these atomic formulas.

Here are a few examples of well-formed sentences that can be written in this language (and might be considered true in specific scenarios). Note, however, that none of them are valid (i.e. true in all models), but can be valid in scenarios where the geometry of objects and possible movements are further restricted in the description of the semantics, or can alternatively be used to prescribe admissible models.

- $FrontOf(a, b) \wedge \mathbf{F} \neg FrontOf(a, b) \longrightarrow \mathbf{F}(a \rightsquigarrow b \vee a \leftarrowtail b \vee b \rightsquigarrow a \vee b \leftarrowtail a)$ 'If a is in front of b, but ceases to be so in the future, then sometime in the future, either a or b must move with respect to the other object's original position';
- $Above(a, b) \wedge \mathbf{G} a \mid\circ b \longrightarrow \mathbf{G} Above(a, b)$ 'If a is above b and never moves relative to b, it will be always above b.' Note that this sentence is not valid: consider e.g. that a circles around b with constant distance. However, it holds if for example a and b always stay on the same line (that is, their relative movement is 1D only);
- $DC(a, b) \wedge \mathbf{G} a \leftarrowtail b \longrightarrow \mathbf{G} DC(a, b)$ 'If a is disconnected to b and always moves away from it, it will always stay disconnected to b.' This is actually a validity.

4.2.4.2 The Semantics of ISL^{FOL}

The combined logic ISL^{FOL} is interpreted spatially over regions in $\mathbb{R}^3$ and temporally over the real line. Note that continuous time is needed in order to interpret QTC properly.

An interpretation (model) M consists of:

- a non-empty set M_{Object}, which is the universe of discourse,
- the fixed interpretation M_{Region} as set of all subsets of $\mathbb{R}^3$,[4]
- the fixed interpretation M_{Path} as set of all paths in 3D space, i.e. of all continuous functions $[0,1] \to \mathbb{R}^3$,
- a function $f_M : M_w \to M_s$[5] for each rigid function symbol $f : w \to s \in F_r$,
- a function $f_M : \mathbb{R} \times M_w \to M_s$ for each flexible function symbol $f : w \to s \in F_f$,
- a relation $p_M \subseteq M_w$ for each rigid predicate symbol $p : w \in P_r$,
- a relation $p_M \subseteq \mathbb{R} \times M_w$ for each flexible predicate symbol $p : w \in P_r$,
- a function $occupies_M : \mathbb{R} \times M_{Object} \to M_{Region}$, mapping each object to the region it occupies (at a certain time).

Given a set of variables $X = (X_{Object}, X_{Region}, X_{Path})$, a variable valuation $v : X \to M$ consists of three functions: $v = (v_{Object} : X_{Object} \to M_{Object}, v_{Region} : X_{Region} \to M_{Region}, v_{Path} : X_{Path} \to M_{Path})$.

Given a term $t \in T_s(X)$, a variable valuation $v : X \to M$ and a time point $\tau \in \mathbb{R}$, its evaluation $[t]_{M,v,\tau,s}$ is defined as follows:

- $[Me]_{M,v,\tau,s} = (0,0,0)$
- $[x]_{M,v,\tau,s} = v_s(x)$
- $[f(t_1,\dots,t_n)]_{M,v,\tau,s} = f_M(\tau, [t_1]_{M,v,\tau,s}, \dots, [t_n]_{M,v,\tau,s})$,[6]
- $[t]_{M,v,\tau,Region} = occupies_M(\tau, [t]_{M,v,\tau,Object})$ if $t \in T_{Object}(X)$,
- $[source(t)]_{M,v,\tau,Region} = \{[t]_{M,v,\tau,Path}(0)\}$,
- $[goal(t)]_{M,v,\tau,Region} = \{[t]_{M,v,\tau,Path}(1)\}$.

Given a formula φ, a variable valuation $v : X \to M$ and a time point $\tau \in \mathbb{R}$, its satisfaction $M, v, \tau \models \varphi$ is defined as follows. If φ is an atomic formula, then we define

- $M, v, \tau \models t = u$ if $[t]_{M,v,\tau,s} = [u]_{M,v,\tau,s}$,
- $M, v, \tau \models p(t_1,\dots,t_n)$ if $(\tau, [t_1]_{M,v,\tau,s}, \dots, [t_n]_{M,v,\tau,s}) \in p_M$,[7]
- If R is an RCC-8 relation, $M, v, \tau \models R(t,u)$ holds if $[t]_{M,v,\tau,Region}$ is in relation R with $[u]_{M,v,\tau,Region}$, following the RCC-8 semantics in Randell et al. (1992). Here, a path tacitly converts into its image in $\mathbb{R}^3$ in order to get a region.
- if R is a cardinal direction relation, then

    - $M, v, \tau \models Left(t,u)$ holds if $\inf\{x \mid (x,y,z) \in [u]_{M,v,\tau,Region}\} \geq \sup\{x \mid (x,y,z) \in [t]_{M,v,\tau,Region}\}$.
    $M, v, \tau \models Right(t,u)$ holds if $M, v, \tau \models Left(u,t)$ holds.
    - $M, v, \tau \models FrontOf(t,u)$ holds if $\inf\{y \mid (x,y,z) \in [u]_{M,v,\tau,Region}\} \geq \sup\{y \mid (x,y,z) \in [t]_{M,v,\tau,Region}\}$.
    $M, v, \tau \models Behind(t,u)$ holds if $M, v, \tau \models FrontOf(u,t)$ holds.

---

[4] Usually, RCC-8 is restricted to regular closed sets. However, for the current purposes it should cover images of paths and source and target points of paths as well, and these are not regular closed.

[5] If $w = s_1 \dots s_n$, then $M_w = M_{s_1} \times \cdots \times M_{s_n}$.

[6] The argument τ needs to be dropped for rigid function symbols.

[7] The argument τ needs to be dropped for rigid predicate symbols.

- $M, v, \tau \models Above(t, u)$ holds if $\inf\{z \mid (x, y, z) \in [t]_{M, v, \tau, Region}\} \geq \sup\{z \mid (x, y, z) \in [u]_{M, v, \tau, Region}\}$.
  $M, v, \tau \models Below(t, u)$ holds if $M, v, \tau \models Above(u, t)$ holds.

- QTC$_{B1D}$ formulas are interpreted as in (Weghe et al., 2006), but over regions as moving objects. More specifically, distance between objects is calculated from their defined geometric centre. For $R \in M_{Region}$, set $C_R = (c_x, c_y, c_z)$, where

$$c_x = \tfrac{1}{2}(\inf\{x \mid (x, y, z) \in R\} + \sup\{x \mid (x, y, z) \in R\})$$
$$c_y = \tfrac{1}{2}(\inf\{y \mid (x, y, z) \in R\} + \sup\{y \mid (x, y, z) \in R\})$$
$$c_z = \tfrac{1}{2}(\inf\{z \mid (x, y, z) \in R\} + \sup\{z \mid (x, y, z) \in R\})$$

Then, for regions $R, S \in M_{Region}$, their distance is the Euclidean distance between the centres

$$d(R, S) = d(c_R, c_S).$$

Then, given terms t and u, exactly one of three cases occurs:

- $M, v, \tau \models t \rightsquigarrow u$ iff t (a potentially moving object) is moving towards u (a non-moving region), that is, if[8]
  $\exists \tau_1 (\tau_1 < \tau \wedge \forall \tau^- (\tau_1 < \tau^- < \tau \to d([t]_{M, v, \tau^-, Region}, [u]_{M, v, \tau, Region}) > d([t]_{M, v, \tau, Region}, [u]_{M, v, \tau, Region}))) \wedge$
  $\exists \tau_2 (\tau < \tau_2 \wedge \forall \tau^+ (\tau < \tau^+ < \tau_2 \to d([t]_{M, v, \tau, Region}, [u]_{M, v, \tau, Region}) > d([t]_{M, v, \tau^+, Region}, [u]_{M, v, \tau, Region})))$

- $M, v, \tau \models t \leftarrow u$ iff t is moving away from u, that is, if
  $\exists \tau_1 (\tau_1 < \tau \wedge \forall \tau^- (\tau_1 < \tau^- < \tau \to d([t]_{M, v, \tau^-, Region}, [u]_{M, v, \tau, Region}) < d([t]_{M, v, \tau, Region}, [u]_{M, v, \tau, Region}))) \wedge$
  $\exists \tau_2 (\tau < \tau_2 \wedge \forall \tau^+ (\tau < \tau^+ < \tau_2 \to d([t]_{M, v, \tau, Region}, [u]_{M, v, \tau, Region}) < d([t]_{M, v, \tau^+, Region}, [u]_{M, v, \tau, Region})))$

- $M, v, \tau \models t \mid\!\circ\, u$ iff t is of stable distance with respect to u, that is, in all other cases. Note that stable distance does not imply absence of relative movement. For example, consider that t moves around u but keeps the distance stable (e.g. a satellite moves around the earth).

Satisfaction of complex formulas is inherited from LTL:

- for atomic p, $M, v, \tau \models p$ has been defined above
- $M, v, \tau \models \neg \varphi$ iff not $M, v, \tau \models \varphi$
- $M, v, \tau \models \varphi \wedge \psi$ iff $M, v, \tau \models \varphi$ and $M, v, \tau \models \psi$
- $M, v, \tau \models \varphi U \psi$ iff for some $\rho > \tau$, $M, v, \rho \models \psi$ and $M, v, \sigma \models \varphi$ for all $\sigma \in [\tau, \rho)$.
- $M, v, \tau \models \exists x. \varphi$ if there exists some valuation $\xi : X \to M$ differing from v at most for x, such that $M, \xi, \tau \models \varphi$.

---

[8] Recall that $[t]_{M, v, \tau, Region} = occupies_M(\tau, [t]_{M, v, \tau, Object})$.

Finally, φ holds in M, denoted $M \models \varphi$, if for all time points $t \in \mathbb{R}$ and all valuations $v : X \to M$, then $M, v, \tau \models \varphi$.[9]

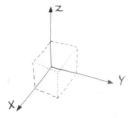

Fig. 4.3: Illustration of Euclidean space.

ISL^{FOL} is introduced as a formal language for image schemas that can be used to describe both spatial and temporal dimensions of the image schemas independently or jointly. Next this logic will be demonstrated by presenting the formalisation of the Two-Object family, followed by a formalisation of some of the members in the PATH family.

4.3 Formalising the Two-Object Family

In Chapter 3 the Two-Object family was properly introduced as a method to formally structure the image schemas that encompass two objects and their physical relationship to one another.

In that chapter, Figure 3.1 illustrates how the image schemas involving two objects can be formally developed by adding specifications such as above orientation and force. The illustration shows how both CONTACT and LINK can be further developed and interconnected with one another.

In the next section, these notions will be formally represented using ISL^{FOL}.

4.3.1 Formalising CONTACT, SUPPORT and LINK

CONTACT:

As previously demonstrated, CONTACT is the most general image schema in which two objects have a (physical) connection to each other. While there exists disagreement to as whether OBJECT should be considered an image schema in itself or rather

---

[9] Note, that in order to keep the semantics simpler and in a first-order paradigm, only quantification over rigid objects is allowed.

THE TWO-OBJECT FAMILY: **an excerpt capturing different** SUPPORT

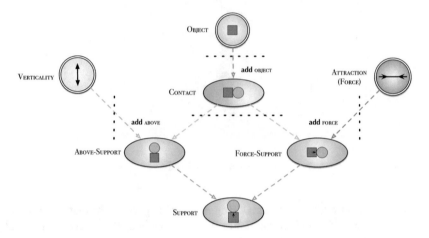

Fig. 4.4: Subset of the Two-Object Family: Constructing the different SUPPORT schemas.

a spatial primitive (Mandler and Cánovas, 2014; Santibáñez, 2002), it needs to be part of the formal representation.

For CONTACT, the relationship is without any force dynamics, neither does it contain any topological or orientational requirements.

CONTACT is formalised as two regions, here represented by object names (O_1 and O_2) touching, which is represented in RCC-8 as:

$$\forall O_1, O_2 : Object \ (\text{CONTACT}(O_1, O_2) \leftrightarrow \neg DC(O_1, O_2))$$

This must also be defined for the relationship between objects and regions:

$$\forall O : Object, \forall R : Region \ (\text{CONTACT}(O, R) \leftrightarrow \neg DC(O, R))$$

Alternatively, it is possible to use $EC(O_1, O_2)$ instead of the $\neg DC(O_1, O_2)$. However, saying that objects are in contact with each other when they are not disjoint also includes overlapping objects. Which naturally is important in many scenarios. For instance, it can be argued as to whether objects present inside a room are in CONTACT with the room or not. However, for now the region an object occupies is a good enough approximation to use when describing relationships such as CONTACT.

SUPPORT:

Following the branching in Figure 3.3, SUPPORT offers a slightly more complicated formalisation as either ATTRACTION and 'force' and/or VERTICALITY and 'above'-ness are involved to keep one object in contact with the other object. Visualise a table that offers counter-force for books on top of it, or a wall that offers SUPPORT for any object resting on the wall.

In order to properly differentiate between CONTACT and SUPPORT it is essential to introduce 'above' and 'force' as conceptual primitives.

Formalising Above and Force:

VERTICALITY in terms of above (and below) orientation is expressed with the following predicate (where the first argument is above the second):

$$Above(\dots,\dots)$$

The spatial relationship in 'the book is on the table' can be described writing *Above(book,table)* together with CONTACT(*book,table*) (see Section 4.2.4.2 for details).

In order to continue with the image schemas, ATTRACTION or 'force' is essential to include for many of the image schemas, including SUPPORT (see Figure 4.4). From a developmental psychology perspective, it goes against intuition to include correctly represented physical laws and forces that are present in our world in a formalisation of image schemas. However, even children early understand that forces are part of how objects relate to one another and their environment. An inaccurate but fairly straightforward way to approach 'force' would be to look at how force relates to movement, e.g. how gravity pulls the book towards the centre of the planet and how the table simply hinders this movement, in other words, SUPPORTs it. However, it is unlikely that children have any comprehension of any notion in which a book is 'moving towards the centre of the Earth' as it appears to simply rest on the table. What they do seem to comprehend is that a table will offer the book a surface to rest on.

Following the introduced notion of image schema primitives the force relation is written as follows (where the first argument puts force on the second):

$$forces(\dots,\dots)$$

Advancing down in the hierarchy of the CONTACT side of the Two-Object family the two weaker SUPPORT versions are formalised: Above-SUPPORT and Force-SUPPORT.

$$\forall O_1, O_2{:}Object\ (Above\text{-}\textsc{Support}(O_1, O_2) \leftrightarrow EC(O_1, O_2) \wedge Above(O_1, O_2))$$
$$\forall O_1, O_2{:}Object\ (Force\text{-}\textsc{Support}(O_1, O_2) \leftrightarrow EC(O_1, O_2) \wedge \mathsf{forces}(O_1, O_2))$$

When these two image-schematic structures are merged together the union corresponds to the universal and more complete image schema of SUPPORT.

$$\forall O_1, O_2{:}Object\ (\textsc{Support}(O_1, O_2) \leftrightarrow$$
$$EC(O_1, O_2) \wedge Above(O_1, O_2) \wedge \mathsf{forces}(O_1, O_2))$$

LINK:

In order to formalise LINK to the full complexity that is involved, a richer logic than that presented in this chapter is needed. However, the core of LINKage is not the flexibility in terms of how a link can be bent, stretched, etc. but rather that there is a link in the first place. As motivated in the previous chapter there are several kinds of LINKs (see Figure 4.5). For now, the formalisation of LINK is limited to those that are part of the CONTACT branching, glue-LINK and its predecessor in the hierarchy, Attraction-LINK.

THE TWO-OBJECT FAMILY: **an excerpt capturing different** LINK

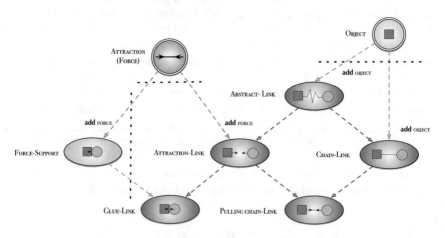

Fig. 4.5: Subset of the Two-Object Family: Constructing the different LINK schemas.

$$\forall O_1, O_2{:}Object\ (Attraction\text{-}\textsc{Link}(O_1, O_2) \leftrightarrow \mathsf{forces}(O_1, O_2) \wedge \mathsf{forces}(O_2, O_1))$$

By adding this to the Force-SUPPORT image schema you find yourself in the LINKage that has primitives of CONTACT and bi-directional force, see below.

$$\forall O_1, O_2 : Object \ (Glue\text{-}\text{LINK}(O_1, O_2) \leftrightarrow$$
$$\text{CONTACT}(O_1, O_2) \wedge Attraction\text{-}\text{LINK}(O_1, O_2))$$

Now that the static Two-Object relation image schemas have been introduced both in terms of their family as well as in their formalisation, the next section will be devoted to some of the members of the PATH-following family.

4.4 Formalising the PATH Family

The Two-Object family looked at static object relations. The PATH family instead deals with the movement of objects (Figure 3.3). Below, the required prerequisites are highlighted.

4.4.1 Required Spatial Primitives

From an ontological point of view, there might exist scenarios in which there exists movement without any objects. However, this goes against intuition from a cognitive perspective. This means that for all kinds of movement, at least one object is needed. Additionally, the movement needs to take place in a spatial 'region' which takes the form of a PATH. This means that for all members of the PATH family at least the spatial primitives OBJECT and PATH are present. While there is no physical need for the PATH to be connected to the OBJECT in order to follow the introduced logic it is presupposed that by using the described CONTACT schema, which implies 'not DC' (disconnected) from the RCC-8 calculus, it is possible to represent the dynamic image schema of PATH-following using an object that proceeds to move along that path.

As movement represents a change in position over time the formalisation must take the temporal dimension into account. As discussed in the previous chapter on the different conceptualisations of SOURCE_PATH_GOAL, Mandler and Cánovas (2014) argue for the existence of a conceptual primitive called 'move.' For the formalisation of movement of an object without a relative point of reference (i.e. another object or location, both discussed as early learned spatial primitives in Mandler and Cánovas (2014)) this spatial primitive is put to use. This is intended to be entirely purpose-free movement in which an object is present at one location (L_1) and as a consequence of the movement at some point will have another location (L_2) in the future. This is a weak form of movement, as the object can move back and forth. In order to be able to use the spatial primitive MOVE in the remainder of the

PATH family it first needs to be formalised. As the logic used is two-sorted, 'paths' are differentiated from 'objects.' Move is here defined by the relative movement in relation to the perceiver positioned at point *Me*.

$$\forall O{:}Object \, \big(Move(O) \leftrightarrow$$
$$(\exists y{:}Region \, (O \rightsquigarrow y)))$$

MOVEMENT_OF_OBJECT:

As it was argued to be unintuitive to speak of movement without objects, there is no difference in formal representation between the spatial primitive MOVE and the first member of the PATH-family, namely MOVEMENT_OF_OBJECT. Hence the formalisation is simplified by assuming that $\forall O{:}Object \, \big(\text{MOVEMENT\_OF\_OBJECT}(O) \leftrightarrow Move(O)\big)$.

MOVEMENT_ALONG_PATH:

Following how the PATH-following family branches out, the second step in the formalisation is to add a particular path, or trajectory that the object moves along. Just like objects are referred to as O_n the Paths are written P_n.

MOVEMENT_ALONG_PATH: O moves in the space, while remaining in contact with the path P.

$$\forall O{:}Object, \forall P{:}Path \, \big(\text{MOVEMENT\_ALONG\_PATH}(O,P) \leftrightarrow$$
$$Move(O) \wedge \text{CONTACT}(O,P) \, \mathbf{U}(\neg(Move(O) \vee \text{CONTACT}(O,P))))$$

SOURCE_PATH and PATH_GOAL:

As the family gets increasingly more specific, additional spatial primitives are required. First speaking of only source, then of only a goal, only to add them together to create a full SOURCE_PATH_GOAL structure.

First, SOURCE_PATH is modelled in which O moves along P from P's source. Second, PATH_GOAL is modelled with O moving towards a goal on P.

$$\forall O{:}Object, \forall P{:}Path \, \big(\text{SOURCE\_PATH}(O,P) \leftrightarrow$$
$$NTTP(Source(P) \wedge O \hookleftarrow Source(P) \wedge$$
$$\text{MOVEMENT\_ALONG\_PATH}(O,P)))$$

$$\forall O{:}Object, \forall P{:}Path \; \big(\text{PATH\_GOAL}(O,P) \leftrightarrow$$
$$NTPP(Goal(P) \wedge O \rightsquigarrow Goal(P) \wedge$$
$$\text{MOVEMENT\_ALONG\_PATH}(O,P))\big)$$

SOURCE_PATH_GOAL:

Merged together the union of these two formalisations forms the most classic form of the image schema, namely SOURCE_PATH_GOAL.

SOURCE_PATH_GOAL is modelled as the union of SOURCE_PATH and PATH_GOAL, with the restriction that the source of P cannot equal the goal of P.

$$\forall O{:}Object, \forall P{:}Path \; \big(\text{SOURCE\_PATH\_GOAL}(O,P) \leftrightarrow$$
$$(Source(P) \neq Goal(P)) \wedge \text{SOURCE\_PATH}(O,P) \wedge \text{PATH\_GOAL}(O,P)\big)$$

SOURCE_PATH_VIA_GOAL:

The path family becomes increasingly complex with additional segments, such as that found when SOURCE_PATH_GOAL is enhanced by the addition of a middle stop/point to pass. This means that while there is an overall goal of the movement, there is also a distinct point on the PATH that needs to be reached. In the PATH family, this was referred to as SOURCE_PATH_VIA_GOAL.

SOURCE_PATH_VIA_GOAL is modelled as two successive SOURCE_PATH_GOAL in which the middle location is initially the goal and then takes the place of the source for the movement.

$$\forall O{:}Object, \forall P{:}Path, \forall R{:}Region \; \big(\text{SOURCE\_PATH\_VIA\_GOAL}(O,P,R) \leftrightarrow$$
$$\text{SOURCE\_PATH\_GOAL}(O,P) \wedge DC(Source(P),R) \wedge$$
$$DC(Goal(P),R) \wedge NTPP(R,P)\big)$$

CLOSED_PATH_MOVEMENT, MOVEMENT_IN_LOOPS and REVOLVE_AROUND:

In the case of circular movement, the SOURCE and the GOAL are simply allowed to be the same entity. This also describes scenarios in which objects move back and forth, such as objects thrown up in the air.

CLOSED_PATH_MOVEMENT is the form of SOURCE_PATH_GOAL in which the goal and the source are in the same position.

$$\forall O{:}Object, \forall P{:}Path \ \big(\text{CLOSED\_PATH\_MOVEMENT}(O,P) \leftrightarrow$$
$$(Source(P) = Goal(P)) \wedge \text{SOURCE\_PATH}(O,P) \wedge \text{PATH\_GOAL}(O,P)\big)$$

CLOSED_PATH_MOVEMENT also resembles MOVEMENT_IN_LOOPS, with the difference that the latter does not have a defined end but continues. As ISL^{FOL} has no possibility to write continuous movement at the moment other than what is implied in the semantics of QTC, this is not possible to express using the logic. Similarly, it is possible for one object to revolve around another object that it has no relative movement towards/from. As this also is a form of continuous movement, the logic (for the time being) falls short of describing these scenarios.

The PATH-following family is one of the most important image schemas and there are undeniably more members than those considered and formalised in this chapter. The logic presented provides a stepping stone to how this can be approached further. In the upcoming Chapter 5 the image schemas will be combined with one another to demonstrate how this formal language can model simple events and more complicated image-schematic concepts.

4.5 A Critical Account on ISL^{FOL}

The first problem concerns movement when only one object is present. Building on the Qualitative Trajectory Calculus (QTC) (Weghe et al., 2006), in particular, its variant QTC$_{B1D}$, only one-dimensional movements *between* objects are considered. This means that using only QTC it is not possible to describe absolute movement. When representing the PATH-following family, where only one OBJECT is involved, this becomes a significant problem. However, ISL^{FOL} does not only take OBJECT into account in its semantics, also regions and paths are possible to define. This means that absolute movement of an object can be defined as 'there exists a region to which the object moves.' From a more cognitive perspective, an additional point of reference was given, *Me*. This is the point from which a perceiver is observing an image schema event. For the current uses of ISL^{FOL}, *Me* has not been given a concrete function. However, the concept has great importance for the future extension of ISL^{FOL} to allow image-schematic transformations such as SCALE, which is involved in the perception of movement coming closer and going further away, and SELF_MOVEMENT, the image schema that denotes the initiation of movement without any external force. Additionally, by centring an image-schematic event around a perceiver, *Me*, scenarios in which the perceiver is moving/transforming together with the object in question can be taken into account. For instance, a person sitting inside a car would not perceive the car as moving, but would rather argue that the 'landscape is flying by.'

A second problem concerns the relationship between objects. QTC presupposes 'moving point objects' whereas the spatial dimension represented using RCC (Randell et al., 1992) presuppose regions. As image schemas demonstrate how objects can be in CONTACT, go INto other objects etc., it is important to address how to calculate the centre of an object. As was argued previously this can and must be done in different ways. For an image schema such as CONTACT, it might be enough to calculate the minimal distance between two objects, but not for other image schemas such as CONTAINMENT. In its current version, ISL^{FOL} only calculates the distance between objects based on their geometric centre of the occupied region. However, dependent on the level of detail the shape of the object possesses in the model, this can become a problem. For instance, if one 'takes the jelly out of the doughnut,' the geometric centre does not change much. Likewise, with the current state of the model, it is possible to sail into Florida, while actually never disembarking as the geometric centre of the occupied region lies in the Gulf of Mexico. Naturally, the state of ISL^{FOL} and the current formalisations are based on a much more abstract level in which the exact spatial details of the logic hold little importance. However, if ISL^{FOL} is used to model real-life scenarios rather than abstract conceptualisations, these restrictions need to be addressed. This would also include restrictions on the size of the regions and the objects as, at least physically, a larger object cannot be contained within a smaller object (Galton, 2010).

Another challenge for ISL^{FOL} is the temporal dimension. Time is difficult to conceptualise as well as to capture formally and often the temporal dimension is simply conceptually mapped onto a spatial dimension (Boroditsky, 2000; Lambalgen and Hamm, 2005). In ISL^{FOL}, linear temporal logic (LTL) over the reals is used to describe the sequence of states. In the upcoming Chapter 5 the simplicity of using sequential steps will be put to the test by describing scenarios such as BLOCK-AGE, CAUSED_MOVEMENT and BOUNCING. Naturally, LTL, which presupposes a one-dimensional timeline, is perfectly suited for such scenarios. However, for increasingly complex scenarios in which time is branching or non-linear the current temporal representation in ISL^{FOL} needs to be revised. Here, inspiration can be found in the large variety of temporal logics that have been proposed to model various temporal aspects of natural language (Benthem, 1983; Prior, 1967). However, for the time being, the current state of ISL^{FOL} provides a satisfactory solution to this problem.

4.6 Chapter Conclusion

This chapter introduced ISL^{FOL} which is a logical language to represent the spatiotemporal aspects of conceptual building blocks such as image schemas. Inspired by previous formalisations of image schemas (e.g. Bennett and Cialone (2014); Galton (2010)), the logic deals with the spatial dimensions through the Region Connection Calculus (RCC) together with the cardinal directions according to Ligozat (1998). For dealing with relative movement between objects and regions, the logic uses Qualitative Trajectory Calculus (QTC) which is simplified to formally represent how one object relates to another object in terms of movement. The temporal dimension of image schemas is handled with Linear Temporal Logic (LTL) as it arguably is enough to present the sequence of events in the image schemas.

As a proof of concept, the logic was used to formally represent the Two-Object family and the PATH family from the previous Chapter 3.

In the upcoming chapter, the logic will be used to express how increasingly more complicated scenarios and simple events can be formally expressed. This is done by looking more closely at what it means when different image schemas are combined with one another. For that, the dynamic aspects of CONTAINMENT are formalised as well as the simple events BLOCKAGE, CAUSED_MOVEMENT and BOUNCING.

References

W. Aguilar and R. Pérez y Pérez. Dev E-R: A computational model of early cognitive development as a creative process. *Cognitive Systems Research*, 33:17–41, 2015.

J. A. Bateman, J. Hois, R. Ross, and T. Tenbrink. A Linguistic Ontology of Space for Natural Language Processing. *Artificial Intelligence*, 174(14):1027–1071, 2010.

B. Bennett and C. Cialone. Corpus Guided Sense Cluster Analysis: a methodology for ontology development (with examples from the spatial domain). In P. Garbacz and O. Kutz, editors, *8th International Conference on Formal Ontology in Information Systems (FOIS)*, volume 267 of *Frontiers in Artificial Intelligence and Applications*, pages 213–226. IOS Press, 2014.

J. V. Benthem. *The Logic of Time: A Model-Theoretic Investigation into the Varieties of Temporal Ontology and Temporal Discourse*. D. Reidel Publishing Company, Dordrecht, Holland, 1983.

L. Boroditsky. Metaphoric structuring: Understanding time through spatial metaphors. *Cognition*, 75(1):1–28, 2000.

S. H. Chavoshi, B. D. Baets, T. Neutens, M. Delafontaine, G. D. Tré, and N. V. de Weghe. Movement Pattern Analysis Based on Sequence Signatures. In *ISPRS Int. J. Geo-Inf.*, volume 4, pages 1605–1626, 2015.

A. G. Cohn, B. Bennett, J. Gooday, and N. Gotts. RCC: a calculus for region based qualitative spatial reasoning. *GeoInformatica*, 1:275–316, 1997.

M. Finger and D. M. Gabbay. Adding a Temporal Dimension to a Logic System. *Journal of Logic, Language and Information*, 1:203–233, 1993.

A. U. Frank and M. Raubal. Formal specification of image schemata – a step towards interoperability in geographic information systems. *Spatial Cognition and Computation*, 1(1):67–101, 1999.

H. U. Fuchs. From image schemas to narrative structures in sciences. contribution to the symposium on conceptual metaphor and embodied cognition in science learning. In *Science Education Research For Evidence-based Teaching and Coherence in Learning (Proceedings of the ESERA Conference)*, pages 216–228, Nicosia, Cyprus, 2013.

A. Galton. Some problems in temporal knowledge representation. In *Logic and Change, GWAI-92*, Bonn, Germany, September 1992.

A. Galton. The Formalities of Affordance. In M. Bhatt, H. Guesgen, and S. Hazarika, editors, *Proceedings of the workshop Spatio-Temporal Dynamics*, pages 1–6, 2010.

M. M. Hedblom, O. Kutz, T. Mossakowski, and F. Neuhaus. Between contact and support: Introducing a logic for image schemas and directed movement. In F. Esposito, R. Basili, S. Ferilli, and F. A. Lisi, editors, *AI*IA 2017: Advances in Artificial Intelligence*, pages 256–268, 2017.

M. Knauff, R. Rauh, and J. Renz. A cognitive assessment of topological spatial relations: Results from an empirical investigation. In S. C. Hirtle and A. U. Frank, editors, *Spatial Information Theory: A Theoretical Basis for GIS*, volume 1329 of *Lecture Notes in Computer Science*, pages 193–206. Springer, 1997.

F. Kröger and S. Merz. *Temporal Logic and State Systems (Texts in Theoretical Computer Science. An EATCS Series)*. Springer, 2008.

W. Kuhn. Modeling the Semantics of Geographic Categories through Conceptual Integration. In *Proceedings of GIScience 2002*, pages 108–118. Springer, 2002.

W. Kuhn. An Image-Schematic Account of Spatial Categories. In S. Winter, M. Duckham, L. Kulik, and B. Kuipers, editors, *Spatial Information Theory*, volume 4736 of *Lecture Notes in Computer Science*, pages 152–168. Springer, 2007.

O. Kutz, J. A. Bateman, F. Neuhaus, T. Mossakowski, and M. Bhatt. E pluribus unum: Formalisation, Use-Cases, and Computational Support for Conceptual Blending. In T. R. Besold, M. Schorlemmer, and A. Smaill, editors, *Computational Creativity Research: Towards Creative Machines*, Thinking Machines. Atlantis, 2014.

G. Lakoff and R. Núñez. *Where Mathematics Comes From: How the Embodied Mind Brings Mathematics into Being*. Basic Books, New York, 2000.

M. V. Lambalgen and F. Hamm. *The Proper Treatment of Events*. Explorations in Semantics. Wiley, 2005.

F. Lehmann and A. G. Cohn. The EGG/YOLK reliability hierarchy: Semantic data integration using sorts with prototypes. In *Proceedings of the Conference on Information Knowledge Management*, pages 272–279. ACM Press, 1994.

G. Ligozat. Reasoning about cardinal directions. *J. Vis. Lang. Comput.*, 9(1):23–44, 1998.

J. M. Mandler and C. P. Cánovas. On defining image schemas. *Language and Cognition*, 6(4):510–532, May 2014.

L. Morgenstern. Mid-Sized Axiomatizations of Commonsense Problems: A Case Study in Egg Cracking. *Studia Logica*, 67:333–384, 2001.

S. Nayak and A. Mukerjee. Concretizing the image schema: How semantics guides the bootstrapping of syntax. In *2012 IEEE International Conference on Development and Learning and Epigenetic Robotics, ICDL 2012*, 2012.

A. Oltramari. *An Introduction to Hybrid Semantics: The Role of Cognition in Semantic Resources*, pages 97–109. Springer, Berlin, Heidelberg, 2012.

C. Pagán Cánovas. Erotic Emissions in Greek Poetry: A Generic Integration Network. *Cognitive Semiotics*, 6:7–32, 2010.

A. N. Prior. *Past, Present and Future*. Oxford University Press, Oxford, 1967.

D. A. Randell, Z. Cui, and A. G. Cohn. A spatial logic based on regions and connection. In *Proceedings of the 3rd International Conference on knowledge representation and reasoning*, 1992.

T. Regier. *The Human Semantic Potential: Spatial Language and Constrained Connectionism*. MIT Press, 1996.

M. Reynolds. The complexity of temporal logic over the reals. *Annals of Pure and
Applied Logic*, 161(8):1063 – 1096, 2010.

F. Santibáñez. The object image-schema and other dependent schemas. *Atlantis*, 24
(2):183–201, 2002.

A. Scivos and B. Nebel. The Finest of its Class: The Natural, Point-Based Ternary
Calculus $\mathscr{LR}$ for Qualitative Spatial Reasoning. In *Spatial Cognition*, pages
283–303, 2004.

R. St. Amant, C. T. Morrison, Y.-H. Chang, P. R. Cohen, and C. Beal. An image
schema language. In *International Conference on Cognitive Modeling (ICCM)*,
pages 292–297, 2006.

M. Steedman. Formalizing affordance. In *Proceedings of the 24th annual meeting
of the cognitive science society*, pages 834–839, 2002.

N. V. D. Weghe, A. G. Cohn, G. D. Tré, and P. D. Maeyer. A qualitative trajectory
calculus as a basis for representing moving objects in geographical information
systems. *Control and cybernetics*, 35(1):97–119, 2006.

Part III
Putting Formalised Image Schemas to Use

Chapter 5
Modelling Conceptualisations: Combining Image Schemas to Model Events

Abstract The notion that image schemas are used as conceptual building blocks in language and conceptualisations as a whole has been repeatedly pushed. It was repeatedly demonstrated that the qualification for image-schematic concepts and the identification between the different image schemas are problems for the research field. It was suggested that more complex image schemas could be viewed as combinations of simpler image-schematic structures, or components from different families. This chapter explores this by looking specifically at image schema combinations. After introducing three different types of image-schematic combinations it also aims to demonstrate how these combinations can be considered to construct the conceptualisation of complex image schemas and simple events as in 'image schema profiles'. This is placed into the framework of formalising image schemas by discussing their usefulness in commonsense reasoning problems as well as an ISL^{FOL} formalisation of the dynamic aspects of CONTAINMENT and the simple image-schematic events BLOCKAGE, CAUSED_MOVEMENT and BOUNCING. The chapter includes considerations and discussions on :

- Commonsense reasoning with image schemas
- Simple vs. complex image schemas
- Three types of image schema combinations
- Formalising the Dynamic Aspects of CONTAINMENT
- Formalising BLOCKAGE, CAUSED_MOVEMENT and BOUNCING

5.1 Motivation

5.1.1 Commonsense Reasoning with Image Schemas

One of the reasons why it matters to look at image schemas not only from an individual instance point of view but also what they mean in conceptualisations of events and narrative is the potential impact it may have for commonsense reasoning problems.

For instance, in Morgenstern's [2001] solution to Davis' prototypical *Egg Cracking problem*[1], Morgenstern uses no fewer than 66 axioms to describe the process of cracking an egg into a bowl. In more complex scenarios, such as making an omelette or preparing pancakes, the number of needed axioms and designed knowledge increases. While artificial intelligence research has recently dramatically advanced with new technologies and methodologies concerning neural networks and machine learning, many AI systems that strive for modelling human commonsense reasoning still rely on hard-coded formal representations of basic aspects of cognition. Indeed, for humans, understanding and executing scenarios, such as egg cracking, are automatic processes, and whatever script underlies these actions, little mental effort is required. Imagine if it was possible to use some of the human automation also in artificial intelligence more generally.

For this combinations of image schemas as a means not only to express affordances but also to express narratives can come to play an important part. Image schemas have been repeatedly demonstrated to be an important part of analogical reasoning. For computational commonsense reasoning, this form of information transfer holds promise as it does not reject the classic knowledge representation format, and therefore allows for integration into already built systems such as the analogy engine HDTP (Schmidt et al., 2014) or the conceptual blender HETS (Mossakowski et al., 2007), more on this in the upcoming Chapter 6.

5.1.2 Simple vs. Complex Image Schemas

Some important characteristics of image schemas are that they exist as both static and dynamic concepts (Cienki, 1997; Tseng, 2007), and in both simple and more complex forms (Mandler and Cánovas, 2014). As was demonstrated in previous chapters with the identification problem, there appears to be no clear border for when one image schema ends and another begins (Grady, 2005). This implies that the borders between image schemas are blurred if not directly overlapping. Simple image schemas tend to be more straightforward than complex image schemas. One major differentiation between simple and complex image schemas is that complex image schemas arguably can be described as higher-level concepts within the image schema family, basically approaching the identification problem through a hierarchy of increasing complexity. However, for this to be possible, complex image schemas often inherit spatial primitives from other image-schematic families (Santibáñez, 2002), turning them into combinations of different image schemas. For instance, Lakoff and Núñez (2000) demonstrate how the combination of CONTAINMENT and SOURCE_PATH_GOAL forms the conceptual structure in prepositions and verbs such as 'into' and 'entering,' which then transfer to more complex natural language ex-

---

[1] See commonsensereasoning.org/problem_page.html for the problem description.

pressions such as 'to get into trouble.' Likewise, take the spatiotemporal events of 'pouring coffee into a cup' or 'going into the house,' both of these scenarios are traditionally considered to be part of the CONTAINMENT schema through the subcategory of the IN schema. In Section 5.3, this will be further analysed as the dynamic aspects of CONTAINMENT will be formally unravelled.

5.2 Image Schema Combinations

It is clear that image schemas can be combined with one another in many different ways. In order to pinpoint the nature of image schema combinations, a few examples will be provided. First, the combination between the image schemas LINK and PATH into a new image-schematic structure: LINKED_PATH, appears as cognitively intuitive. It follows from how easy it is to visualise two objects that move together and react to external stimuli in the same way (or through transitivity). The conceptual blend that takes place in the merge follows naturally. Based on the information transfer that underlies image schemas, this combination is also used as a means to explain abstract concepts. A real-life example is the conceptualisation of the concept 'marriage,' where two individuals are perceived to go through life together (Mandler, 2004).

Similarly, PATH can be combined with SUPPORT (or CONTAINMENT), resulting in the conceptualisation behind 'transportation' (Kuhn, 2007). This is particularly interesting because it illustrates how image schemas become part of the definition of what concepts are[2].

Another metaphorical example is the idiom 'to hit the wall.' In many contexts, this does not mean to physically crash into a wall but instead implies some form of mental breakdown, often preceded by long-term stress or exhausting efforts. The idiom captures the image schema of BLOCKAGE. It is clear that BLOCKAGE is not an atomic image schema but rather a temporal combination of several ones. Breaking it down, there are at least two OBJECTs, at least one member of the PATH-family, and at least one time point when the two objects are in CONTACT. Translating it to the linguistic expression: The OBJECTs represent the person and the abstract time point and/or scenario with which the person 'crashed,' so to speak, and this moment captures an abstract version of the image schema CONTACT. Additionally, as was previously demonstrated, PATHs often describe time and processes. In this case, the PATH present in the idiom captures the time and processes that precede the 'crash.'

As demonstrated, this kind of image-schematic breakdown can be done not only on concrete scenarios but also on many abstract natural language expressions. These mentioned examples lead primarily to three different ways in which image schemas can be combined with one another. These three methods are introduced and discussed under the names: *Merge*, *collection* and *structured* (see Figure 5.1).

---

[2] This as an idea was empirically investigated and the results are presented in Chapter 7

5.2.1 The Three Different Types of Image Schema Combinations

Fig. 5.1: Illustration of the three different types for how image schemas can be combined with one another.

Merging: is an operation that takes a number of image schemas and merges them (non-commutatively) into newly created primitive concepts. These primitives are not yet logically analysed, but carry strong cognitive semantics. This process can be iterated to create ever more complex primitives, as happens in the cognitive development of children. This is the case with LINKED_PATH, which is a conceptual merge of two image-schematic notions. It would correspond to the intersections in the image schema families in which multiple families are contributing with image-schematic components.

Collection: technically corresponds to the formation of an unsorted multiset of atomic and merged image schemas used to describe scenes or objects in a complex scenario. A collection of image schemas does not per se alter the Gestalt properties of a particular spatiotemporal relationship, but instead functions as a joint representation for a particular concept. Most representations of concepts and non-linear events fit into this category. A previously mentioned example is the conceptualisation of 'transportation' as the combination of PATH and SUPPORT and/or CONTAINMENT.

Structured: covers the case where, on the one hand, merged image schemas receive a formal semantics, and on the other hand, the temporal interaction that is absent in the 'collection' scenario is formally made explicit using temporal logic. This means that structured combinations most often conceptualise processes and events (usually with a clear linear structure) rather than static concepts. In the upcoming sections, this will be looked at in the cases of formalisation of BLOCKAGE, CAUSED_MOVEMENT and BOUNCING[3].

5.2.1.1 Merges: Atomic Combinations turn into Complex Image Schemas

The idea in Chapter 3 captures a way to address complex image schemas that involve spatial (and temporal) primitives originating from different image schema families. When image schemas are sorted into such graphs, there are intersections where dif-

---

[3] Note that BOUNCING is not an image schema, but can be described as an image-schematic event.

ferent schema families overlap. For instance, even though Going_IN is often conceptualised as an atomic image schema in its own right, it is arguably better analysed as
a SOURCE_PATH_GOAL that results in an instance of CONTAINMENT. This in fact
gives a good example for the non-commutative nature of the 'merge' operation, here
denoted by $\mathbb{M}$. Given the primitives $s, c \in \mathfrak{A}$ (for SOURCE_PATH_GOAL and CON-
TAINMENT), one obtains the merges $s \mathbb{M} c$ and $c \mathbb{M} s$ creating two new primitives that
take the sum of the arguments of the component image schemas, but where the first
corresponds to Going_IN and the latter to Going_OUT.

Likewise, the more advanced image schema REVOLVING_MOVEMENT is part
of the SOURCE_PATH_GOAL family, yet it can be argued that it inherits the revolving pattern from the image schema CYCLE and the spatial proportions of CEN-
TER_PERIPHERY.

This line of combining image schemas to build new ones can be interpreted as a
particular instance of the theory of conceptual blending, introduced in Fauconnier
and Turner (1998) (see Eppe et al. (2018) for a more formal computational treatment) which will be discussed in Chapter 6.

5.2.1.2 Collections: Classic Image Schema Profiles

The second form of image schematic combination, here called **collection**, is where
image schemas co-exist to describe a concept, distinct from their own properties. For
instance, it describes how the concept *transportation* actualises the image schemas
SOURCE_PATH_GOAL and SUPPORT (or CONTAINMENT) (Kuhn, 2007), but the
image schemas themselves are not merged, they are simply grouped together to capture the conceptualisation of the concept; that is, they each provide relevant properties for the overall schema. Experiments have been performed to demonstrate this
phenomenon of using image schemas to describe the essence of objects, for instance,
in (Gromann and Macbeth, 2019) and Chapter 7. In (Oakley, 2010), these profiles
are specifically described to be without any particular structure or order. Instead,
they are thought to correspond to the gathered experience a person has with a particular concept. For instance, when presented with a familiar scenario, e.g., *going to
the supermarket* or *borrowing a book at the library*, we have a mental generalisation
based on all previous (explicit and implicit) experiences with that particular scenario
and have a mental space for that concept that we use to verbalise our thoughts when
conversing and interacting with other people. In the more generic, often-experienced
situations, human conceptualisations can be argued to be greatly overlapping across
people. For instance, despite strong cultural differences, it is likely that all humans
share the same, or essentially indistinguishable, conceptualisation of the concepts of
being hungry and *going to sleep* as they are fundamentally embodied in their nature.
For events such as *going to war* or *preparing Turducken*[4] which many of us never
experience first hand, our conceptualisations are based on the accounts of others.
This is one of the strengths of the human mind. Namely, that a person who never

---

[4] A dish prepared through the iterative stuffing of a chicken into a duck, and the duck into a turkey.

cooked *Turducken* can still create an image schema profile to capture the process of preparing the dish. One such conceptualisation could consist of: going IN—as the chicken goes into the duck, and the duck goes into the turkey; CONTAINMENT—as the animals remain inside 'each other;' ITERATION—as this process is repeated three times; and SCALE—as the chicken, the duck, and the turkey are treated in their respective sizes. Naturally, an expert chef frequently preparing the dish might understand that there is more at work. This form of combining image schemas behaves like **collections** as they are without any internal structure and temporal or hierarchical order.

5.2.1.3 Structured: Sequential Image Schema Combinations

A metaphorical example for a structured combination is the idiom *to hit a wall*. In many contexts, this does not mean to physically crash into a wall but instead implies some form of mental or physical breakdown, often preceded by long-term stress or exhausting efforts. The idiom captures the image schema of BLOCKAGE. It is clear that BLOCKAGE is not an atomic image schema but rather a **sequential** combination of several ones. It would not be inaccurate to describe BLOCKAGE as a merge of other image schemas, as it is built on primitives from several image schema families (among others SOURCE_PATH_GOAL and CONTACT) but it is more useful to acknowledge the sequential dimension of the image schema; basically, the presence of a cause-and-effect relationship. The structured sequences of image schemas used to model events resemble Schankian scripts (Schank and Abelson, 1975), but with the crucial difference that each scene in the sequence is defined by a potentially different image-schematic structure. This is an important distinction as the image schemas are inherently meaningful and would as such be the core meaning of a particular present situation. Therefore, one could assume that a particular event segment (i.e., a scene) remains the same as long as there is no alteration in the image-schematic structure.

5.2.2 Defining Events

Throughout this chapter, events[5] are to be understood as defined, for instance, by Galton (2012) who defines an event as:

> "(...) a temporally bounded occurrence typically involving one or more material participants undergoing motion or change, usually with the result that at least one partipant [sic!] is in a different state at the end of the event from the beginning."

---

[5] The precise ontological nature and status of events has for a long time been, and still is, an open question and lies outside the focus of the present book. For instance, the reader may look more closely at the work by Bach (1986) for a classic account on the classification of events and their internal structure. Alternative proposals have also been made by Lambalgen and Hamm (2005); Mourelatos (1981); Pustejovsky et al. (2005), among others.

This notion of event is also well-suited to an embedding in the context of narratives (which are to be understood as reports of connected events presented in a sequential manner as mental images, written or spoken words, visual scenes, and/or similar), particularly when allowing for participants that only exhibit a 'derived materiality.'

The next sections will demonstrate how a few complex image schemas and simple events can emerge as consequences of combinations of simpler image schemas. These combinations will build on the family representation in Chapter 3 and the logic presented in Chapter 4. First the dynamic aspects of CONTAINMENT are introduced, as they represent good examples of image schemas merging together, followed by the somewhat more complex scenarios BLOCKAGE, CAUSED_MOVEMENT and BOUNCING, which represent a structured combination of image schemas (collections of image schemas will be empirically investigated in Chapter 7).

5.3 Formally Modelling the Dynamic Aspects of CONTAINMENT

5.3.1 Requirements of CONTAINMENT

5.3.1.1 Objects, Containers and Openings

While image schemas can often be described without direct reference to objects, it might be seen as unintuitive to speak of spatiotemporal relationships without considering the spatial primitive OBJECT (Mandler and Cánovas, 2014). For CONTAINMENT, a minimum of two objects is required: a container and a containee. In the context of the logic described above, it is the atomic names O_i that represent objects (here: considered subsets of 3D Euclidean space). Given the lack of restrictions on the interpretations of the O_i, these objects can also cover the 'openings' of containers or other, not strictly physical interpretations of objects. Only finitely many objects (actually rarely more than 3 or 4) participate in a given scenario, and therefore direct quantification over objects is intentionally avoided with the motivation that it is cognitively inadequate.

The kinds of entities that are clearly relevant from an image-schematic point of view on CONTAINMENT are: (i) (physical) objects, (ii) insides and outsides (of objects), (iii) openings (of objects), and (iv) paths ('carrying' the movement of objects). These need not be analysed further topologically, and therefore the language is augmented with the following primitive predicates:

- inside(O): is a function to denote the *inside* of O
- opening_of(op, O): op is an opening of O,
- cavity_of(cav, O): cav is a cavity of O

Here, it is supposed that all objects may only have one inside(I), but they may have several openings opening_of(op, O) and cavities cavity_of(cav, O). Imagine for example a cabinet, it usually has several drawers each with its own hatch, yet objects are inside the cabinet regardless of in which drawer they are. A bowl on the other hand has only one inside with one cavity, but in some cases the borders of the 'inside' can extend outside of the physical borders. For instance, in an overflowing fruit bowl, even the apples that are 'outside' of the container are still inside the bowl. Here the inside is larger than the bowl's cavity. Rather than further analysing these predicates topologically, they are assumed to be fixed by the model, with appropriate interpretation functions. Solutions for defining these notions in detail can be found in the literature (Casati and Varzi, 1997; Davis et al., 2017), and are omitted here to focus on the high-level commonsense modelling of the dynamics of CON-TAINMENT. Notice that an opening can be both an object, or a path, and vice versa, therefore, no restrictions on the interpretations are meaningful in general. Further, as evidenced by examples such as "And he said, Call her. And when he had called her, she stood in the door"[6], or an expression like "He got stuck in the revolving door," openings can be containers of objects at the same time.

Thus three different kinds of containers can be distinguished regarding the role of openings, for examples see Figure 5.2. While all types of containers per definition have an inside, an outside and a border (Johnson, 1987), these kinds can be differentiated by the nature of the realisable dynamic aspects, namely how objects can move IN and OUT of them.

This means that the border's characteristics are highly relevant for the dynamic aspects of CONTAINMENT insofar as they relate to openings, just as the characteristics of the containee and the container are essential to the nature of the static representation of CONTAINMENT (e.g. a contained liquid is more likely to correspond to a tight-fitted container). However, from an image-schematic point of view, it is the affordance-centred characteristics of openings regarding possible movements, rather than the mereotopological analysis of the border, which is central to the basic understanding of the dynamics of containers.

Fig. 5.2: Examples of the three different kinds of containers considered: a cup, a building and a lake.

One opening: These are the most prototypical containers, in which objects go in
and out through the same entry point. A coffee cup fits this category.

---

[6] 2 Kings 4:15, King James Bible

Two or more openings: These are the containers in which an object may exit at
   another point than the entry. Tunnels, buildings and colanders belong to this category.

Flexible openings: These containers have 'liquid' borders in which no directly
   specified openings exist, but where objects can (essentially) leave the containment through any part of the border. Spatial regions, liquids and more abstract
   concepts are examples of this kind of container.

While an opening is arguably most often part of the object's border (when understood in the commonsense meaning of the word rather than topologically), which in
turn can be argued to be part of the conceptualisation of a container any opening has
two potential states. The opening may either be bi-directional, as in a cup in which
coffee can both go in and out, or uni-directional in which objects can only move
in one direction (or simply only move through once) such as normally found when
eating and swallowing.

5.3.1.2 Representation of Static CONTAINMENT

Despite distinguishing between three different kinds of containers in relation to their
openings, the nature of the actual containment, such as the eight found CONTAIN-
MENT relationships presented by Bennett and Cialone (2014), is not considered.
Simplified as illustrated in Figure 5.3, it is presupposed that if something is contained within another object, it does not (at the moment) matter if they touch the
border or not, whether they are tight (NTPP) or loose (TPP) forms of CONTAIN-
MENT. Following the ISL^{FOL} language in Chapter 4, the formalisation of the state
of one object being contained within another by first establishing the relationship of
a proper part (PP):

$$\forall x,y\text{:}Region \left(PP(x,y) \leftrightarrow TPP(x,y) \vee NTPP(x,y) \right)$$

$$\forall O_1,O_2\text{:}Object \left(\text{Contained\_Inside}(O_1,O_2) \leftrightarrow PP(O_1,\text{inside}(O_2)) \right)$$

As it is possible also for objects to be inside regions and for regions to be inside
objects two additional versions are needed:

$$\forall O\text{:}Object, \forall R : Region \left(\text{Contained\_Inside\_Region}(O,R) \leftrightarrow PP(O,\text{inside}(R)) \right)$$

And analogously:

$$\forall O\text{:}Object, \forall R : Region \left(Region\text{\_Contained\_Inside}(R,O) \leftrightarrow PP(R,\text{inside}(O)) \right)$$

Fig. 5.3: Illustration of Contained_Inside(x,y)

Next, as a first approximation, the outside is defined as the complement of the object together with its inside, based on assumed Boolean region terms, as studied in the case of RCC8 in detail in (Wolter and Zakharyaschev, 2000).

$$\forall O_1, O_2 : Object \left(\text{outside\_of}(O_1, O_2) \leftrightarrow \right.$$
$$\left. DC(O_1, \text{inside}(O_2)) \vee EC(O_1, \text{inside}(O_2)) \right)$$

5.3.1.3 Related Object Movement

After introducing the state of being contained, one of the central foci is how to represent relative movement between the containee to-be and the container, see Figure 5.4. While the SOURCE_PATH_GOAL schema was thoroughly introduced in Chapter 3, for this purpose the movement dimension is simplified by talking exclusively of relative object movement following the ISL^{FOL} language. This is represented in the following manner:

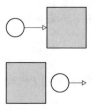

Fig. 5.4: Illustration of $x \rightsquigarrow y$ respectively $x \leftarrow y$

$$\forall O_1, O_2 : Object \left(\text{On\_PATH\_Toward}(O_1, O_2) \leftrightarrow \right.$$
$$\left. (O_1 \rightsquigarrow O_2 \wedge \text{outside\_of}(O_1, O_2)) \right)$$

As with Contained_Inside above, two additional formalisations are needed to take into account when objects are moving towards regions, respectively when regions are moving towards objects.

Note that in the case that the objects are externally connected (EC) the distance between the objects needs to be calculated based on the geometric centre, rather than the shortest possible distance.

$$\forall O\text{:}Object, \forall R\text{:}Region \ (\text{On\_PATH\_From\_}Region(O,R) \leftrightarrow$$
$$(O \hookleftarrow R \wedge \text{outside\_of}(O,R)))$$

$$\forall O\text{:}Object, \forall R\text{:}Region \ (Region\text{\_On\_PATH\_Toward}(R,O) \leftrightarrow$$
$$(R \rightsquigarrow O \wedge \text{outside\_of}(R,O)))$$

Enforced by the entailments of image schemas, transitivity is an essential aspect of not only the static aspects but also the dynamic aspects of CONTAINMENT (Johnson, 1987). This means that if the container moves, the containee must move as well. This is true for all 'true containers'[7] namely that:

$$\forall O_1, O_2, O_3\text{:}Object \ ((\text{Contained\_Inside}(O_1, O_2) \wedge$$
$$\text{On\_PATH\_From}(O_2, O_3)) \implies$$
$$\text{On\_PATH\_From}(O_1, O_3))$$

5.3.1.4 Entering the Opening

Dynamic aspects of image schemas can be dissected into smaller building blocks. First is the scenario of one object entering the container's opening, or 'crossing its border.' To avoid temporal confusion, the formalisations assume continuity of time and space and therefore omit some of the logical steps of the sequence in order to better model human cognition following the results in (Bogaert et al., 2008).

Simplified, one can argue that an object is contained as long as it has entered the container, and not left it. The formalisation below can easily be translated to crossing the border by substituting the opening for a border. Formalised it reads:

$$\forall O_1, O_2\text{:}Object, \forall op\text{:}Region \ (\text{Crossing\_Opening}(O_1, O_2, op) \leftrightarrow$$
$$\text{opening\_of}(op, O_2) \wedge (\text{On\_PATH\_Toward}(O_1, op) \ \mathbf{U} \ PO(O_1, op)))$$

In this variation, it is the opening of object O_2 that is doing the moving.

---

[7] In opposition, a non-true container would not entail this transitivity and could for example simply denote 'overlap.' For example, 'being in the shade' would demonstrate a non-true container.

$$\forall O_1, O_2 : Object, \forall op : Region \ (Opening\_Crossing(O_1, O_2, op) \leftrightarrow$$
$$\textsf{outside\_of}(O_1, O_2) \wedge \textsf{opening\_of}(op, O_2) \wedge$$
$$(On\_Path\_Toward(op, O_1) \ U \ PO(O_1, op)))$$

Now that these formal building blocks are introduced, let us proceed to see what three of the most basic dynamic aspects of CONTAINMENT look like: *going* IN, *going* OUT and *going* THROUGH.

5.3.2 Dynamics of CONTAINMENT

Going IN:

The most obvious dynamic aspects of CONTAINMENT are the movements of entering and exiting. As it has already been formalised what crossing the opening looks like, the difference lies in the end state. Entry/going into:

$$\forall O_1, O_2 : Object, \forall op : Region \ \big(Going\_IN(O_1, O_2, op) \leftrightarrow$$
$$On\_Path\_Toward(O_1, op)$$
$$U \ PO(O_1, op)$$
$$U \ Contained\_Inside(O_1, O_2)\big)$$

There is also the scenario in which it is the container that takes the active role in 'something becoming contained.' Here it is presented as 'Swallowed_By' to illustrate the active role of the container:

$$\forall O_1, O_2 : Object, \forall op : Region \ \big(Swallowed\_By(O_1, O_2, op) \leftrightarrow$$
$$(\textsf{outside\_of}(O_1, O_2) \wedge On\_Path\_Toward(O_2, O_1))$$
$$U \ On\_Path\_Toward(op, EO_1)$$
$$U \ PO(O_1, op)$$
$$U \ Contained\_Inside(O_1, O_2)\big)$$

Going OUT:

Similarly, there are two forms of exit. One dominated by the containee and one by the container. The second scenario is particularly interesting as it implies a weakened LINK-state between the containee and the container, as the container 'leaves' or ejects the containee behind. Previously it was pointed out that these are not necessarily 'true containers,' but regardless humans still use similar linguistic expressions for them.

$$\forall O_1, O_2 : Object, \forall op : Region \ (Going\_OUT(O_1, O_2, op) \leftrightarrow$$
$$Contained\_Inside(O_1, O_2)$$
$$\mathbf{U} \ On\_PATH\_Toward(O_2, O_1)$$
$$\mathbf{U} \ PO(op, O_1)$$
$$\mathbf{U} \ outside\_of(O_1, O_2))$$

When the container moves away from the containee[8]:

$$\forall O_1, O_2 : Object, \forall op : Region \ (Container\_Leaving(O_1, O_2, op) \leftrightarrow$$
$$Contained\_Inside(O_1, O_2) \wedge$$
$$\mathbf{U} \ On\_PATH\_Toward(O_2, O_1)$$
$$\mathbf{U} \ PO(op, O_1)$$
$$\mathbf{U} \ outside\_of(O_1, O_2))$$

Going THROUGH:

In Section 5.3.1, three different kinds of containers were distinguished, based on their number of openings. Naturally, in order to go THROUGH something, one cannot exit at the entry point. It is therefore essential to not only go IN and OUT, but to go out at another location, basically following the idea that "when a door closes, a window opens." Thus, the two openings are part of the conceptualisation of 'going THROUGH:'

$$\forall O_1, O_2 : Object, \forall op_1, op_2 : Region \ (Going\_THROUGH(O_1, O_2, op_1, op_2) \leftrightarrow$$
$$opening\_of(op_1, O_2) \wedge opening\_of(op_2, O_2) \wedge (op_1 \neq op_2) \wedge$$
$$(Going\_IN(O_1, O_2, op_1)$$
$$\mathbf{U} \ Contained\_Inside(O_1, O_2)$$
$$\mathbf{U} \ Going\_OUT(O_1, O_2, op_2)$$
$$\mathbf{U} \ (outside\_of(O_1, O_2))))$$

The dynamic aspects of CONTAINMENT are only one of the areas in which combinations of image schemas can be formalised. In the next section, this will be extended upon by formalising the conceptualisation of events.

---

[8] In the case of actual 'ejection of the containee,' a formal representation of force and agency is needed.

5.4 Formally Modelling BLOCKAGE, CAUSED_MOVEMENT and BOUNCING

In order to explain how image schema combinations model events, the PATH family will be combined with the Two-Object Family to model the complex image schemas BLOCKAGE and CAUSED_MOVEMENT as well as the conceptually similar event BOUNCING.

5.4.1 Formalising BLOCKAGE

BLOCKAGE, or 'blocked movement,' is a commonly mentioned image schema in the literature as children early learn to predict how one object may hinder the movement of another. This is a common phenomenon that may have many different outcomes and in the following sections, (some of) these outcomes will be explored. Needed first, however, is the most general form of BLOCKAGE.

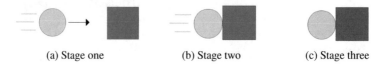

(a) Stage one   (b) Stage two   (c) Stage three

Fig. 5.5: Illustrations of the three time intervals of BLOCKAGE. a) O_1 On_PATH_Toward O_2. b) O_1 Blocked_By O_2. c) O_1 In_CONTACT with O_2.

The simplest form of blocked movement is the scenario in which the movement of an object simply ceases to exist. While BLOCKAGE is considered an image schema in its own right, it is also possible to describe blockage using a sequential series of simple image schemas: MOVEMENT_OF_OBJECT, CONTACT and 'force'[9], followed by the lack of MOVEMENT_OF_OBJECT. Figure 5.5 illustrate these three image-schematic stages.

Following the formalisation language ISL^{FOL} that was introduced in Chapter 4 these three stages demonstrated in Figure 5.5 can individually be represented as[10]:

---

[9] In Chapter 3, force is introduced as a conceptual primitive from the force group of image schemas, more specifically, the ATTRACTION image schema. However, it can also be described as a non-spatial component that should not be included under image schemas (Mandler and Cánovas, 2014). Regardless, as it is not in itself an image schema it is presented in lower case letters.

[10] Note that the formalisation of On_PATH_Toward(O_1, O_2) differs from that above, as it now is no longer relevant to speak of 'insides' and 'outsides.' Instead the RCC relation DC is implied in the semantics.

$$\forall O_1, O_2 : Object \; \big(\text{On\_PATH\_Toward}(O_1, O_2) \leftrightarrow$$
$$O_1 \rightsquigarrow O_2 \wedge \text{outside\_of}(O_1, O_2) \big)$$

$$\forall O_1, O_2 : Object \; \big(\text{Blocked\_By}(O_1, O_2) \leftrightarrow$$
$$(O_1 \mid \circ \, O_2 \wedge O_2 \mid \circ \, O_1 \wedge Force\text{-SUPPORT}(O_1, O_2)) \big)$$

$$\forall O_1, O_2 : Object \; \big(\text{CONTACT}(O_1, O_2) \leftrightarrow$$
$$(O_1 \mid \circ \, O_2 \wedge O_2 \mid \circ \, O_1 \wedge EC(O_2, O_1)) \big)$$

Using these building blocks to model the temporal scenario of BLOCKAGE with the ISL^{FOL} results in the following formalisation[11]:

$$\forall O_1, O_2 : Object \; \big(\text{BLOCKAGE}(O_1, O_2) \leftrightarrow$$
$$(\text{On\_PATH\_Toward}(O_1, O_2) \; \textbf{U} \; \text{Blocked\_By}(O_1, O_2)$$
$$\textbf{U} \; \text{In\_CONTACT}(O_1, O_2)) \big)$$

Here, the time operator guarantees that these events happen in the correct temporal order.[12]

As these first steps until contact between two objects happen in all the subsequent scenarios, the defined predicates of On_PATH_Toward(O_1, O_2) and Blocked_By(O_1, O_2) will be repeatedly put to use.

One interesting thing to note here is that formalised and in combination with motion, BLOCKAGE works much like Force-SUPPORT. Compare the axiom for SUPPORT and the axiom for Blocked_By.

$$\forall O_1, O_2 : Object \; \big(Force\text{-SUPPORT}(O_1, O_2) \leftrightarrow$$
$$EC(O_1, O_2) \wedge \text{forces}(O_1, O_2) \big)$$

$$\forall O_1, O_2 : Object \; \big(\text{Blocked\_By}(O_1, O_2) \leftrightarrow$$
$$(O_1 \mid \circ \, O_2 \wedge O_2 \mid \circ \, O_1 \wedge$$
$$Force\text{-SUPPORT}(O_1, O_2)) \big)$$

The only difference is the addition of a temporal aspect through the lack of movement $(O_1 \mid \circ \, O_2 \wedge O_2 \mid \circ \, O_1)$. This is an interesting observation, as our experience is effected by our physical world, meaning that gravitational pull could be viewed as a sort of 'downward' movement and that all SUPPORT is simply BLOCKAGE of movement in that direction. In an alternative universe with different physical laws, either through science fiction or artificial simulation, it is likely that there would be other distinctions for these image schema structures.

---

[11] Note that the semantics of ISL^{FOL} includes QTC which presupposes disjoint objects. Therefore, all representations need to take this into account.

[12] In the case of animated objects, this would behave differently.

5.4.2 *Formalising* CAUSED_MOVEMENT

There are more scenarios that can follow from BLOCKAGE than the static relation of CONTACT between the moving object and the blocking object, that was presented above. One of the more 'complex' image schemas that appears in the literature is CAUSED_MOVEMENT. Namely the spatiotemporal relationship that comes to be as one object crashes into another and causes it to move.

Simplified, this particular image schema comes in three different forms. First, in the scenario in which the hitting object comes to rest while the hit object continues onward (e.g. as in a well-executed billiards shot), referred to as 'Pure_CM.' Second, in which both objects continue in disjoint forward movement, 'Pursuit_CM.' Thirdly, in the scenario in which the objects together continue forward, 'Joint_CM.' This scenario holds an important distinction from the other CAUSED_MOVEMENTS. The reason for this is that there are limited natural scenarios in which an inanimate object will proceed to push another object. Children early learn to distinguish the role agency has in objects (including animals and people) and how this affects the movement pattern of the object. For instance, children learn how to distinguish between SELF_MOVEMENT and CAUSED_MOVEMENT at an early age and associate SELF_MOVEMENT with agency and animated life. In the case of pushing, there is an underlying understanding that the first object has some power to maintain the force and direction throughout the action of the pushing which could be considered to be a sign for agency, here referred to as the conceptually weaker 'Joint_CAUSED_MOVEMENT' (Joint_CM).

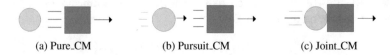

(a) Pure_CM   (b) Pursuit_CM   (c) Joint_CM

Fig. 5.6: Illustrations of the three alternative endings of CAUSED_MOVEMENT. a) O_2 moves away from O_1. b) O_1 and O_2 move forward. c) O_1 and O_2 move together.

As focus lies on the second object, it is for the image schema itself irrelevant whether the first object is in movement or not. However, for the sake of completeness, all three scenarios will be individually formalised to pinpoint the complexity of properly formalising the minor differences that exist in simple events and image-schematic structures.

As presented above, the first two steps which will be consistently repeated are defined as follows. First that O_1 is on a path toward O_2 which is then followed by O_1 being blocked by O_2. The first of the three alternative endings of CAUSED_MOVEMENT, Pure_CM (see Figure 5.6a) is formalised below:

$$\forall O_1, O_2 : Object \ (\text{Pure\_CM}(O_1, O_2) \leftrightarrow O_2 \leftarrow O_1 \wedge O_1 \,|\circ O_2)$$

The second of the three alternative endings of CAUSED_MOVEMENT, Pursuit_CM, (see Figure 5.6b) differs from Pure_CM as both objects move forward:

$$\forall O_1, O_2 : Object \ (\text{Pursuit\_CM}(O_1, O_2) \leftrightarrow O_1 \rightsquigarrow O_2 \land O_2 \hookleftarrow O_1)$$

In the third alternative ending for CAUSED_MOVEMENT, Joint_CM, both objects move forward while in CONTACT (see Figure 5.6c):

$$\forall O_1, O_2 : Object \ \big(\text{Joint\_CM}(O_1, O_2) \leftrightarrow$$
$$Force\text{-SUPPORT}(O_1, O_2) \land O_1 \rightsquigarrow O_2 \land O_2 \mid \circ O_1\big)$$

These three scenarios are the most obvious scenarios that are involved in CAUSED_MOVEMENT. In full temporal representation, the scenarios looks as follows:

$$\forall O_1, O_2 : Object \ \big(\text{CAUSED\_MOVEMENT}(O_1, O_2) \leftrightarrow$$
$$\text{On\_PATH\_Toward}(O_1, O_2)$$
$$\textbf{U} \ \text{Blocked\_By}(O_1, O_2)$$
$$\textbf{U} \ (\text{Pure\_CM}(O_1, O_2) \ \underline{\vee} \ \text{Pursuit\_CM}(O_1, O_2) \ \underline{\vee} \ \text{Joint\_CM}(O_1, O_2))\big)$$

It is here noteworthy that is it possible that the movement of O_2 is in fact not a CAUSED_MOVEMENT. It could be SELF_MOVEMENT that simply by coincidence happened at the same time that another object was blocked by it.

5.4.3 Formalising BOUNCING

Another natural scenario that happens as one object hits another, is BOUNCING. In comparison to CAUSED_MOVEMENT, the object of interest here is not the object that is hit but rather the object that is doing the hitting.

The formalisation below correspond to the end result of BOUNCES, as depicted in Figure 5.7a.

$$\forall O_1, O_2 : Object \ \big(\text{BOUNCES}(O_1, O_2) \leftrightarrow O_1 \hookleftarrow O_2 \land O_2 \mid \circ O_1\big)$$

In full temporal representation the scenario looks as follows:

$$\forall O_1, O_2{:}Object \left(\text{BOUNCING}(O_1, O_2) \leftrightarrow\right.$$
$$\text{On\_PATH\_Toward}(O_1, O_2)$$
$$\textbf{U} \text{ Blocked\_By}(O_1, O_2)$$
$$\textbf{U} \text{ BOUNCES}(O_1, O_2))$$

5.4.4 The Combination of CAUSED_MOVEMENT and BOUNCING

Another event that might take place is the scenario in which CAUSED_MOVEMENT is merged with the event of BOUNCING. In this scenario, the hitting object O_1 bounces on O_2 while at the same time the impact pushes the blocking object away. Formalised the end result reads (see Figure 5.7b):

$$\forall O_1, O_2{:}Object \left(Bouncing\_CM(O_1, O_2) \leftrightarrow O_1 \leftarrow O_2 \wedge O_2 \leftarrow O_1\right)$$

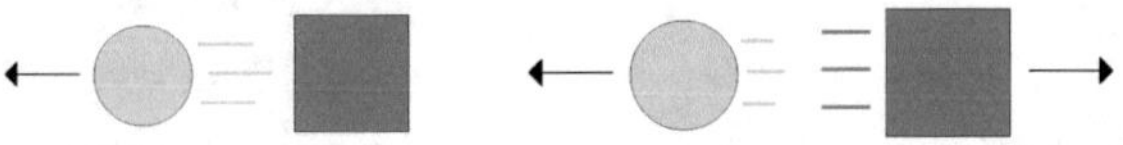

(a) BOUNCING   (b)   BOUNCING   and
                            CAUSED_MOVEMENT

Fig. 5.7: Illustrations of the results of BOUNCING respectively the result of the combination of CAUSED_MOVEMENT and BOUNCING. a) O_1 BOUNCES on O_2. b) O_1 BOUNCES and O_2 moves forward.

The full event is then formalised as follows:

$$\forall O_1, O_2{:}Object \left(Bouncing\_CM(O_1, O_2) \leftrightarrow\right.$$
$$\text{On\_PATH\_Toward}(O_1, O_2)$$
$$\textbf{U} \text{ Blocked\_By}(O_1, O_2)$$
$$\textbf{U} \text{ Bouncing\_CM}(O_1, O_2))$$

5.5 Chapter Conclusion

It is non-trivial to represent events, not only from the perspective of developmental psychology, but also for cognitive systems and natural language comprehension in computational systems. Following the presented approach with image schemas as the conceptual building blocks, this chapter showed how the ISL^{FOL} language introduced in Chapter 4 can not only be used to represent the image schema families from Chapter 3 but also be used to model complex image schemas, events and image schema profiles.

In the introduction of the Chapter, Morgenstern's [2001] solution to Ernie Davis's [1997] *Egg Cracking problem* was mentioned as an example to demonstrate the difficulty of formally capturing a real-life scenario relating to some of the CONTAINMENT aspects. For egg cracking some immediate CONTAINMENT notions are: how the egg is inside the shell, how it is 'poured' OUT from the crack and INto the bowl. In Hedblom et al. (2019a,b) a more image-schematic approach to breaking down the scenes in egg cracking is introduced. The argument presented there is that a change in image-schematic state constitutes an ontologically sound point for event segmentation. However, still further work is needed to validate to which extent the integration of formalised image schemas can reduce the required number of axioms as well as making better inferences in commonsense reasoning problems. The idea behind image-schematic formalisations is, in their role as conceptual building blocks, to use them as design patterns when describing scenarios and events (Besold et al., 2017; Hedblom et al., 2019a; St. Amant et al., 2006).

The approach in this chapter represents some of the initial steps towards a more substantial formalisation of image schemas that can be used not only in representation of commonsense problems, but also in analogy engines (e.g. HDTP (Schmidt et al., 2014)) and similar systems such as those for conceptual blending (e.g. HETS (Mossakowski et al., 2007) as demonstrated by Gómez-Ramírez (2015); Neuhaus et al. (2014)). The next chapter will particularly look at the role image schemas could play in computational conceptual blending.

References

E. Bach. The algebra of events. *Linguistics and Philosophy*, 9(1):5–16, 1986.

B. Bennett and C. Cialone. Corpus Guided Sense Cluster Analysis: a methodology for ontology development (with examples from the spatial domain). In P. Garbacz and O. Kutz, editors, *8th International Conference on Formal Ontology in Information Systems (FOIS)*, volume 267 of *Frontiers in Artificial Intelligence and Applications*, pages 213–226. IOS Press, 2014.

T. R. Besold, M. M. Hedblom, and O. Kutz. A narrative in three acts: Using combinations of image schemas to model events. *Biologically Inspired Cognitive Architectures*, 19:10–20, 2017.

P. Bogaert, R. M. Emile van der Zee, N. V. de Weghe, and P. D. Maeyer. Cognitive and linguistic adequacy of the qualitative trajectory calculus. In *Proceedings van de Internationale Workshop "From Natural to Formal Language" (In association with "GIScience")*, pages 1–7, 2008.

R. Casati and A. C. Varzi. *Spatial Entities*, pages 73–96. Springer, Dordrecht, 1997.

A. Cienki. Some properties and groupings of image schemas. In M. Verspoor, K. D. Lee, and E. Sweetser, editors, *Lexical and Syntactical Constructions and the Construction of Meaning*, pages 3–15. John Benjamins Publishing Company, Philadelphia, 1997.

E. Davis, G. Marcus, and N. Frazier-Logue. Commonsense reasoning about containers using radically incomplete information. *Artificial Intelligence*, 248:46–84, 2017.

M. Eppe, E. Maclean, R. Confalonieri, O. Kutz, M. Schorlemmer, E. Plaza, and K.-U. Kühnberger. A computational framework for conceptual blending. *Artificial Intelligence*, 256:105–129, 2018. ISSN 0004-3702. doi: https://doi.org/10.1016/j. artint.2017.11.005. URL http://www.sciencedirect.com/science/article/pii/S000437021730142X.

G. Fauconnier and M. Turner. Conceptual integration networks. *Cognitive Science*, 22(2):133—187, 1998.

A. Galton. States, processes and events, and the ontology of causal relations. In *Formal Ontology in Information Systems*, volume 239 of *Frontiers in Artificial Intelligence and Applications*, pages 279–292, 2012.

D. Gómez-Ramírez. Conceptual Blending as a creative meta-generator of mathematical concepts: Prime ideals and Dedekind domains as a blend. In *Proceedings of the 4th international workshop on computational creativity, concept invention, and general intelligence (C3GI), Publications of the Institute of Cognitive Science*, volume 2, pages 1–11, 2015.

J. E. Grady. Image schemas and perception: Refining a definition. In B. Hampe and J. Grady, editors, *From Perception to Meaning: Image Schemas in Cognitive Linguistics*, pages 35–55. Mouton de Gruyter, Berlin, 2005.

D. Gromann and J. C. Macbeth. Crowdsourcing image schemas. In *Proceedings of TriCoLore*, volume 2347 of *CEUR-WS*, Bolzano, Italy, 2019.

M. M. Hedblom, O. Kutz, R. Peñaloza, and G. Guizzardi. What's Cracking: How image schema combinations can model conceptualisations of events. In *Proceedings of TriCoLore*, volume 2347 of *CEUR-WS*, Bolzano, Italy, 2019a.

M. M. Hedblom, O. Kutz, R. Peñaloza, and G. Guizzardi. Image Schema Combinations and Complex Events. *KI - Künstliche Intelligenz*, 33:279–291, 2019b.

M. Johnson. *The Body in the Mind: The Bodily Basis of Meaning, Imagination, and Reason*. University of Chicago Press, 1987.

W. Kuhn. An Image-Schematic Account of Spatial Categories. In S. Winter, M. Duckham, L. Kulik, and B. Kuipers, editors, *Spatial Information Theory*, volume 4736 of *Lecture Notes in Computer Science*, pages 152–168. Springer, 2007.

G. Lakoff and R. Núñez. *Where Mathematics Comes From: How the Embodied Mind Brings Mathematics into Being*. Basic Books, New York, 2000.

M. V. Lambalgen and F. Hamm. *The Proper Treatment of Events*. Explorations in Semantics. Wiley, 2005.

J. M. Mandler. *The Foundations of Mind: Origins of Conceptual Thought: Origins of Conceptual Though*. Oxford University Press, New York, 2004.

J. M. Mandler and C. P. Cánovas. On defining image schemas. *Language and Cognition*, 6(4):510–532, May 2014.

L. Morgenstern. Mid-Sized Axiomatizations of Commonsense Problems: A Case Study in Egg Cracking. *Studia Logica*, 67:333–384, 2001.

T. Mossakowski, C. Maeder, and K. Lüttich. The Heterogeneous Tool Set. In O. Grumberg and M. Huth, editors, *TACAS 2007*, volume 4424 of *Lecture Notes in Computer Science*, pages 519–522. Springer, 2007.

A. P. D. Mourelatos. Events, processes, and states. In *Tense and Aspect*, pages 191–212. Academic Press, 1981.

F. Neuhaus, O. Kutz, M. Codescu, and T. Mossakowski. Fabricating Monsters is Hard - Towards the Automation of Conceptual Blending. In *Proceedings of Computational Creativity, Concept Invention, and General Intelligence (C3GI-14)*, volume 1-2014, pages 2–5, Prague, 2014. Publications of the Institute of Cognitive Science, Osnabrück.

T. Oakley. Image schema. In D. Geeraerts and H. Cuyckens, editors, *The Oxford Handbook of Cognitive Linguistics*, pages 214–235. Oxford University Press, Oxford, 2010.

J. Pustejovsky, I. Mani, and R. Gaizauskas, editors. *The Language of Time: A Reader*. Oxford University Press, 2005.

F. Santibáñez. The object image-schema and other dependent schemas. *Atlantis*, 24 (2):183–201, 2002.

R. C. Schank and R. P. Abelson. Scripts, plans, and knowledge. In *IJCAI*, pages 151–157, 1975.

M. Schmidt, U. Krumnack, H. Gust, and K.-U. Kühnberger. Heuristic-Driven Theory Projection: An Overview. In H. Prade and G. Richard, editors, *Computational Approaches to Analogical Reasoning: Current Trends*, volume 548 of *Computational Intelligence*. Springer, 2014.

R. St. Amant, C. T. Morrison, Y.-H. Chang, P. R. Cohen, and C. Beal. An image schema language. In *International Conference on Cognitive Modeling (ICCM)*, pages 292–297, 2006.

M.-Y. Tseng. Exploring image schemas as a critical concept: Toward a critical-cognitive linguistic account of image-schematic interactions. *Journal of literary semantics*, 36:135–157, 2007.

F. Wolter and M. Zakharyaschev. Spatial reasoning in RCC-8 with boolean region terms. In W. Horn, editor, *Proceedings of the 14th European Conference on Artificial Intelligence (ECAI)*, pages 244–248, Berlin, Germany, 2000. IOS Press.

Chapter 6
Generating Concepts: Guiding Computational Conceptual Blending with Image Schemas

Abstract In the previous chapters, the formal aspects of representing image schemas were dealt with. Likewise, the role of image schemas in conceptualisations was investigated in the previous chapter. This chapter advances the work on concept invention by suggesting how image schemas can be integrated into conceptual blending, introduced in Chapter 1 as a theoretical framework for creativity. It includes two different approaches. The first focuses on giving image-schematic information higher priority to be inherited into the blended space. The second is to use image schemas as the foundation in the generic space. In addition to providing a series of examples of how this would look, the chapter also goes into details on how the family structure from Chapter 3 can be used during the blending to either strengthen or weaken the image-schematic structure in the input spaces, if needed. The chapter includes considerations and discussion on:

- Problems with computational blending
- Previous work on formalising conceptual blending
- Using image schemas in conceptual blending: i) As priority heuristics, ii) In the generic space, iii) Blending with the family hierarchy
- Examples of image schemas in conceptual blending

6.1 Image-Schematic Information Skeletons

6.1.1 Hypotheses and Motivation

One of the main research assumptions is that image schemas construe the smallest building blocks that are used by humans to understand their world, to comprehend linguistic expressions, including abstract expressions such as metaphors, and for event conceptualisation, and also that they provide an information skeleton upon which analogical reasoning can be performed. In the previous chapters, some theoretical work was presented that aims to strengthen these hypotheses.

© Springer Nature Switzerland AG 2020

M. M. Hedblom, *Image Schemas and Concept Invention*, Cognitive Technologies,
https://doi.org/10.1007/978-3-030-47329-7_6

Based on these results, another hypothesis follows, namely, that if it is through image-schematic skeletons that humans gain knowledge from analogical transfer, it follows as a natural consequence that image schemas ought to play a central role in the generation of new concepts as well (Forceville, 2016).

In Chapter 1, conceptual blending was introduced as a framework for concept invention, in which conceptual spaces, or ontologies in formal domains, are merged together under certain criteria to generate novel concepts and conceptual spaces. As image schemas represent building blocks, this chapter will discuss how image schemas can be integrated into conceptual blending and consequently also provide a useful tool for computational creativity (Falomir and Plaza, 2019; Kutz et al., 2014a; Schorlemmer et al., 2014).

Before introducing the different ways image schemas can be used in conceptual blending, some linguistic motivation is presented. This is followed by a brief introduction to the utilised formal framework for computational conceptual blending (Fauconnier and Turner, 2003; Lakoff and Núñez, 2000; Turner, 2007) set in the context of the similar computational frameworks found in analogy engines.

6.1.2 Examples of Image Schemas as Analogy and Blending Skeletons

In Chapter 2 image schemas were discussed in their role in conceptual metaphors and analogical reasoning. Here one suggestion was that image schemas could play a central role in the invariance principle, which states that the information transfer in all analogies is built on structure similarity (Turner, 1992). In this section, this will be linguistically demonstrated. One of the most focused-on image schemas is the SOURCE_PATH_GOAL schema, or as it was presented in Chapter 3, the PATH family. To demonstrate how SOURCE_PATH_GOAL often constructs the conceptual skeleton, this section looks more closely at how time and processes often are mapped to the spatial domain in the image schema.

6.1.2.1 Time and Processes as PATHs

The conceptualisation of time has been investigated by Boroditsky (2000). Following suit, this section looks at how members of the PATH-following image schema family are widely used as conceptual metaphors for time. Several examples are considered and the role of PATH-following image schemas for the conceptualisation of processes is discussed.

One popular way to conceptualise time is as MOVEMENT_ALONG_PATH. Often, time is conceptualised as having a beginning, a START_PATH; this may be the Big Bang or the moment of creation in a religious context. Depending on the cosmological preferences, time may also be conceptualised to have an end, an END_PATH: the Big Rip or the Apocalypse.

Other religious traditions embrace the notion of a 'Wheel of Time,' that is, time as a cyclic repetition of different aeons. The underlying image schema involves a CYCLE and as wheels are associated with physical movement, it can be extended to MOVEMENT_IN_LOOPS. The same image schema is used in the conceptualisation of time within calendars: the seasons are a continuous cycle where any winter is followed by a new spring. Similarly, the hours of the day are represented on analogue clocks as 12 marks on a cycle, and the passing of time is visualised as MOVEMENT_IN_LOOPS of the hand of the clock.

The conceptualisation of time, in itself, is an interesting example of the usage of image schemas. However, the real significance is that these image schemas can be seen as providing the conceptual skeletal structure for the understanding of processes. Imagine a desire to understand a complex process, for instance, the demographic development of a country, the acceleration of a falling object, or the economic situation of a country. In these situations, humans often use two-dimensional coordinate systems where the vertical axis represents the property in question (e.g. population, speed, GDP, respectively) and the horizontal axis represents time, to transfer the information. These coordinate systems are so useful and so widely applicable because humans can conceptualise arbitrary processes as MOVEMENT_ALONG_PATH, where the paths represent some important dimension or aspect of the process.

PATH similes:

In Chapter 3, the PATH-following family was introduced and for each family member, linguistic examples were offered. In this section, this linguistic manifestation is used to motivate how this image-schematic skeleton can be used in analogical information transfer through PATH similes.

If a target domain X from the first column and a source domain Y from the second column in Table 6.1 are picked randomly, the resulting simile X *is like* Y will make sense. Of course, depending on the choice of X and Y, the simile may be more or less intuitive and interesting. Note that the target domains have little or nothing in common. Thus, at least at first glance, one would not expect that one can compare them meaningfully to one and the same source domain.

Table 6.1: PATH similes: <target> is like <source>.

Target Domain	Source Domain
Watching the football game	the swinging of a pendulum
Their marriage	a marathon
The story	escaping a maze
This piece of music	a sailboat during a hurricane
Bob's career	a roller coaster ride
Her thoughts	a Prussian military parade
Democracy in Italy	stroll in the park

The similes work because all of the concepts in the second column involve physical MOVEMENT_ALONG_PATH, which have some pertinent characteristics. These characteristics may concern the shape of the path itself. For instance, the path of a roller coaster involves many ups and downs and tight curves, the path out of a maze involves many turns, the path of a pendulum is regular and between two points. Or the characteristics can concern the way the movement is performed. For instance, the movement of a sailboat during a storm is erratic and involuntary, a stroll in the park is done leisurely. Or the characteristics can concern the effects the movement may have. For instance, running a marathon is exhausting, a Prussian military parade may be perceived as threatening. In each of the similes, some of the pertinent characteristics of the MOVEMENT_ALONG_PATH in the source domain are used to describe the process in the target domain. For example, in the simile 'Bob's career is like a Prussian military parade' the career is conceptualised as movement along a 'time path,' with career-related events like promotions as sites, or locations, on the path, and transfer characteristics from the movement of a Prussian military parade to this path. Thus, one way to read the simile is that Bob moves through the stages of his career in an exceptionally predictable fashion. The example illustrates how the similes work: first, the process is conceptualised in the target domain as MOVEMENT_ALONG_PATH, where the events of the process are ordered by time, and then some pertinent characteristic(s) of the MOVEMENT_ALONG_PATH of the source domain is transferred to the target domain following the rules of conceptual metaphors. This pattern is not just applicable to the concepts in Table 6.1. As was discussed above, any process can be conceptualised as MOVEMENT_ALONG_PATH, thus, any process could be added as target domain in Table 6.1. Further, any concept that involves interesting physical movement along some path could be added as source domain. Hence, the use of the image schema MOVEMENT_ALONG_PATH enables the mechanical generation of similes for processes.

CONTAINMENT similes:

To demonstrate that this phenomenon is not exclusive to PATH image schemas, consider the concepts 'Spaceship,' North Korea,' 'Spacetime,' 'Marriage' and 'Bank account.' While all these concepts differ significantly, they can all be argued to be construed as various kinds of containers. For physical containers such as spaceships, which may contain passengers and cargo, the CONTAINMENT schema is without a doubt. Likewise, geopolitical entities like North Korea instantiate the CONTAINMENT schema, as well since countries and spatial regions in general, have a two-dimensional boundary that people may either be inside or outside of. For more complex concepts such as 'Spacetime,' it is conceived as a container as not only space is a container, but time as well. Despite being a great simplifications of the laws involved within the Theory of Relativity (DiSalle, 2016), it does not prevent science fiction writers from construing spacetime as a container for planets, stars and other things. For example, in many fictive stories, it is possible to leave and return to the universe (e.g. by visiting a 'parallel universe'). While the first three examples are physical entities, 'Marriage' is an abstract and social entity. Thus, in the literal physical sense marriage cannot be a container. Nevertheless, humans use vocabulary that is associated with containers to describe marriage. In the conceptual space, one can 'enter' and 'leave' a marriage, marriages can be both 'open' and 'closed' which adds specifications to the IN and OUT movements, and people may find happiness 'in' their marriage. Similarly, a 'bank account' may *contain* funds, and if it is 'empty' it is possible to add additional funds 'into' the account in order to later take them 'out' again. This shows that while bank accounts and marriages are conceptually very different entities, it is still possible to say that the CONTAINMENT schema is essential for these concepts.

Similarly, as with the PATH similes above, the CONTAINMENT schema can also be used in similes. The first column (target domain) of Table 6.2 contains the mentioned concepts. The second column (source domain) contains various examples of concrete and physical containers that highlight some possible features of containers: a container may leak, be hard to get out of or have a flexible boundary. Randomly choosing an element from the first column and combining it with a random element in the second column with the structure *X is like a Y*, generates similes. For example, 'The universe is like a treasure chest,' 'Their marriage is like a prison,' 'My bank account is like a leaky pot.' Note that all of the resulting similes are cognitively meaningful. Some of them will intuitively have more appeal than others, which may only be meaningful within a particular context. For example, 'This spaceship is like a bottomless pit' may sound odd in isolation, but in the context of 'I have already 20.000 containers in storage, and there is still empty cargo space' the simile works.

Table 6.2: CONTAINMENT similes: <target> is like a <source>.

Target Domain	Source Domain
This spaceship	leaky pot
North Korea	prison
The universe	treasure chest
Their marriage	bottomless pit
My bank account	balloon

The fact that Table 6.2 can be used to randomly produce similes is linguistically interesting because the target concepts vary significantly. The concepts 'spaceship,' 'marriage' and 'North Korea' seem to have nothing in common. Therefore, the fact that they can all be compared meaningfully to the same concepts requires an explanation. Just like with the PATH similes, one answer is found if the notion is accepted that all concepts in the first column share the same underlying image schema, in this case CONTAINMENT. For this reason, they can be blended with the container concepts from the second column. Each simile projects some feature of CONTAIN-MENT in the source domain via analogical transfer onto the container aspect of the target domain. Thus, Table 6.2 provides evidence that image schemas can help us to identify or construe shared structures between concepts. This follows the invariance principle which argues that for conceptual metaphors to be possible, the same conceptual skeleton is needed.

The shared structure of concepts can be utilised in conceptual blending. For example, it is possible to conceptually blend the concepts 'universe' and 'balloon' into a 'balloon-universe,' here with the interpretation that the universe is continuously expanding and eventually will burst. Blending 'spaceship' with 'prison' could lead to various interesting concepts, for instance, a spaceship that is used as a prison.

It is also possible to attempt to blend two different concepts from the first column from Table 6.2. However, since these concepts contain more prominent aspects than CONTAINMENT, these blends may not involve the CONTAINMENT as shared structure. For example, in a blend of 'Spaceship' and 'North Korea' probably other aspects of the concept of North Korea would be more dominant such as that a 'North Korean Spaceship' may be, trivially, a spaceship built in North Korea. Only by providing some additional context one can prime the CONTAINMENT aspect of North Korea into the desired format.

Another example is the blend between 'marriage' and 'bank account' which may yield a concept such as a 'marriage account.' This new concept could be used in sentences like the following: 'Marcus and Susie have just spent a long and happy holiday together, this was a big 'investment' into their marriage account, it is now full of love' or 'Jim needs to watch the way he treats Jill, their marriage account is draining quickly and is nearly empty. She is probably going to leave him.' In this blend, the 'marriage account' is a container which contains positive feelings between the spouses rather than money. The blend inherits the domain from 'marriage,' with the major difference that the spouses themselves are no longer inside the container. Some main contributions of 'bank account' to the blend are the ability to 'invest' and 'check the balance' of the content in the 'marriage account.'

In Chapter 5 it was discussed how concepts and events are conceptualised in terms of image schema combinations. One important thing to acknowledge is that the combination is not a fixed variable, but rather how something is conceptualised depends greatly on the context. For example, surgeons may conceptualise people as containers of organs, blood, and various other anatomical entities, but in most contexts, humans are not conceptualised in this way. By choosing the appropriate context, an image schema may be pushed from the background into the conceptual forefront. In most contexts, a 'mother' is not conceptualised as a kind of container. However, in selected contexts, it is possible to generate similes for 'mother' reusing the source domains from Table 6.2, such as in 'The mother is pregnant with twins, she looks like a balloon' or 'The mother is like a prison for the unborn child.'

These examples show how the PATH family and the CONTAINMENT image schema are part of analogical reasoning in their role in similes. In the next section, some formal approaches to analogy and conceptual blending will be introduced before sketching a few examples of how image schemas can be integrated into conceptual blending.

6.2 Analogy Engines and Computational Conceptual Blending

One computational analogy framework is the Structure Mapping Theory and the associated implementation that can perform analogical transfer, the Structure Mapping Engine (SME) (Gentner, 1983). By trying to find common relationships in the analogy's source and target domain, the system performs generalisations to identify the involved structures. Similarly, the analogy engine Heuristic Driven Theory Projection (HDPT) computes a 'least general generalisation' of two input spaces through anti-unification[1] (Schmidt et al., 2014). Both of these systems rely on a purely syntactic approach without any consideration of the involved information in the domains, thus often performing poorly by making inappropriate and incorrect inferences.

Also for computational concept invention image schemas could play an important role (Confalonieri et al., 2016). Conceptual blending, a cognitive framework for concept invention, builds on the idea that creative generation comes from the blending of already known information and takes generalisations such as image schemas into account (Fauconnier and Turner, 1998). When building novel concepts through combination, there are several aspects that need to be taken into account to make sure that the resulting concept is not inconsistent. Confalonieri et al. (2016) propose a formal model for blending image schemas with the objective of concept invention. Their computational model captures the process by using logical operators such as anti-unification and a knowledge representation language called *feature terms*.

6.2.1 The Major Problem with Computational Conceptual Blending

One problem for computational conceptual blending, and related work such as analogy engines (e.g. Structure Mapping Engine (SME) (Forbus et al., 1989; Gentner, 1983) and Heuristic-Driven Theory Projection (HDPT) (Schmidt et al., 2014)) is the generation of a 'sensible' blend. In Chapter 1, this was discussed in relation to the example with the gryphon, where less successful blends of a lion and an eagle would be equally possible. In a completely automatised system, there is currently no simple way to distinguish the blends that a human would consider meaningful from those that lack cognitive value in the context of the input spaces. This problem grows exponentially in relation to the size of the input spaces. The larger the input spaces, the more combinations can be generated, resulting in a multitude of possible blends, most of which will make little sense if evaluated by humans. In real-life scenarios, the amount of information in the input spaces can be vast, complicating the process for successful concept invention tremendously when looked at as a formal, combinatorial problem.

---

[1] In computer science anti-unification is a process in which two symbolic expressions are searched for a common generalization.

A proposal to explain the ease with which humans perform blending is given via the ideas of *packing and unpacking*, as well as *compression and expanding* of conceptual spaces, as outlined by Turner (2014). These terms aim to capture how we mentally carry around ideas as compressed 'idea packages' that we can 'unpack' and utilise in different contexts on the fly. These packages are designed to be hooked into our surroundings to be used appropriately there. The process of packing and unpacking ideas is important for the contextualised usage of conceptual blends in various situations. Generally, the idea of *Optimality Principles* in blending theory is meant to account for an evaluation of the quality and appropriateness of the resulting blends (Fauconnier and Turner, 2003).

However, there is currently no general formal proposal for how such optimality principles could be implemented computationally, apart from some work on turning such principles into metrics for rather lightweight formal languages (Goguen and Harrell, 2004; Pereira and Cardoso, 2003).

The problem is not just one of applying enough forward constraints and optimality principles. In the CRIME-model found in (Veale et al., 2013), this problem is approached by constraining the search. The authors argue that blending must be considered in a task-specific context, simultaneously working forward from the input spaces and backward from the desired elements of the blended space.

6.2.2 Formalisation of Conceptual Blending

The approach to formalising conceptual blending is based on Goguen's (1999) work on *Algebraic Semiotics* in which certain structural aspects of semiotic systems are logically formalised in terms of algebraic theories, sign systems, and their mappings. In (Goguen and Harrell, 2010) algebraic semiotics has been applied to user interface design and conceptual blending. Algebraic semiotics does not claim to provide a comprehensive formal theory of blending. Indeed, Goguen and Harrell admit that many aspects of blending, in particular concerning the meaning of the involved notions, as well as the optimality principles for blending, cannot be captured formally. However, the structural aspects *can* be formalised and provide insights into the space of possible blends. The formalisation of these blends can be formulated using languages from the area of algebraic specification, for instance OBJ3 (Goguen and Malcolm, 1996).

Hois et al. (2010) and Kutz et al. (2012, 2014b) present an approach to computational conceptual blending, based on the tradition of Goguen's proposal (see Figure 6.1). In this approach, the input spaces were suggested to be represented as ontologies, for example, in the Web Ontology Language (OWL)[2]. Here also the structure that is shared across the input spaces, namely the generic space, is also represented as an ontology, which is linked by mappings to the input spaces. As proposed by Goguen, the blending process is modelled by a colimit computation, a

---

[2] 'OWL' refers to OWL 2 DL, see http://www.w3.org/TR/owl2-overview/

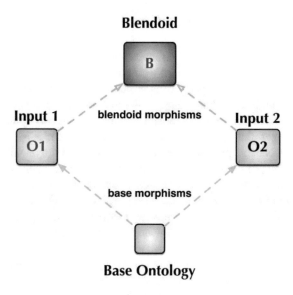

Fig. 6.1: The blending process using ontologies as input spaces and as the generic space, here referred to as the base ontology.

construction that abstracts the operation of disjoint union modulo the identification of certain parts specified by the base and the interpretations, as discussed in detail by Goguen (2003) and Kutz et al. (2010, 2012).

Regarding blending diagrams as displayed in Figure 6.1, notice the following discrepancy in terminology and in the way the basic blending process is visualised. In the cognitive science literature, following Fauconnier and Turner (1998), conceptual blending is visualised as shown in Figure 1.6, with a *generic space* at the top identifying commonalities. In the technically oriented literature following Goguen and Harrell (2010), the formalisation of this process is represented as a diagram as shown in Figure 6.1 with the generic space, or base ontology, at the bottom. This kind of diagram is, on the one hand, an upside-down version of the first illustration, following a tradition in mathematical diagrams where simpler concepts are often placed at the bottom. On the other hand, it replaces the term 'generic space' with 'base space.' partly because of a clash with mathematical terminology. The formalisation of blending presented makes no technical difference between 'generic space' and 'base space' and treats them as synonymous.

The inputs for a blending process, namely, input concepts, generic space and mappings, can be formally specified in networks, sort of *blending diagrams*, in the Distributed Ontology, Model, and Specification Language (DOL).

6.2.3 *Identifying the Structure in the Base Space*

As illustrated with the examples of similes in Section 6.1.2, a critical step in the blending process is the identification of the common structure of the generic space and its mapping to the input spaces. The structural similarity between conceptual blending and analogical thinking suggests the investigation and application of approaches to analogical reasoning as tools for computational conceptual blending.

One way to determine what is common to the input spaces is by means of looking at the cross-space mapping between them. Hence, structural mapping techniques that identify isomorphic substructures of the inputs might be useful to create an abstraction of this substructure. Here, cross-space mappings are established by means of the HDTP algorithm (Schmidt et al., 2014), which computes a restricted higher-order anti-unification of two input spaces represented as first-order logical theories. This anti-unification then serves as a generic space for the blend of the original first-order theories.

The algorithm is built on the Structure Mapping Theory (Gentner, 1983) which argues that analogical reasoning is characterised by the relationships between objects in the different domains rather than their attributes. HDTP computes a 'least general generalisation' B of two input spaces I_1 and I_2. This is done by anti-unification to find common structure in both input spaces I_1 and I_2. HDTP's algorithm for anti-unification is, analogously to unification, a purely syntactical approach that is based on finding matching substitutions. Another method for finding generalisations is presented in the *Analogical Thesaurus* which uses *WordNet*[3] to identify common categories for the source and target spaces (Veale, 2003).

While these are interesting approaches, they have a major disadvantage. Typically, for any two input spaces there exists a large number of potential generalisations. Thus, the search space for potential base spaces and potential conceptual blends is vast. HDTP implements heuristics to identify interesting anti-unifiers. In other words, it prefers anti-unifiers yielding rich theories over anti-unifiers yielding weak theories. However, since anti-unification is a purely syntactical approach, there is no way to distinguish cognitively relevant from irrelevant information. As a result, an increase in the size of the two input ontologies leads to an explosion of possibilities for anti-unifications, which is the major problem for computational conceptual blending.

6.3 Image Schemas in Conceptual Blending

Instead of relying on a purely syntactical approach to blending, the semantic content found in image schemas can be employed to help guide the blending process. The

---

[3] "WordNet is a large lexical database of English. Nouns, verbs, adjectives and adverbs are grouped into sets of cognitive synonyms (synsets), each expressing a distinct concept. Synsets are interlinked by means of conceptual-semantic and lexical relations." See https://wordnet.princeton.edu for more information.

basic idea here is that in order to identify common structure sufficient for defining a useful generic space for two, or more, given input spaces, it is possible to search for shared image-schematic information rather than arbitrary structure. Given the powerful role that image schemas generally seem to play in human conceptual (pre-linguistic) development, the working hypothesis is that the semantic content and cognitive relevance given by identifying shared image schemas will provide valuable information for constructing and selecting the more substantial or interesting possible blends.

Two methods will be discussed in which image schemas can improve the computational blending process. Image schemas can provide heuristics for, first, detecting conceptually valuable information from each input space and, second, for identifying suitable base spaces. In the upcoming sections, these methods will be discussed in more detail. In addition, the structuring of image schemas into family hierarchies presented in Chapter 3 will be demonstrated to be a valuable asset in these processes. To provide support for the usefulness of these methods, a series of examples will be presented.

6.3.1 Method One: Image Schema Prioritisation

The first method is rather straightforward. The presumption that image schemas are conceptual building blocks pushes the hypothesis that they are valuable pieces of information that surpass the information present in other properties such as visual cues. As argued for in Chapter 2 image schemas are tightly connected to affordances, which connects the objects and concepts to the 'uses' they afford, e.g. a cup affords actions involving CONTAINMENT such as 'pouring coffee IN/OUT' or 'containing liquid.' When novel concepts are created through conceptual blending, it is reasonable to assume that these affordances play a central role also in the emerging blend.

6.3.1.1 The Houseboat Example

The benefit of inheriting image schemas can be demonstrated with the classic blends, the 'Houseboat' and the 'Boathouse.' Both blended concepts are generated from the merge of the conceptual spaces 'house' and 'boat' (see Goguen (1999); Kutz et al. (2014b) for formalisations of the Houseboat example). Taking a closer look at the 'houseboat' example, which consists of a house to live in that also functions as a boat, the idea of giving higher priority to image-schematic content can be illustrated.

One of the most apparent image schemas associated with the input space 'house' is CONTAINMENT. One lives 'in' houses, houses 'contain' rooms and furniture, it is possible to go 'into,' 'out of' and 'through' a house, basically embodying both the static and the dynamic aspects of CONTAINMENT presented in Section 5.3. While

boats also can be containers, and therefore follow the structure of the CONTAIN-
MENT similes above, the most prominent feature of boats is that they can transport
people and goods from one point to another along a water-based path, capturing the
SOURCE_PATH_GOAL image schema. Consequently, one of the most cognitively
interesting blends that can arise from this merge is the 'houseboat' as it contains
both of these essential image schemas (see Figure 6.2 for an illustration).

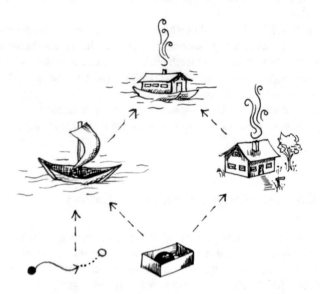

Fig. 6.2: The Blending of Houseboat. Here, both input spaces share the CONTAIN-
MENT schema, but only the input space 'boat' contains the SOURCE_PATH_GOAL
schema. For the blended space 'houseboat' both image schemas are present.

The blend 'boathouse' is another 'sensible' merge that can take place, but it contains a distinct difference. Here the mapping is not between the conceptual spaces
houses and boats as a whole, but between particular aspects, or subsets, of the inputs. Instead of making the boat a house and the house a boat, as in 'houseboat,'
the 'boathouse' remains entirely a house. The information transfer is based on a
conceptual mapping between 'people' and 'boats.' This means that the blending
process maps 'people *live_in* houses' to 'boats *live_in* boathouses.' As the blend
behaves more like a conceptual metaphor in which a CONTAINMENT-related affordance from the conceptual space 'house' is mapped directly to the conceptual space
'boat,' the SOURCE_PATH_GOAL schema is disregarded as it is not included in the
part of the input space that is responsible for the information transfer. This means
that for each input space that is blended the present image schemas play a central
role in the information transfer. Figure 6.3 shows the blending diagram made by
HETS to illustrate the relationships between the input spaces and the blended concepts 'houseboat' and 'boathouse.'

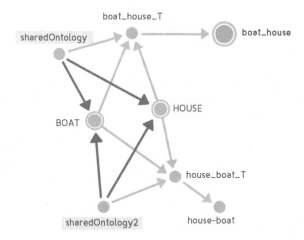

Fig. 6.3: The blending diagram of houseboat and boathouse created with HETS on Ontohub.

6.3.2 Method Two: Image Schema Projection

Another way to use image schemas in blending is to identify them as the prime ingredient for the construction of a generic space. When performing the search for common structure in the different input spaces, the search can be guided by mapping (parts of) the content of the input spaces to nodes in a library of formally represented image schemas. As image schemas hold semantic value in the form of spatial relationships, the blends would be based on the same content. In theory, this is similar to classic structure mapping that preserves relationships, but as image schemas model affordances (Kuhn, 2007) such as 'live_in' (CONTAINMENT) in the example of 'boathouse' in Section 6.3.1, which by definition have higher cognitive value, the blend will inherit such information as well.

6.3.2.1 The Mothership Example

The mothership example relies on the idea that image schemas can successfully constitute the generic space in the conceptual blending process as both the input concepts 'spaceship' and 'mother' share the CONTAINMENT schema.

In Chapter 5, CONTAINMENT was formally represented using ISL^{FOL}. In this section, the static form of CONTAINMENT will be put to use to describe the search for a generic space, see below.

$$\forall O_1, O_2 : Object\ (Contained\_Inside(O_1, O_2) \leftrightarrow PP(O_1, \mathsf{inside}(O_2)))$$

Here containers are defined as objects that have an inside, and for something to be Contained_Inside, it, more precisely the space input O_1 occupies, needs to be a proper part of that inside.

As previously mentioned, many conceptual spaces contain an information-rich structure. Naturally, no attempt is made to provide a full axiomatisation of the input spaces 'mother' nor 'spaceship,' but we simply focus on some salient points for the sake of illustrating the blending process.

In Section 6.1.2, it was argued that 'Mother' realises the CONTAINMENT schema since women can 'contain' unborn children. More specifically, woman have insides and a proper part of that inside is a 'uterine cavity,' which, in the case of (biological) mothers, at some point contained some child. For adult children, the pertinent relationship between mother and child is 'parent_of.'

Mothers, M, are described as females that are parents of humans, K, and have a UterineCavity, U, that is Contained_Inside the Mother.

$$\forall M{:}Object \; (Mother(M) \rightarrow$$
$$\exists K{:}Object, \exists U{:}Region \; (Female(M) \wedge Human(K) \wedge$$
$$Parent\_of(M,K) \wedge \textsf{cavity\_of}(U,M) \wedge \textsf{Contained\_Inside}(U,M)))$$

As Spaceships are a subcategory of vehicles, these need to be defined first. Vehicles are defined as objects with an inside, basically defining them as containers, as well as given the SOURCE_PATH_GOAL image schema. While vehicles may be at rest, the SOURCE_PATH_GOAL schema requires a path for 'potential' movement. From this, is it possible to define spaceships, which are described as vehicles Contained_Inside space, rather than on Earth, and that may have CargoSpace as a cavity_of that is a proper part of the inside of the vehicle.

Vehicles, V, are described as objects that have the image schema SOURCE_PATH_GOAL[4], and have an inside, I.

$$\forall V{:}Object \; (Vehicle(V) \rightarrow$$
$$\exists I{:}Region \; (has\_\textsc{Source\_Path\_Goal}(V) \wedge$$
$$\textsf{Contained\_Inside}(I,V)))$$

Spaceships, S, are described as vehicles, and thus inherit the image schema SOURCE_PATH_GOAL, they are Contained_Inside space rather than on Earth and have a CargoSpace, C, that is Contained_Inside the Spaceship.

---

[4] Gathered from the formalisations in Chapter 4, having the image schema is defined as follows:
$\forall O{:}Object, (has\_\textsc{Source\_Path\_Goal}(O) \leftrightarrow \exists P{:}Path(\textsc{Source\_Path\_Goal}(O,P)))$

$$\forall S{:}Object\ (SpaceShip(S) \rightarrow$$
$$\exists C, Space{:}Region\ (Vehicle(S) \wedge Contained\_Inside(S, Space) \wedge$$
$$CargoSpace(C)\ \wedge\ \mathsf{cavity\_of}(C,S)\ \wedge Contained\_Inside(C,S)))$$

During the blending into 'mothership,' the CONTAINMENT structure of both input spaces is preserved, see below. The uterine cavity and the cargo space are both mapped to the docking space. The 'mothership' inherits some features from both input spaces, while others are dropped. Obviously, a mothership is a space travelling vessel. But like a mother, it is a 'parent' to some smaller entities of the same type. These smaller vessels can be contained within the mothership, they may leave its hull (a process analogous to a birth) and are supported and under the authority of the larger vessel.

MotherShips, *MS*, are described as the union of SpaceShips, *S*, and Mothers. In this example, in addition to CONTAINMENT, both the image schema SOURCE_PATH_GOAL from the SpaceShip input, as well as the Parent_of relationship from the Mother input is inherited by the blend.

$$\forall MS{:}Object(MotherShip(MS) \rightarrow$$
$$\exists S{:}Object, \exists D, Space{:}Region\ (Vehicle(MS) \wedge$$
$$Contained\_Inside(D, MS)\ \wedge DockingPlace(D)\ \wedge \mathsf{cavity\_of}(D, MS) \wedge$$
$$Contained\_Inside(MS, Space)\ \wedge$$
$$Parent\_of(MS, S) \wedge SpaceShip(S)))$$

To summarise, in this example the input spaces of 'mother' and 'spaceship' are blended. Instead of trying to utilise a syntactic approach like anti-unification to search for a base space, it is recognised that both input spaces have cavities and, thus, are containers. Using the base space CONTAINMENT in the blending process yields a blended concept of 'mothership' (see Figure 6.4). Here, the precise mappings from the base space axiomatisation of CONTAINMENT to the two input spaces regulate the various properties of the blended concept. Note also that the principle of image schema prioritisation can also be applied in cases when an image schemas is only present in one of the input spaces. For instance, one can argue that mothers also have the SOURCE_PATH_GOAL schema, as they have the capacity for SELF_MOVEMENT, a high-level image schema capturing not only SOURCE_PATH_GOAL but also agency. In the next section, a method will be discussed to use the image schema family structure presented in Chapter 3, as a tool to identify members of the same family in several input spaces.

6.3.2.2 Blending with the Family Hierarchy

Chapter 3 presents in detail the idea that image schemas should be formally approached as interconnected families of theories, that are partially ordered by gen-

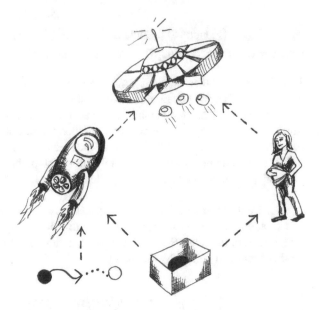

Fig. 6.4: In the blending of mothership the blend inherits properties and characteristics from each input space. As both input spaces have the CONTAINMENT schema, this is automatically inherited. Additionally, the SOURCE_PATH_GOAL image schema found in the spaceship is also given priority in the blending process.

erality. This section demonstrates the formal benefits of using a family structure to represent image schemas and how this also has benefits when performing computational conceptual blending.

Figures 6.5 and 6.6 show two basic ways of using image schemas within the conceptual blending workflow. In both cases, the image-schematic content takes priority over other information the input concepts might contain. In Figure 6.5, following the core model of blending described in Section 1.6, the different spatial structures are first identified within the same image schema family in the input concepts. They are then generalised to the most specific, common version within the image schema family to identify a generic space, using the pre-determined graph of image schemas (i.e. the least upper bound in the family hierarchy is computed).

The second case, Figure 6.6, illustrates the situation in which we first specialise or complete the (description of the) image schemas found in the input concepts, before performing a generalisation step and identifying the generic space. This means moving down in the graph of the image schema family and choosing a more specified member. Of course, also a mix of these two basic approaches is reasonable, in other words, where one input's image schema is specialised within a family whilst the other is generalised in order to identify a generic space based on image-schematic content.

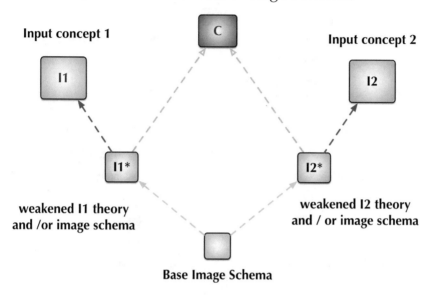

Fig. 6.5: Blending using common image schemas through theory weakening.

6.4 Complicated Problems: Recognising and Generalising Image Schemas

To implement computationally the idea of using image schemas as generic spaces, two independent algorithmic problems have to be solved. Namely, 1. the *Recognition Problem*: to identify an image-schematic theory within an input theory, and 2. the *Generalisation Problem*: to find the most specific image schema common to both inputs.

To address the recognition problem, suppose a theory graph $\mathfrak{F}$ encoding an image schema family is fixed. For simplicity, it is assumed that elements of $\mathfrak{F}$ will be logical theories in a fixed formal logic, say ISL^{FOL} with first-order logic elements[5]. Given an input theory I_1 and $\mathfrak{F}$, solving the recognition problem means finding a member $f \in \mathfrak{F}$ that can be *interpreted* in I_1, that is, such that a renaming σ of the symbols in f (called a signature morphism) is found and such that $I_1 \models \sigma(f)$ (also

---

[5] Note that none of the ideas presented here depends on a particular, fixed logic. Indeed, heterogeneous logical specification is central to formal blending approaches, see Kutz et al. (2014a).

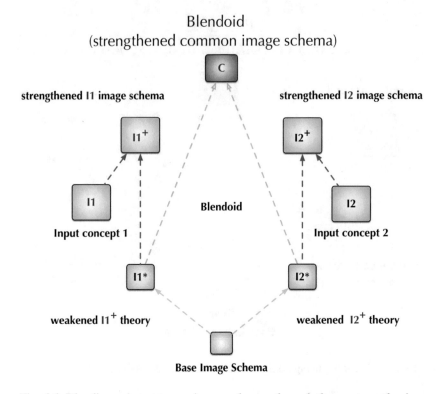

Fig. 6.6: Blending using common image schemas through theory strengthening.

written $I_1 \models_\sigma f$).[6] Note that this is a more general statement than claiming the inclusion of the axioms of f (modulo renaming) in I_1 (the trivial inclusion interpretation) since establishing the entailment of the sentences in $\sigma(f)$ from I_1 might in fact be non-trivial, and the axioms needed for this quite different from the ones in f.

Computational support for automatic theory-interpretation search in first-order logic is investigated in (Normann, 2008), and a prototypical system was developed and tested as an add-on to the Heterogeneous Tool Set (HETS) (Mossakowski et al., 2007). Experiments carried out in (Kutz and Normann, 2009; Normann and Kutz, 2009) showed that this works particularly well with more complex axiomatisations in first-order logic, rather than with simple taxonomies expressed in, for instance, OWL. This is because in the latter case too little syntactic structure is available to control the combinatorial explosion of the search task. From the point of view of interpreting image schemas into non-trivial axiomatised concepts, this can be seen as an encouraging fact, as image schemas are, despite their foundational nature, complex objects to axiomatise, and the main reason why Chapter 4 introduces ISL^{FOL}.

---

[6] In more detail: a theory interpretation σ is a signature morphism renaming the symbols of the image schema theory f and induces a corresponding sentence translation map, also written σ, such that the translated sentences of f, written $\sigma(f)$, are logically entailed by I_1.

Once the recognition problem has been solved in principle, the given theory graph structure of the image schema family $\mathfrak{F}$ provides a simple handle on the generalisation problem. Namely, given two input spaces I_1, I_2, and two image schemas f_1, f_2 from the same family $\mathfrak{F}$ (say, 'CONTAINMENT') such that $I_1 \models_{\sigma_1} f_1$ and $I_2 \models_{\sigma_2} f_2$, compute the most specific generalisation $G \in \mathfrak{F}$ of f_1 and f_2, that is their least upper bound in $\mathfrak{F}$. Since the signature of G will be included in both signatures of f_1 and f_2, one obtains that $I_1 \models_{\sigma_1} G$ and $I_2 \models_{\sigma_2} G$. $G \in \mathfrak{F}$ is, therefore, an image schema common to both input spaces and can be used as a generic space.

In order to implement this idea, a sufficiently comprehensive library of formalised image schemas like those presented in Chapters 3, 4 and 5 needs to be made available for access by a blending engine.

6.5 Examples: Blending with Image Schema Families

6.5.0.1 Example One: The Spacestation

Imagine the blended concept that can arise when the previously blended 'mothership' is yet again blended, this time with a 'moon.' Disregarding astronomical definitions, let us allow a moon to be constrained to be defined as a celestial body that is part of some solar system, consists of stone, and orbits around a planet (see below). Of course, many people would associate additional information with the concept 'moon,' but even with these limited aspects, there are already enough different possibilities on how these two concepts can be blended. For instance, a structure mapping approach would likely first try to identify the parthood relationship between the docking station and the mothership on one hand with the parthood relationship between the moon and the solar system. This may lead to the concept of a Moon/DockingPlace that is part of a SolarSystem/MotherShip. While this is not incorrect, it does not provide for a particularly useful concept.

Moons, *Mo*, are defined as CelestialBodies that have the image schema REVOLVE_AROUND by circling a Planet, *P*. Both planets and moons are Contained_Inside a SolarSystem, *So*.

$$\forall Mo{:}Object, \big(Moon(Mo) \rightarrow$$
$$\exists P, Stone{:}Object, \exists So{:}Region \; (Consists\_of(Mo, Stone) \wedge$$
$$has\_shape(Mo, Spherical) \wedge CelestialBody(Mo) \wedge$$
$$CelestialBody(P) \wedge \text{REVOLVE\_AROUND}(Mo, P)$$
$$\wedge SolarSystem(So) \wedge Contained\_Inside(Mo, So) \wedge$$
$$Contained\_Inside(P, So)\big)\big)$$

In contrast, if one utilises shared image schemas as heuristics for conceptual blending, it is quite natural to look at a different place for blending opportunities. As a mothership is a kind of vehicle, it has the capability to move things or people from one place to another along a path (CONTAINMENT and SOURCE_PATH_GOAL). A moon also moves along a path, namely, an orbit around a planet, its focal point (REVOLVING_MOVEMENT). Both SOURCE_PATH_GOAL and REVOLVING_MOVEMENT are part of the introduced PATH family, therefore, this information can be utilised in the blending process despite them not instantiating the same image-schematic structure.

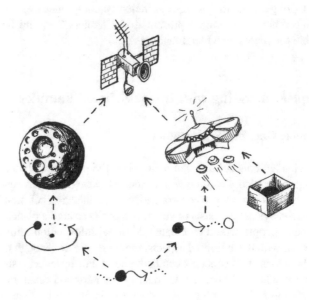

Fig. 6.7: In the blending process of spacestation, the blend inherits RE-VOLVE_AROUND from the input space moon. It is possible to identify that both input spaces share the SOURCE_PATH_GOAL movement by backtracking in the PATH family. The spacestation also inherits the CONTAINMENT schema from the mothership input space.

As discussed in Chapter 3, image schemas can be enriched by adding additional spatial primitives; the image schemas instantiated by the movement of a vessel and of a moon, respectively, are different (and mutually exclusive) refinements of MOVEMENT_OF_OBJECT. For the purpose of blending, the important lesson is that image schemas do not exist in isolation, but they are members of *families of image schemas*. The members of these image schema families are variants of some root conceptualisation (e.g. movement) and can be partially ordered by their strength.

One can utilise this observation as a heuristic for conceptual blending: if two concepts involve two different image schemas, which are within the same image schema family, then a good candidate for the base space for blending both concepts is the *least general* member of the image schema family that generalises the image

Fig. 6.8: An illustration of what a 'moonship' blend could look like.

schemas in the input spaces. In this case, the least general member of the PATH family that is common to both input spaces is MOVEMENT_ALONG_PATH. This idea is further motivated as the blended concept should probably include only one member of each image schema family. In this example, it is possible to create a new concept that inherits the salient features of the mothership but replaces its ability to travel from one place to another by some orbital movement. The resulting theory describes a 'spacestation,' which orbits around a planet (see formalisation below and Figure 6.7). Alternatively, it is possible to think of a moon-like concept that is given the SOURCE_PATH_GOAL instead of REVOLVE_AROUND as hypothesised in Figure 6.8. One concept resulting from such a blending outcome would be a 'meteor' that travels on a path from a point in space into the atmosphere and potentially also the surface of a planet. A more 'creative' concept would be a spacefaring moon. This is a kind of 'moon ship' that while being 'a moon' has the capability to move from a location of origin along a path to a destination.

Spacestations, Sa, are defined as vehicles, thus they have the image schema SOURCE_PATH_GOAL, additionally this has been strengthened to the image schema REVOLVE_AROUND from the input space moon as both circle around a planet, P. Both planets and spacestations are Contained_Inside in a SolarSystem, So.

$$\forall Sa{:}Object \; \big(Spacestation(Sa) \rightarrow$$
$$\exists P{:}Object, \exists D, So{:}Region \; (Vehicle(Sa) \wedge Planet(P) \wedge$$
$$SolarSystem(So) \wedge \text{REVOLVE\_AROUND}(Sa,P) \wedge$$
$$\text{cavity\_of}(D,Sa) \wedge DockingPlace(D)$$
$$\wedge Contained\_Inside(D,Sa) \wedge Contained\_Inside(Sa,So) \wedge$$
$$Contained\_Inside(P,So)))$$

Moonships, *MoS*, are defined as Vehicles, thus they have the image schema SOURCE_PATH_GOAL from the input space moon they inherit the material *Stone* as well as that they are Contained_Inside a solarsystem, *So*.

$$\forall MoS{:}Object \; (MoonShip(MoS) \rightarrow$$
$$\exists So{:}Region \; (Vehicle(Mos) \; \wedge \; has\_shape(Mo, Spherical) \; \wedge$$
$$SolarSystem(So) \; \wedge \; \text{Contained\_Inside}(MoS, So)))$$

6.5.0.2 Example Two: The Stream of Consciousness vs. the Train of Thought

As outlined in Section 6.1.2.1, processes can easily be combined with a variety of more specific PATH-following schemas. More specifically, this section explores the basic idea of how to combine the input space of 'thinking process,' which involves only an underspecified kind of 'movement of thoughts,' with a second input space that carries a clearly defined PATH-following image schema. This leads intuitively to a number of more or less well-known conceptual metaphors, including 'train of thought,' 'line of reasoning,' 'derailment,' 'flow of arguments,' or 'stream of consciousness,' amongst others. Indeed, a central point this section stresses is that these blends work well and appear natural because of the effectiveness of the following heuristics, derived from the formal considerations in Section 6.4:

1. given two input spaces I_1 and I_2, search for the strongest version G of some image schema that is *common to both*, according to the organisation of a particular image schema family $\mathfrak{F}$;
2. use G as generic space; and
3. use $\mathfrak{F}$ again to identify the stronger version of G, say G', inherent in one of the two inputs, and use the semantic content of G' to steer the overall selection of axioms for the blended concept.

This process will be informally illustrated. Let us briefly consider the concepts of 'stream of consciousness,' 'train of thought,' and 'line of reasoning'[7].

On a first inspection, the image schema of movement related to 'thinking' might be identified as MOVEMENT_OF_OBJECT, as there is not necessarily a PATH that can be identified. Indeed, in Figure 3.3, MOVEMENT_OF_OBJECT is marked as an 'entry point' to the PATH-following family.

The *stream of consciousness* may be seen as an unguided flow of thoughts, in which topics merge into each other without any defined steps, but rather in a continuous manner. It lacks a clear START_PATH and has no guided movement towards a particular END_PATH. It resembles the more basic form of PATH-following that, according to Mandler and Cánovas (2014), simply is movement in any trajectory.

---

[7] The examples presented here are chosen to illustrate the basic ideas of how to employ families of image schemas in blending. It is not intended to capture fully the meaning of these terms as they

Fig. 6.9: The picture aims to visualise a conceptual difference between the idioms train of thought and stream of consciousness.

Like any conceptual metaphor, 'train of thought'[8] can be conceptualised in various ways. It differs from a 'stream of consciousness' by having a more clear direction, often with an intended END_PATH, see Figure 6.9. It is possible to say that one 'lost their train of thought,' or that 'it was hijacked' or how 'it reversed its course.' The 'train' may be understood as a chain-like spatial object, in which case 'losing the train' decodes to 'disconnecting the chain,' or more plainly as a locomotive. In the Pixar film 'Inside Out' (2015), the 'Train of Thought' is an actual train that travels the mind of the fictional character Riley Anderson, and delivers daydreams, facts, opinions, and memories.

A 'line of reasoning' might be seen as a strengthening of this blend, where the imposed PATH is linear. Although a 'line,' mathematically speaking, has no beginning nor end, the way this expression is normally understood is as a discrete succession of arguments, following logical rules, leading to an insight or truth. Therefore, this blend might be analysed to correspond to the SOURCE_PATH_GOAL as described by Lakoff and Núñez (2000), in which there are both a clear path and a defined trajectory of the 'thought' (the trajector).

In order to understand how blending can result in these concepts, and how image schemas are involved, a closer look at the input spaces and their relationship to the PATH-following image schemas will be presented. Relevant input spaces include line (perhaps analysed as 'discrete interval'), stream/river, train/locomotive, and, as secondary input space, 'thinking process.'

---

are used in the psychological or linguistic literature, or indeed the subtle meaning they might carry in natural language.

[8] The expression 'train of thoughts' appears to have been first used by Thomas Hobbes in his book Leviathan (1651): "By 'consequence of thoughts' or 'TRAIN of thoughts' I mean the occurrence of thoughts, one at a time, in a sequence; we call this 'mental discourse,' to distinguish it from discourse in words."

'Thinking' as an input space is difficult to visualise. However, when 'thinking' is understood as a process it can be easily combined with various PATH-following notions. As thoughts (in the form of OBJECT) are moved around, the simplest form of thinking is MOVEMENT_OF_OBJECT. There is no START_PATH nor an END_PATH. Intuitively, it does not appear to have any particular PATH (in the sense of a spatial primitive).

A stream is characterised by a continuous flow along a PATH. Whilst a START_PATH and END_PATH can be part of a stream-like concept, like in the fleshed-out concept of a river with a source and a mouth, they do not constitute an essential part of the concept of a stream.

For a train (understood as 'locomotive'), the concepts of a START_PATH and END_PATH have a much higher significance. The affordances found in trains are primarily those concerning going from one place to another. A train ride can also be seen as a discrete movement in the sense that for most train rides, there are more stops than the final destination. This results in a discrete form of the image schema SOURCE_PATH_VIA_GOAL.

When blending such forms of movement with the thinking process, what happens is that the unspecified form of movement found in 'thinking process' is specialised to the PATH-following characteristics found in the second input space. The result is the conceptual metaphors for the different modes of thinking listed above, where the generic space contains just MOVEMENT_OF_OBJECT and the blended concepts inherit the more complex PATH-following from 'train,' 'stream,' or 'line.'

In more detail, Figure 6.10 shows two specialisations of the basic image schema of MOVEMENT_OF_OBJECT. The first, shown on the left, specialises to a discrete version of the schema SOURCE_PATH_GOAL with a designated element and discrete movement, supporting the 'train of thought' blend. The second, shown on the right, specialises to a continuous version of MOVEMENT_ALONG_PATH, where specialisation for gapless movement is added to the MOVEMENT_ALONG_PATH image schema to support the 'flow of consciousness' blend. A third possibility, in 'line of reasoning,' would be to impose additionally a linear (and perhaps discrete) path onto 'thinking.'

6.6 Chapter Conclusion

This chapter discussed how formalised image schemas can be used in computational concept invention through the framework of conceptual blending. This was done by looking more closely at how image schemas structure the conceptual skeleton for similes and conceptual metaphors and how this could be translated into computational conceptual blending.

Regarding the integration of image schemas into conceptual blending, two different methods were highlighted. First, a method in which the image schemas should have higher priority as being inherited in the blend. Second, following the invariance

PATH: specialisation (and generalisation) of image schemas in the path family

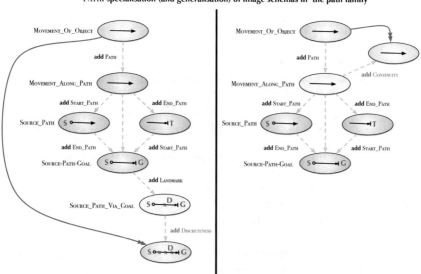

Fig. 6.10: How 'thinking' transforms into 'train of thought' respectively 'stream of consciousness' by specialising arbitrary movement inherent to 'thinking' to discrete SOURCE_PATH_GOAL respectively to continuous PATH-following.

principle, the image schemas could be the foundation for the generic space/base ontology.

Simultaneously, suggestions on how to integrate the family hierarchy into the blending framework were formally introduced as both strengthening and weakening of the input spaces. This was illustrated through a series of examples.

References

L. Boroditsky. Metaphoric structuring: Understanding time through spatial metaphors. *Cognition*, 75(1):1–28, 2000.

R. Confalonieri, E. Plaza, and M. Schorlemmer. A process model for concept invention. In *Proceedings of the 7th International Conference on Computational Creativity (ICCC)*, 2016.

R. DiSalle. Space and time: Inertial frames. In E. N. Zalta, editor, *The Stanford Encyclopedia of Philosophy*. Metaphysics Research Lab, Stanford University, winter 2016 edition, 2016.

Z. Falomir and E. Plaza. Towards a model of creative understanding: deconstructing and recreating conceptual blends using image schemas and qualitative spatial descriptors. *Annals of Mathematics and Artificial Intelligence*, pages 1–21, 2019.

G. Fauconnier and M. Turner. Conceptual integration networks. *Cognitive Science*, 22(2):133—187, 1998.

G. Fauconnier and M. Turner. *The Way We Think: Conceptual Blending and the Mind's Hidden Complexities*. Basic Books, 2003.

K. D. Forbus, B. Falkenhainer, and D. Gentner. The structure-mapping engine. *Artificial Intelligence*, 41:1–63, 1989.

C. Forceville. Theories of conceptual metaphor, blending, and other cognitivist perspectives on comics. In N. Cohn, editor, *The Visual Narrative Reader*. Bloomsbury, London, 2016.

D. Gentner. Structure mapping: A theoretical framework for analogy. *Cognitive Science*, 7(2):155–170, 1983.

J. Goguen and D. F. Harrell. Style as a choice of blending principles. *Style and Meaning in Language, Art Music and Design*, pages 49–56, 2004.

J. Goguen and G. Malcolm. *Algebraic Semantics of Imperative Programs*. MIT Press, 1996.

J. A. Goguen. An Introduction to Algebraic Semiotics, with Applications to User Interface Design. In *Computation for Metaphors, Analogy and Agents*, number 1562 in Lecture Notes in Computer Science, pages 242–291. Springer, 1999.

J. A. Goguen. Semiotic Morphisms, Representations and Blending for Interface Design. In *Proceedings of the AMAST Workshop on Algebraic Methods in Language Processing*, pages 1–15. AMAST Press, 2003.

J. A. Goguen and D. F. Harrell. Style: A Computational and Conceptual Blending-Based Approach. In S. Argamon and S. Dubnov, editors, *The Structure of Style: Algorithmic Approaches to Understanding Manner and Meaning*, pages 147–170. Springer, Berlin, 2010.

J. Hois, O. Kutz, T. Mossakowski, and J. A. Bateman. Towards Ontological Blending. In *Proceedings of the The 14th International Conference on Artificial Intelligence: Methodology, Systems, Applications (AIMSA-2010)*, Varna, Bulgaria, September 8th–10th, 2010.

W. Kuhn. An Image-Schematic Account of Spatial Categories. In S. Winter, M. Duckham, L. Kulik, and B. Kuipers, editors, *Spatial Information Theory*, volume 4736 of *Lecture Notes in Computer Science*, pages 152–168. Springer, 2007.

O. Kutz and I. Normann. Context Discovery via Theory Interpretation. In *Proceedings of the IJCAI Workshop on Automated Reasoning about Context and Ontology Evolution (ARCOE-09)*, Pasadena, California, 2009.

O. Kutz, T. Mossakowski, and D. Lücke. Carnap, Goguen, and the Hyperontologies: Logical Pluralism and Heterogeneous Structuring in Ontology Design. *Logica Universalis*, 4(2):255–333, 2010. Special Issue on 'Is Logic Universal?'.

O. Kutz, T. Mossakowski, J. Hois, M. Bhatt, and J. A. Bateman. Ontological Blending in DOL. In T. Besold, K.-U. Kühnberger, M. Schorlemmer, and A. Smaill, editors, *Computational Creativity, Concept Invention, and General Intelligence, Proceedings of the 1st International Workshop C3GI@ECAI*, volume 01-2012, Montpellier, France, August 27 2012. Publications of the Institute of Cognitive Science, Osnabrück.

O. Kutz, J. A. Bateman, F. Neuhaus, T. Mossakowski, and M. Bhatt. E pluribus unum: Formalisation, Use-Cases, and Computational Support for Conceptual Blending. In T. R. Besold, M. Schorlemmer, and A. Smaill, editors, *Computational Creativity Research: Towards Creative Machines*, Thinking Machines. Atlantis, 2014a.

O. Kutz, F. Neuhaus, T. Mossakowski, and M. Codescu. Blending in the Hub— Towards a collaborative concept invention platform. In *Proceedings of the 5th International Conference on Computational Creativity*, Ljubljana, Slovenia, June 10–13 2014b.

G. Lakoff and R. Núñez. *Where Mathematics Comes From: How the Embodied Mind Brings Mathematics into Being*. Basic Books, New York, 2000.

J. M. Mandler and C. P. Cánovas. On defining image schemas. *Language and Cognition*, 6(4):510–532, May 2014.

T. Mossakowski, C. Maeder, and K. Lüttich. The Heterogeneous Tool Set. In O. Grumberg and M. Huth, editors, *TACAS 2007*, volume 4424 of *Lecture Notes in Computer Science*, pages 519–522. Springer, 2007.

I. Normann. *Automated Theory Interpretation*. PhD thesis, Department of Computer Science, Jacobs University, Bremen, 2008.

I. Normann and O. Kutz. Ontology Correspondence via Theory Interpretation. In *Proceedings of the Workshop on Matching and Meaning (@AISB)*, Edinburgh, UK, 2009.

F. C. Pereira and A. Cardoso. Optimality Principles for Conceptual Blending: A First Computational Approach. *AISB Journal*, 1(4), 2003.

M. Schmidt, U. Krumnack, H. Gust, and K.-U. Kühnberger. Heuristic-Driven Theory Projection: An Overview. In H. Prade and G. Richard, editors, *Computational Approaches to Analogical Reasoning: Current Trends*, volume 548 of *Computational Intelligence*. Springer, 2014.

M. Schorlemmer, A. Smaill, K.-U. Kühnberger, O. Kutz, S. Colton, E. Cambouropoulos, and A. Pease. COINVENT: Towards a Computational Concept Invention Theory. In *Proceedings of the 5th International Conference on Computational Creativity*, Ljubljana, Slovenia, June 10–13 2014.

M. Turner. Language is a Virus. *Poetics Today*, 13(4):725–736, 1992.

M. Turner. The Way We Imagine. In I. Roth, editor, *Imaginative Minds - Proceedings of the British Academy*, pages 213–236. OUP, Oxford, 2007.

M. Turner. *The Origin of Ideas: Blending, Creativity, and the Human Spark*. Oxford University Press, 2014.

T. Veale. The analogical thesaurus. In J. Riedl and R. Hill, editors, *Proceedings of the 15th Innovative Applications of Artificial Intelligence Conference*, pages 137–142. AAAI Press, 2003.

T. Veale, K. Feyaerts, and C. Forceville. E unis pluribum: Using mental agility to achieve creative duality in word, image and sound. In *Creativity and the Agile Mind: A Multi-Disciplinary Study of a Multi-Faceted Phenomenon (Applications of Cognitive Linguistics)*, pages 37–57. 2013.

Part IV
Image Schema Experiments

Chapter 7
Defining Concepts: The Role of Image Schemas in Object Conceptualisation

Abstract Chapter 5 introduced the idea that combinations of image schemas represent the underlying conceptualisations of temporally complex image schemas and simple events. Likewise, Chapter 6 relied on the idea that concepts could be partly defined by their involved image schemas. In this chapter, these ideas are further investigated empirically by presenting an experimental study that investigates the image schemas behind a series of common objects.

7.1 Image Schemas Behind Conceptualisations

In Chapter 5 the role of image schemas in event conceptualisation was investigated formally. This idea can be stretched further by backtracking from the complex conceptualisation of events to objects and concepts in the first place.

For instance, Kuhn (2007) proposed that the concept underlying the term 'transportation' can be described just considering the behaviour of the two image schemas CONTAINMENT and SOURCE_PATH_GOAL. Likewise, abstract concepts such as 'marriage' could, in a limited sense, be described using a combination of the image schemas LINK and SOURCE_PATH_GOAL, as a common conceptualisation of marriage is that of two 'parts' moving together on the axis of time (Mandler, 2004).

So far, to the best of the author's knowledge, little empirical work has been devoted to identifying to what degree image schemas truly are the conceptual building blocks for everyday concepts (e.g. Gromann and Macbeth (2019)). To improve on this, this chapter contains an experimental study that investigates the relationship between a series of image schemas and the conceptualisation of everyday objects.

The experiment takes a closer look at a few commonly mentioned image schemas and their relationship to a series of everyday objects. The experimental set-up uses illustrations of eight of the most mentioned image schemas in the literature[1] to describe a series of everyday objects.

---

[1] Naturally, it would be more accurate to present a complete list of all image schemas, however, two problems hinder this: First, there exists no coherent and agreed upon list of all the image schemas.

© Springer Nature Switzerland AG 2020

M. M. Hedblom, *Image Schemas and Concept Invention*, Cognitive Technologies,
https://doi.org/10.1007/978-3-030-47329-7_7

7.1.1 Related Work on Conceptualisation

The classic work on conceptualisation is that of Kellman and Spelke (1983), who investigated infants' understanding of objects through a series of experiments on object occlusion. Their work shows that infants, already in the early months, understand the relationship between 'behind' and 'in front.' In terms of image schemas, their work demonstrated also that children at this early age have a conceptualisation of LINK as they can register that two parts moving in unison behind an occlusion belong to the same object.

A study that highlights the difference between concept definitions and conceptualisations is the work by Vinner (1983). Vinner performed a survey with pupils in tenth and eleventh grade on their conceptualisation of mathematical functions. The work demonstrated how conceptualisations often varied more than the concept definition, indicating a difference between the internal conceptualisation and the linguistic expression used to describe it.

Antović (2009) and Antović et al. (2013) performed experiments on music conceptualisation in relation to cognitive metaphor theory in different settings. Important findings were that musical concepts are often conceptualised by using visuospatial conceptual metaphors.

Looking directly at the link between conceptualisation and image schemas is among others the famous research by Lakoff and Núñez (2000). In their book, they present theoretical support for the notion that image schemas lay the conceptual foundation for mathematical concepts. For instance, addition and subtraction are according to the authors perceived as movement along a path, a weaker form of SOURCE_PATH_GOAL. Also, Venn diagrams used to describe set-theory and discrete mathematics are a direct visual representation of the CONTAINMENT schema. Through their work, they make their way up to increasingly abstract concepts including tracing down the conceptualisation of 'infinity' and 'zero' into embodied experiences and image-schematic structures.

Looking at spatial categories for ontology building, Kuhn (2007) uses ontological properties of image schemas to formally construct concepts' underlying meanings. His work takes a straightforward approach to how image schemas can be used as conceptual building blocks for concept definitions.

7.1.2 Motivation and Hypotheses

The main hypothesis that this chapter rests on is the notion that image schemas are conceptual building blocks that are used in conceptualisation for concepts.

Hypothesis I (H1):   Image schemas are conceptual building blocks that capture the essence of concepts, including abstract ones.

Second, while by definition the image schemas must be of a limited number the current estimate is too vast to feasibly take part in an experiment of the nature proposed.

Following this hypothesis it must be possible to investigate to what degree image schemas are involved in concept generation and understanding. This study challenges that hypothesis by looking at instances of everyday objects and their conceptual connection to the image schemas.

The purpose of the study was twofold. First, the desire to empirically establish if image-schematic thinking plays a pivotal role in conceptualising everyday objects. Second, if this was the case, then to establish if there are any differences in the importance of specific image schemas for different objects.

7.2 Method

7.2.1 Material and Motivation

7.2.1.1 Representing the Image Schemas

The first important obstacle was to select a feasible number of image schemas for the study. This presented two problems. First, which image schemas should be chosen given the large number of image-schematic structures proposed in the literature? Second, as image schemas are used to model abstract conceptual patterns, how can they be investigated in this study?

The selection was made on primarily two criteria. First, their commonality in the literature, with the motivation that the more commonly studied, the more reliable (or at least agreed upon) their image-schematic structure was. Second, the image schemas needed to be presented in such a way that it could be intuitively understood what the image schema entailed. This disqualified for these purposes image schemas that are too abstract and dynamic rather than static.

The representation of the image schemas used two methods, consequently dividing the participants into two groups. First, simply the linguistic phrasing of the image schemas was used and, second, a basic visualisation of each image schema.

The visualisation of the image schemas was approached by aiming to inspire as much abstract thinking as possible. This resulted in a homogeneous design of all illustrations made with graphite pencil on white sketch paper. Figure 7.1 contains the visual illustrations of the eight selected image schemas.

After some contemplation, the following image schemas were selected: BLOCKAGE, SCALE, LINK, SOURCE_PATH_GOAL, SUPPORT, CONTAINMENT, VERTICALITY and CYCLE. Additionally, a 'none' alternative was also included to allow participants the choice of not assigning any image schemas.

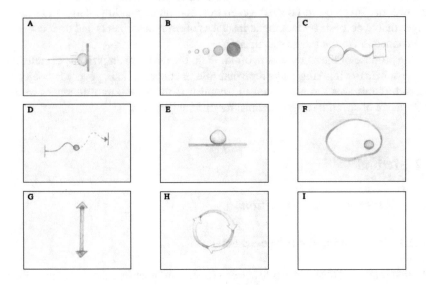

Fig. 7.1: The image schema illustrations as used in the experiment. From $A - I$ as follows: A: BLOCKAGE; B: SCALE; C: LINK; D: SOURCE_PATH_GOAL; E: SUPPORT; F: CONTAINMENT; G: VERTICALITY; H: CYCLE; I: the empty set.

7.2.1.2 Everyday Objects for Assessment

When deciding which objects to choose, it was deemed important that they were objects that children come into contact with early on in conceptual development. This was believed to be important as the conceptual core of the concepts should be sheltered from cultural influence as much as possible and instead represent a more basic conceptualisation. A second aspect was that in order to avoid priming the participants with language, the objects should be presented visually rather than written. Therefore, flashcards for language learning were used[2].

Focusing solely on nouns, the selection process excluded all verbs and adjectives. Likewise, all animate objects, as well as roles, were eliminated as the association and conceptualisation of these categories may be clouded by personal and cultural experience. To get as unbiased a sample as possible, 44 objects were selected at random within the presented restrictions.

---

[2] http://www.kids-pages.com

7.2.2 Expert Assessment of the Objects into Image Schema Categories

Three image schema experts performed the experiment by assigning image schemas to the objects, generating a series of image schema categories.

Table 7.1 shows the objects after they have been sorted into their respective categories. Note that, occasionally, objects occur more than once as a consequence of the experts assigning multiple image schemas per object. The table is also missing three objects that were included in the experiment (camera, lamp, pacifier) since these had not been assigned any particular image schemas by the majority of the experts.

Table 7.1: The objects sorted into an image-schematic category by the majority of the experts.

Image schema category	Objects
VERTICALITY	colour pyramid, stiletto shoes, ladder, plant sprout, sunflower, skyscraper, stairs, tree
CYCLE	clock, screw, sunflower, washing machine
CONTAINMENT	banana, bathtub, boiled eggs, car, cherries, computer, guitar, hat, house, mirror, oven glove, pants, school bag, skyscraper, strainer, wardrobe, washing machine
SOURCE_PATH_GOAL	aeroplane, car, garden path, lightning, ruler, stairs, wheelbarrow
SUPPORT	bed, play blocks, chair, plate, stiletto shoes, sofa, wheelbarrow
LINK	ankle, cherries, computer, lightning, pliers
BLOCKAGE	oven glove, strainer, umbrella
SCALE	colour pyramid, fire, plant sprout, ruler, thermometer

7.2.3 Participants and Experimental Groups

The experiment consisted of 25 participants gathered using a convenience sampling. From these, four participants had to be eliminated due to not following the instructions of the experiment. The remaining 21 participants (females: 28.6 percent, males: 71.4 percent) had a varied cultural background, coming from twelve different mother tongues and ages ranging from 25 to 60 (*mean age:* 36.3, *median age:* 32, *SD:* 10.69, *variance:* 108.78).

As mentioned above, the participants were divided into two groups. Ten participants were presented with the illustrations of the image schemas (see Figure 7.1) and eleven participants were instead presented with the terms of the image schemas.

In order to avoid possibles bias towards particular image schemas based on placement on the sheets, each group was divided into an additional three groups, where the image schemas had been randomly re-arranged. Before all the data was analysed, this data was aligned to make sure that all answers were based on the same material.

7.2.4 Experimental Set-Up

The experiment started with a brief oral introduction including encouraging the participants to carefully read the written instructions. Written instructions had been selected to avoid accidentally providing the participants with different instructions.

The experiment required the participants to familiarise themselves with the alternatives $A - I$ on the image schema sheet, followed by flipping through the 44 flashcards[3] and 'describing' the object on it by matching it to one or more of the abstract image schemas. They were explicitly asked not to focus on visual attributes of the illustrations nor of the objects, but instead to "think holistically about the object." The experiment also required the participants to write a short motivation to explain how they were thinking.

7.2.5 Methods of Analysis

7.2.5.1 Analysis of Method Behind Object Conceptualisation

The study aimed to investigate whether participants used image-schematic thinking to conceptualise the objects. To determine this, only the data in the motivations were used, as the assigned image schemas were considered irrelevant for the mode of thinking.

Presented below are the four major analysis methods estimated to be at work when conceptualising the objects:

Image schemas: if the motivation contained the abstract spatiotemporal motion or relationship found in image schemas. Examples: Stiletto shoes: VERTICAL-ITY and CONTAINMENT, *increase height of person, contain feet*;[4] Umbrella: BLOCKAGE, *blocks rain and sun*.

Association: if the motivation described associations to similar concepts and objects to that on the flashcard. Examples: Lightning: CYCLE, *the water cycle*; Ankle: SOURCE_PATH_GOAL, *running towards a goal*.

Visual/attribute cues: if the motivation made direct visual or attribute connections between the object and the image schemas. Examples: Camera: LINK, *objective is round, picture is square*; Boiled eggs: CONTAINMENT, *illustration looks like an omelette*.

---

[3] Note that the three objects excluded by the experts were still present in the experiment.

[4] Note the structure: IMAGE SCHEMA, *Motivation*

Other: This was used when none of the previous methods were deemed applicable. Examples: Clock: BLOCKAGE, *if it falls it breaks*; Guitar: SUPPORT, *supports a singer.*

7.2.5.2 Analysis of Image Schemas Attributed to Objects

The second research question was to determine if it is possible to assign particular image schemas to certain objects. For this part, the data from both groups were merged, motivated by assuming that the illustrations and the terms could be treated equally. This was approached by, similarly to the expert assessment, generating image-schematic categories from the majority of the participants. At the same time, three other aspects were looked at more closely: First, the objects that had the highest assignment of 'nothing.' Second, the most consistently defined objects; And third, the objects that had more than 50 percent of a *particular combination* of assigned image schemas.

The objects that best matched these criteria were then presented and discussed to find the commonality amongst the objects that had the highest image-schematic structure.

7.3 Results

The results show a great diversity in the number of assigned image schemas between the participants. Some participants made an effort to find image schemas for all objects whereas other applied the 'nothing applies' answer more generously.

Likewise, despite it having been made clear to the participants that they may choose to use more than one image schema to explain particular objects, many participants chose to focus on the most prominent attribute and picked only one image schema. At the same time, there were participants who instead had the opposite approach with results that appeared to cover all possible aspects of the objects and therefore used a more generous assignment of image schemas.

The group presented with illustrations were more inclined to select more than one image schema to describe the objects with an average of 1.41 assigned image schemas per object compared to the group presented with terms, which had an average assignment of 1.22 image schemas per object.

7.3.1 Assignment Method

Table 7.2 shows the distribution in percent between the different assignment methods for respective participation groups.

Table 7.2: Distribution of method for assigning the image schemas to the objects for the two groups.

Assignment method	Illustrations	Terms
Image schemas	70.82	65.48
Association	14.66	14.88
Visual/attribute cues	14.65	7.14
Other	10.23	12.50

The results show a dominance in using a method of abstract image-schematic thinking when describing the everyday objects approximately 2/3 of the time regardless of being presented with illustrations or terms. This result gives a strong indication that the participants were thinking abstractly enough and in line with the goals of the experiment.

7.3.2 The 'Image-Schematic' Structure of the Objects

7.3.2.1 Mapping of Image Schema Group

Table 7.3 shows the image schema categories where at least 50 percent of the participants agreed upon a particular image schema for the same object. While the table demonstrates a great reduction in the number of assigned image schemas compared to those made by the experts (see Table 7.1), it does represent a near perfect mapping. Out of the objects that the participants agreed upon, all but one ('plant sprout') had been assigned the same image schemas by the experts, illustrating that while the participants had no trained knowledge of the concept of image schemas, their intuitions closely align with those of the experts.

Table 7.3: The objects sorted into image-schematic categories by at least 50 percent of the participants.

Image schema category	Objects
VERTICALITY	ladder, skyscraper, stairs, tree
CYCLE	clock, plant sprout, screw, washing machine
CONTAINMENT	bathtub, boiled eggs, house, school bag
SOURCE_PATH_GOAL	aeroplane, car, garden path
SUPPORT	bed, chair, sofa, wheelbarrow
LINK	computer
BLOCKAGE	
SCALE	ruler

7.3.2.2 The Highest Non-Assigned Objects

Whilst the experts could not find an agreement on three objects, this number was higher for the participants. The objects in Table 7.4 demonstrate the object with the highest number of 'no image schema' assigned.

Table 7.4: The objects that the participants found the hardest to describe in image schemas.

Count	Object	Count	Object
9	camera	6	pants
9	lamp	6	strainer
8	fire	5	blocks
8	hat	5	cherries
6	banana	5	mirror
6	guitar	5	pacifier
6	lightning	5	skyscraper
6	oven glove	5	umbrella

7.3.2.3 The Most Consistently Assigned Objects

After counting the number of assessed image schemas to each object and per person, a few objects ranked higher in agreement of the assigned image schema. Table 7.5 shows the objects that had at least 2/3 of the participant agreeing in the assignment task.

Table 7.5: The objects to which more than 2/3 of the participants assigned the same image schemas.

Count	Object	Image schema
18	chair	SUPPORT
16	garden path	SOURCE_PATH_GOAL
16	sofa	SUPPORT
16	ladder	VERTICALITY
15	bathtub	SUPPORT
15	washing machine	CYCLE
14	stairs	VERTICALITY

7.3.2.4 The Image-Schematic Combination Objects

For some objects, the pattern for assigning image schemas was spread widely amongst the different alternatives. However, for several of the objects, the assigned image schemas were occasionally arranged in patterns in which more than one image schema played a central role in its conceptual description. The objects which had two (or on occasion three) assigned image schemas that 'in combination' had been assigned by at least 50 percent of the participants can be seen in Table 7.6.

Table 7.6: The objects which appear to be conceptualised as a combination of image schemas.

Count	Object	Image schemas
8, 7, 6	wheelbarrow	SUPPORT, CONTAINMENT, SOURCE_PATH_GOAL
9, 8	sunflower	VERTICALITY, CYCLE
6, 6	stiletto shoes	SUPPORT, VERTICALITY
6, 5	play blocks	VERTICALITY, SUPPORT
6, 5	ankle	SUPPORT, LINK

7.4 Discussion

7.4.1 Method Discussion

7.4.1.1 Sample

The participants were gathered through a convenience sampling. This resulted in a higher than average level of education of the participants, which in turn could have resulted in unintended 'over thinking.' However, since the experiment had the purpose to tap into the underlying conceptual structure, it is believed that the possible effects of this are minimal and that they can be disregarded.

Likewise, the gender distribution is uneven. However, since the experiment does not presume any gender difference in cognitive conceptualisation (supported by e.g. Richardson et al. (1997)) and the cognitive mechanisms investigated ought not to be influenced by any potentially existing gender-cultural differences, it is believed that this uneven distribution can be disregarded as well.

The divergence in nationality, consequently also in native language, and the varied age of the participants are thought to produce a fairly solid sample. Naturally, the sample size lies in the lower margin with only 21 participants whose performance could be counted into the analysis of the results. In order to properly assess the generalisability of the results, further studies need to be conducted.

7.4.1.2 Material

Regarding the image schema illustrations, the results illuminated a few issues with some of the them. The biggest challenge of making the illustrations was to capture the whole family of notions involved in the image schemas, meaning that CONTAINMENT should also include the notions of IN and OUT, and VERTICALITY should include vertical movement and/or relative position in either direction of UP-DOWN. Likewise, SOURCE_PATH_GOAL was required to cover not only movement but the source and the goal as well, supported by the family representation of image schemas presented in Chapter 3. The experiment used a set-up with static illustrations, suppressing the dynamic aspects of the image schemas. To balance this issue, the instructions contained an explanatory text: *"The nine illustrations are meant as capturing a mental 'idea' and while this abstract content should remain you may perform transformations to apply it to the context of the object"*. However, it is not clear whether these clarifications were interpreted in the intended way. For instance, one of the participants violated the VERTICALITY principle by transforming it into 'horizontality,' rather than preserving the verticality through other means of transformations.

Additionally, the results indicated that the image schema illustrations might have been a bit too abstract. The participants' written motivations occasionally demonstrated misapprehension of some of the illustrations, where LINK was the illustration to gain the most incoherent interpretations. Naturally, this had negative effects on the results, producing outliers.

For further and similar experiments, the image schema illustrations presented in this study may be used as a guide, but ought to be mildly modified in order to better capture the dynamics of the underlying spatiotemporal relationships.

As previously motivated, the objects had been chosen because of their commonality in everyday life, varying from simple (e.g. chair, house) objects to increasingly complex objects (e.g. camera, washing machine). Their visual representation utilised pre-designed flashcards to have a homogeneous design. The goal of choosing objects with a coherent visual representation was to reduce the possible problems due to participants being distracted and associating the objects on the cards with particular visual characteristics. While most of the pictures caused no misapprehension in the subjects, two of the illustrations appeared to have been borderline cases: the 'skyscraper,' to which several participants asked what the picture portrayed, and the 'ankle' which some participants (as illuminated in the participants' motivation) had interpreted as a 'foot.'

7.4.2 Result Discussion

7.4.2.1 Method Behind Object Conceptualisation

With approximately 2/3 of the image schema assignments determined through abstract image-schematic thinking, the result provides strong support towards objects being conceptualised in accordance with the main hypothesis of this experiment, namely that image schemas lie at the foundation and give structure to the meaning of concepts (Johnson, 1987; Lakoff, 1987; Turner, 1993).

The findings show similar results to those found in the related work on music conceptualisation and image-schematic structures performed by Antović et al. (2013), who showed that music conceptualisation is often based on visuospatial metaphors.

7.4.2.2 Image Schemas Assigned to Objects

The results show a near perfect correlation between the expert assessment (taken as a gold standard) and the most commonly assigned image schemas per object. While the experts demonstrated a superior level of detail in terms of which image schemas were assigned, among the objects where the majority of the participants assigned the same image schema, there was only one instance that did not correspond to the experts' choice. While this is an encouraging result underpinning that image schemas can be seen as conceptual building blocks, the rather large variance in choices needs attention. One reason for this might be due to the image schemas not being comprehended completely. A second reason could also lie in the observed high reluctance among the participants to assign more than one image schema per object. Naturally, this resulted in a smaller set of image schemas being distributed over the objects than in the more generously assigned image schemas found amongst the experts.

Regarding why some objects had a higher number of 'no image schema assigned,' this might be a consequence of the objects being perceived as more complex. For example, the underlying conceptualisation of an object such as a 'camera' might be far more affected by associations and the 'complex' usage than far more straightforward objects such as a 'chair.' Indeed, complex technical artefacts have low image-schematic content in an expert assessment, too. Perhaps it is no longer appropriate to speak of objects such as these as image-schematic alone, after all, they are also concepts that humans usually fail to comprehend in early childhood, but rather are learned throughout life-experience and through cultural expression.

Likewise, objects such as 'banana' and 'cherries' whose primary function (for humans) is to be eaten may also not carry clear image-schematic content in terms of spatiotemporal relationships as used in this study, but rather have other affordance-based conceptual primitives associated, relating to nutrition and providing physical energy[5].

The objects that were most coherently assigned image schemas were those objects where the usage of the object, and people's contextual experience, are more or less homogeneous amongst individuals. The possible uses and experiences a person has with a 'chair' are more or less identical in all (adult) individuals. Likewise, different modes of transportation are heavily associated with the notion of going from one place to another; therefore, concepts such as car, aeroplane and garden path are associated to the SOURCE_PATH_GOAL schema in accordance with the ideas presented by Kuhn (2007).

7.5 Chapter Conclusion

The notion of 'image schema' is central to conceptual metaphor theory, has been an influential idea in cognitive linguistics for decades and is increasingly being used in cognitive AI approaches. This study has provided empirical support that strengthen the hypothesis (H1) that image schemas can serve as core conceptual building blocks for everyday objects. With this in mind, the study investigated different aspects of image schemas in object conceptualisation for the purpose of identifying general patterns in conceptualisation and their relationships to image schemas.

The first research question addressed to what degree abstract conceptualisations can be considered to be based on image-schematic thinking. The results of this study show that for the variables used in this study, roughly 2/3 of the participants' conceptualisations were based on the abstract nature found in the spatiotemporal relationships captured by image schemas. This gives good grounds for the experiment and suggests that image schemas are involved in the conceptualisation of objects.

The second research purpose was to determine whether some objects are thought to be more image-schematic than others. The results provide support that this is indeed the case. It can be argued that the differences found may depend on sociocultural influences associated with the objects, as the more complex objects often were more inconsistently assessed, and objects with more straightforward affordances associate with them (e.g. 'chair' which affords 'sit_on' associated with the image schema SUPPORT) had higher consistency in assigned image schemas.

In summary, one conclusion to be drawn from the study is that the investigation of image schemas as conceptual building blocks is a promising research program to tap into cognitive mechanisms behind conceptualisation.

Future work will have to confirm the findings in more refined set-ups, extend the approach to dynamic presentations of image schemas, and address the multi-modality of image schemas beyond the basic spatiotemporal interpretation.

---

[5] In accordance with embodied cognition and the multi-modal nature of image schemas, it is possible that primitives such as those found in taste and bodily reactions to food should also be included in the research field of image schemas. However, to my knowledge, little such research exists as of yet.

References

M. Antović. Musical Metaphors in Serbian and Romani Children: An Empirical Study. *Metaphor and Symbol*, 24(3):184–202, 2009.

M. Antović, A. Bennett, and M. Turner. Running in circles or moving along lines: Conceptualization of musical elements in sighted and blind children. *Musicae Scientiae*, 17(2):229–245, 2013.

D. Gromann and J. C. Macbeth. Crowdsourcing image schemas. In *Proceedings of TriCoLore*, volume 2347 of *CEUR-WS*, Bolzano, Italy, 2019.

M. Johnson. *The Body in the Mind: The Bodily Basis of Meaning, Imagination, and Reason*. University of Chicago Press, 1987.

P. J. Kellman and E. S. Spelke. Perception of Partly Occluded Objects in Infancy. *Cognitive Psychology*, (15):483–524, 1983.

W. Kuhn. An Image-Schematic Account of Spatial Categories. In S. Winter, M. Duckham, L. Kulik, and B. Kuipers, editors, *Spatial Information Theory*, volume 4736 of *Lecture Notes in Computer Science*, pages 152–168. Springer, 2007.

G. Lakoff. *Women, Fire, and Dangerous Things. What Categories Reveal about the Mind*. University of Chicago Press, 1987.

G. Lakoff and R. Núñez. *Where Mathematics Comes From: How the Embodied Mind Brings Mathematics into Being*. Basic Books, New York, 2000.

J. M. Mandler. *The Foundations of Mind: Origins of Conceptual Thought: Origins of Conceptual Though*. Oxford University Press, New York, 2004.

J. T. E. Richardson, P. J. Caplan, M. Crawford, and J. S. Hyde. *Gender Differences in Human Cognition*. Oxford University Press, 1997.

M. Turner. An image-schematic constraint on metaphor. *Conceptualizations and mental processing in language*, pages 291–306, 1993.

S. Vinner. Concept definition, concept image and the notion of function. *International Journal of Mathematical Education in Science and Technology*, 14(3): 293–305, 1983.

Chapter 8
Identifying Image Schemas: Towards Automatic Image Schema Extraction[1]

Abstract One of the missing pieces before image schemas can be used in conceptual blending and artificial intelligence is a method to automatically identify image schemas in natural language. In order to investigate this problem, the PATH-following family introduced in Chapter 3 will be empirically investigated by using a natural language corpus to detect existing members of the family and detect possible additional candidates. The experiment relies on a method of syntactic pattern matching using words strongly associated with movement and processes. The experiment includes four different languages to strengthen the idea that PATH-following in abstract domains (here finance) is not only found in one language but universal as assumed through their embodied manifestation. The experiment found that approximately 1/3 of extracted words could be image-schematic and could not only provide linguistic support for the members of the PATH family but also provide additional candidates.

8.1 Challenges with Image Schema Identification

One of the most challenging parts of using image schemas in formal systems and artificial intelligence is that there currently exists no comprehensive method to identify them in natural language. If image schemas are to be used in systems dealing with natural language understanding or production, as seen with conceptual blending in Chapter 6, then there needs to exist a method to automatically identify the image schemas in natural language, both expressions that are concrete and abstract. Additionally, by automatically identifying image schemas in natural language it would be possible to expand the number of identified image schemas and place them in their respective family as presented in Chapter 3. As there currently exists no agreed-upon list of the image schemas, any method that extracts image schemas would greatly

---

[1] This chapter is co-authored by Dagmar Gromann and has been published in (Gromann and Hedblom, 2016).

help to build a better comprehension as to which image-schematic entities exist in natural language.

The main purpose of the experiment is to approach this problem by trying to devise a method that can find empirical support for the ideas presented in Chapter 3, in particular regarding the hierarchy of the PATH family.

8.1.1 Motivation and Hypotheses

Detecting spatiotemporal relations in natural language is central to a wide range of Artificial Intelligence (AI) applications, including robotic navigation (e.g. Tellex et al. (2011)), manipulation instructions in human-robot interaction (e.g. Kollar et al. (2014); Misra et al. (2016)), simulation of natural sensorimotor knowledge acquisition of infants (e.g. Guerin (2008)), and any kind of mapping between natural language symbols and their objects in the physical world (e.g. Krishnamurthy and Kollar (2013)). However, the symbol grounding problem, introduced in Chapter 1, remains challenging. The cognitive grounding of spatial language has been investigated in different disciplines, including AI (Misra et al., 2016) and linguistics (Hampe and Grady, 2005).

This chapter rests on the assumption that any mental conceptual system guiding abstract thinking and acting in humans is also the system that communication is based on. Natural language is considered "an important source of evidence of what that system is like" (Lakoff and Johnson, 1980), where that refers to the cognitive system guiding our actions.

The experiment rests on the hypothesis discussed in previous chapters, namely:

Hypothesis I (H1):   Image schemas are conceptual building blocks that capture the essence of concepts, including abstract ones.[2]

Hypothesis II (H2):   Following from H1, image schemas are consistent over languages as a concept's meaning is consistent over languages.

8.2 Method

The method builds on the ontology of the PATH-following family introduced and developed in Chapter 3 and Chapter 4, where linguistic manifestations of image-schematic structures were one of the grounds for differentiating between the members of the family. The experiment extracted potential candidate entries for the PATH schema in English by means of lexico-syntactic patterns and synonym sets. Additionally, this was done for German, Swedish and Italian, as the used natural language corpus consists of multilingual alignment of terminological data. The results were manually analysed by first-language speakers to map them to the different PATH

---

[2] Note that this is the same hypothesis as in Chapter 7.

schemas. The analysis used the structure of the PATH-following ontology (see Figure 3.3 for a smaller version) as well as a graphical representation method.

8.2.1 The Corpus: A Financial Terminological Database

Concept-oriented terminological databases organise multilingual natural language data into terminological entries, so-called 'units of meaning.' A terminology seeks to mitigate ambiguity and polysemy of natural language by limiting its content to a specialised domain of discourse. The use of a given term is specified by means of its salient features and semantic type in a natural language definition. All natural language descriptions associated with the same entry are considered semantically equivalent. Such resources are typically applied to computer-aided translation, information extraction, machine translation, and corporate terminology management to name but a few.

The data set for this experiment was extracted from the InterActive Terminology for Europe (IATE)[3], which classifies its 1.3 million entries in up to 24 European languages by domain and sub-domain. For this experiment, only entries classified into the financial domain and its sub-domains were considered. Likewise, the search was limited to the extraction of entries that existed in all the following languages: English, Swedish, German, and Italian.

8.2.2 Lexico-Syntactic Patterns and Entry Extraction

In order to identify the image schemas, lexico-syntactic patterns were used to identify the spatiotemporal relationships. Inspired by the method presented in (Bennett and Cialone, 2014), in which CONTAINMENT was sought for through identification of similar words (e.g. enclose, surround, contain), a series of PATH-related words (see Table 8.1) were used to automatically identify members of the PATH family.

The lexico-syntactic patterns were initially motivated by the presented members of the PATH-following family, with abstract interpretation to some of the more complex members such as CYCLE and MOVEMENT_IN_LOOPS. Likewise, attention was given to the spatial primitives such as SOURCE and GOAL presented by Mandler and Cánovas (2014) in order to identify the difference between image schema members such as SOURCE_PATH_GOAL, PATH_GOAL and SOURCE_PATH etc. In consequence, this meant that words such as 'from' and 'to' were included in the sought for patterns.

---

[3] http://iate.europa.eu/

Pattern name	Content
From-to	from [...] to
Prepositions	around, across, through, behind, before, earlier
Movement	movement, track, path, transportation, transit, mobility, steps, passage
Process	process, operation, transfer, transferal
Development	development, evolution, progress, progress, progression, chance, migration
Cycle	cycle, course, chain, ring, rotation, circle, circuit, loop, sequel, orbit, wheel
Move	move, transfer, drift, migrate, walk, drive, fly, proceed, etc.
Start	start, commence, begin, etc.
End	end, target, arrive, etc.

Table 8.1: Lexico-Syntactic Patterns for PATH Extractions

8.2.3 Linguistic Mapping of Image-Schematic Structure

The mapping procedure was done on the pattern-extracted entries per language. For each language, one (German, Swedish) or two native/fluent speakers (English, Italian) mapped the concept to the image-schematic structures. The method consisted of mapping the definition of terms to the PATH-family. This was done through using a graphical representation technique that aimed to take the linguistic expression to a more concrete spatiotemporal representation in order to assign the potential candidates the right member of the PATH family. While following the general structure of the family, additional image-schematic components where considered in order to not only strengthen the PATH-family notion but also by analysis improve the PATH-family to match natural language. This allowed for a freer interpretation of the terms which better mapped the intended content. At the end, a comparison of all identified schemas allowed for an evaluation of their cross-lingual persistence.

8.3 Results

The analysis targeted the identification of image-schematic structures of PATH-following in natural language text across four natural languages. The (a)symmetries of such structures across languages were of particular interest as well as the coverage of the predefined schematic structures (see Figure 3.3) within the domain of financial terminology.

From the financial subset of the IATE terminology database, the extraction was restricted to entries containing natural language definitions and a minimum of one of the identified patterns. Thereby, 190 extracted terminological entries for the languages English, Swedish, German and Italian were obtained. A manual analysis of at least one first-language/fluent speaker per language resulted in more than 69 entries or 36 percent containing image-schematic structures related to PATH-following. This was followed by breaking down the results into individual languages through individual interpretation. Here 224 schema structures or 31 percent could be identi-

fied from the 720 natural language definitions across the four languages. The results
separated by language and structure are depicted in Table 8.2 as cumulative fre-
quencies. A majority of extracted entries could be discarded as objects, institutions,
natural or legal persons, strategies, techniques, or measures, that is, not related to
any kind of PATH or movement. Instead, events, processes, and actions provided
excellent candidates for image-schematic structures within a PATH family.

Image-Schematic Structure	Eng	Swe	Ger	Ita	Total
LINK	2	4	2	2	10
SOURCE_PATH_GOAL (SPG)	3	7	6	7	23
SOURCE_PATH	7	6	7	11	31
PATH_GOAL	6	9	10	7	32
SOURCE_PATH_VIA_GOAL (SPVG)	3	2	3	1	9
PATH_VIA_GOAL *	2	1		2	5
SOURCE_PATH_VIA *	1				1
CAUSED_MOVEMENT	1				1
CLOSED_PATH_MOVEMENT	2		1	1	4
MOVEMENT_IN_LOOPS	1	1	1	1	4
PATH_SWITCHING *	1		1	1	3
JUMPING *	1	1			2
BLOCKAGE_AVOIDANCE *	1		1	1	3
PATH_SPLITTING *	4	3	4	3	14
SPG and SPG	1	1	1	1	4
SPVG and SPVG	1	1	1	1	4
SPG OR PATH_SPLITTING		1			1
SPG OR PATH			1		1
SPG OR LINK	1	1	1	1	4
Total	57	54	58	54	224

Table 8.2: Metrics for identified image-schematic structures across languages. * indicate novel finds that were not previously introduced in Chapter 3. 'and' is the
presence of more than one image schema and 'or' determines a distinct uncertainty.

8.3.1 Statistical Results of Patterns

With just above 30 percent the overall precision of the extraction and analysis
method is rather low. This means that only 1/3 of the overall extracted entries actually contained image-schematic structures from the PATH schema. Judging from
the number of identified image schemas for each pattern, nominal structures and
prepositions returned most candidate entries. A total of 67 percent of the 'CYCLE'
synonym set and 59 percent of the 'process' nouns returned image-schematic structures, followed by 'from-to' with 40 percent of the 48 extracted entries. The 37 extracted entries based on prepositions (across, through, around, etc.) and the 7 ones
based on motion verbs resulted in image schema candidates in 30 percent of their

cases. The 'end' pattern with 8 entries contained one schema, 'start' with 3 potential schemas provided no schemas at all. While the movement and development pattern extracted almost 20 entries each, only 19 percent in the former and 18 percent in the latter case contained PATH-related structures.

8.3.2 Image Schema Candidates

All resulting image-schematic structures are ordered by approximate complexity in Table 8.2. Financial entries in the data set most frequently (30 percent of all cases) feature a regular SOURCE_PATH_GOAL schema followed by the similar, yet simpler, pattern PATH_GOAL. On occasion, specific textual references concurrently defined two image-schematic structures that could equally be designated by the same given term. For such cases representation with the logical operator 'OR' was opted for. For instance, an 'interlinking mechanism' (IATE:892281) can designate a cross-border payment procedure 'OR' a technical infrastructure, which was represented as SOURCE_PATH_GOAL 'OR' LINK.

8.3.3 Breaking Down the CLOSED_PATH_MOVEMENT Schema

A graphical representation technique was employed to identify the movements of objects between entities along PATHs for each definition in each language. It turned out that some of the identified image-schematic structures were not present in the predefined structures in Figure 3.3. From all languages, four different scenarios depicted in Figure 8.2 could be identified by means of the graphical representation technique. Additionally, image-schematic structures of a 'double-way' SOURCE_PATH_GOAL movement could be observed in financial definitions. These movements were dependent on two variables: the number of PATHs and the number of OBJECTs that are moved along them. The four resulting image-schematic structures that are differentiated based on those two variables are depicted in Figure 8.1.

In a symmetric SOURCE_PATH_GOAL, one OBJECT moves or is being moved along one path until it returns to its starting point, potentially also passing a distinguished point. For instance, taking out and repaying a loan is the transfer of money from the creditor to the debtor where the same object (money) is returned on the same PATH (e.g. bank transfer) to the original source, that is, the creditor. In cases such as this, the SOURCE and the GOAL coincide, and the concept matches the CLOSED_PATH_MOVEMENT introduced in Chapter 3.

It is also possible, however, that the PATH of returning differs from the initial one, in which case the image-schematic structure specifies two PATHs. If the same OBJECT moves from the SOURCE and back again on a different PATH, this is introduced as a bidirectional SOURCE_PATH_GOAL. In the event of SOURCE and GOAL being identical, the PATH that returns to the SOURCE can either be equivalent to the initial

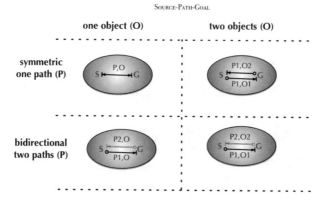

Fig. 8.1: The Returning Object(s) Problem.

PATH (symmetric) or differ from the original PATH (bidirectional). The latter would be considered a bidirectional CLOSED_PATH_MOVEMENT. For instance, 'painting the tape' (IATE: 927775) is an example of several transactions (PATHs) being used in a CLOSED_PATH_MOVEMENT to create the impression of price movement of a financial instrument.

A second dimension that was identified is whether the returning/exchanging OBJECT is identical to the first one. In finance, often the returning object is different from the one initially moved along the PATH, basically capturing any kind of exchange or purchase. The SOURCE for one object becomes the GOAL for the second object and vice versa. The two different OBJECTs moving along the same path are defined as poly-object symmetric SOURCE_PATH_GOAL. If two OBJECTs move along two different PATHs, this is called a poly-object bidirectional SOURCE_PATH_GOAL. A real-life example is the exchange of shares (the first OBJECT) from the stock market (the first PATH) and money (the second OBJECT) from a bank transaction (the returning PATH) between a client and a broker.

8.3.4 Additionally Identified PATH Members

Additionally, four PATH-related structures that did not appear in Figure 3.3 and Chapter 3, could be identified. These four structures are JUMPING, PATH_SWITCHING, PATH_SPLITTING and BLOCKAGE_AVOIDANCE[4]. As they did not already appear in Chapter 3, it can be argued that the PATH family can be extended by these additions. In Figure 8.2 they are depicted. Note that the illustration

---

[4] Note that these members are written in the image schematic caps despite them previously not being introduced as image schemas. This is an active choice as they are here introduced as image schema candidates in the PATH family, not as spatial or conceptual primitives.

of BLOCKAGE only serves the sole purpose to clarify the movement involved in BLOCKAGE_AVOIDANCE.

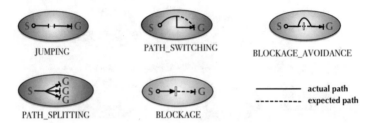

JUMPING   PATH_SWITCHING   BLOCKAGE_AVOIDANCE

PATH_SPLITTING   BLOCKAGE

——————— actual path
- - - - - - - - - expected path

Fig. 8.2: Four kinds of complex PATH structures extracted from the financial domain.

JUMPING:

First, JUMPING[5] represents the temporary discontinuity of a given PATH. For instance, 'bond washing' (IATE:3544441) is a method of obtaining tax-free capital profits by selling the bond immediately before the coupon pays and buying it back right thereafter to avoid tax payments. 'Bond washing' is a classic metaphor based on the notion of 'cleaning,' which indeed captures important aspects of the term. However, while explaining the underlying process behind the term also the PATH-following family can be used. Considering ownership as the PATH from the initial acquisition of the bond (SOURCE) to the gains it generates (GOAL), 'bond washing' leads to this interruption of the PATH and can be seen as an example of JUMPING. The term is taken from the equivalent physical movement that makes the object temporarily lose touch with the path and inevitably leads back to the same path subsequent to the discontinuation, i.e., the jump. While it may be argued that JUMPING is simply a sequential combination of two disjoint SOURCE_PATH_GOALs, JUMPING takes on its own logic as both paths are involved in one particular movement as demonstrated in the conceptualisation example above. Therefore, it can be argued that JUMPING can be justified as a complex image-schematic structure in its own right much like BOUNCING was argued for in Chapter 5.

PATH_SPLITTING:

Second, in the case of PATH_SPLITTING, one object is distributed along a path to several GOALs. It could be argued that this represents merely a type of cardinality. However, since the PATH can be asymmetrical or bidirectional, it can be considered

---

[5] Jumping is not to be confused with the motion verb *to jump*. It refers to a jump in time or space, much like 'teleportation' rather than a temporary elevation.

an image-schematic structure in its own right. For instance, in all kinds of 'tender procedures' (e.g. IATE:887199) the identical piece of information (a call) is sent to several parties, who return their individual pieces of information (the bids). Hence, this is an example of bidirectional PATH_SPLITTING. One example to account for this image-schematic structure in sensory-motor experiences would be the distribution of auditory information to several recipients with varying replies.

PATH_SWITCHING:

Third, in PATH_SWITCHING the expected PATH is fully discontinued and replaced by a new PATH. For instance, the definition of 'refinancing' (IATE:786103) specifies the extending of a new loan and a mutual agreement to discontinue the previous loan. Thus, the original loan PATH is switched to a new loan PATH with altered conditions. It is important to note that the definition clearly specifies the replacement of a debt obligation with a new one and not merely altering the conditions of an existing loan. This explicit switching of the agreed path is an excellent example of PATH_SWITCHING.

BLOCKAGE_AVOIDANCE:

Finally, the active avoidance of a BLOCKAGE can be considered an image-schematic construction that combines a number of pre-existing structures and schemas. The course of the PATH is (intentionally) altered to prevent the discontinuation of the movement of the object due to a BLOCKAGE. A 'Paulian action' (IATE:822870) allows a creditor to take action to avoid potential fraudulent activities of an insolvent debtor, granting the former rights to have a debtor's transaction to that end reversed. Thus, the term as such represents an example of BLOCKAGE_AVOIDANCE.

8.3.5 Image Schemas Across Languages

A slight asymmetry in the distribution of image-schematic structures across languages could be observed. In English and German definitions more structures could be identified than in Swedish and Italian, as shown in Table 8.2. However, those statistical results fail to provide any insights into the differences across languages. In a surprisingly high 45 percent of all 69 entries, the identified schemas were not identical across the languages. However, it has to be taken into consideration that in 27 percent of all cases the differences arise from either an addition or omission of a SOURCE, GOAL, or via a location (VIA), while the general structure is that of a SOURCE_PATH_GOAL. Differences that arise from other sources can be pinned down to 10 percent of all entries. A slight preference for GOAL usage in Swedish and German could be observed as opposed to a heightened use of SOURCE in Italian in the reduced SOURCE_PATH_GOALS.

The method deliberately relied on explicitly described content only. This means that omissions that arise from linguistic or grammatical differences across languages or stylistic choices affected the extraction result. For instance, differences can arise from a heightened use of passive constructions in one language, e.g. German, and an increased utilisation of active SOURCEs and GOALs due to grammatical choices in another. One of the reasons for this choice was the intention to analyse linguistic consistency in relation to schematic persistence across languages.

In a final cross-lingual analysis, it was found that most cross-lingual differences in the identification of schematic structures arise from unnecessarily complicated descriptions, or even inconsistencies, in one language. Semantically identical entries resulted in diverging image schemas for two major reasons: a) the difference in lexical or grammatical choices (e.g. passive vs. active voice), and b) the omission of salient features. While the first difference postulates no difficulty for human users, the second severely distorts the term's understanding for users of that language. For automated methods, both differences lead to a certain degree of difficulty. The method could uncover inconsistencies across languages for both cases, which was considered an added benefit of the linguistic mapping of image schemas.

This approach equally uncovered conceptual inconsistencies across and within languages. For instance, 'equity capital' and 'equity financing' (IATE: 1119090) are modelled as synonymous where in fact the former refers to equity of the company while financing refers to the process of generating such capital. Thus, they should clearly be separated into two entries, a claim that is supported by the fact that the entry's definition consists of two sentences that define both concepts. In view of the potential automation of the approach, it was found that a linguistic analysis of the specification's surface structure would definitely lead to misleading results. For instance, 'lifecycling' (IATE: 3516328) describes a shift of a person's investment approach at a specific moment in life rather than a CYCLE as the term suggests. Furthermore, the manual approach and cross-linguistic analysis revealed (unintentionally) repeated definitions and entries, e.g. 'fine-tuning operation' (IATE: 111402 & 907147).

8.4 Discussion

One of the most important parts of the used method was the extraction of terms and definitions. This was achieved by applying a limited number of lexico-syntactic patterns to the English definitions of terms. The initial patterns resulted in more than 3000 extracted entries that at first analysis contained fewer image-schematic structures than had been expected and desired. A repeated tweaking of the patterns reduced this number to 190 pattern-extracted entries with a precision of only one third. This was partly due to the entries mostly referring to actual objects, such as financial instruments or institutions, rather than processes or events, which was one criterion for the entries to be regarded as a candidate for image schemas. For further experiments, precision of the applied patterns needs to be improved.

A second problem that was disregarded here is the recall of the applied extraction method, that is, the number of potentially missed schemas. It is unlikely that a rich database like the one used for this study should result in so few image-schematic structures. It would be advisable for future replications of the study to make sure that the extraction patterns have a better coverage and higher precision. In fact, the exact choice of patterns and linguistic expressions used for the extraction have a strong influence on the nature of schemas that might be obtained (Lakusta and Landau, 2005). Thus, the extraction method is biased by the choice of vocabulary and the linguistic structures opted for. Naturally, the method also has a strong English bias, since this initial experiment was limited to the extraction of the English definitions and benefited from the multilingual alignment of entries in the database. These biases could definitely be reduced by the cross-linguistic application of abstract lexico-syntactic patterns or even an altogether different approach to information extraction, such as machine learning.

Another issue is the method applied for the analysis. In this study, it was performed by one or two individual(s) fluent in the language. Naturally, this did not represent a particularly large sample and consequently, both potential errors and biases are problems. Although the basic criteria for definitions to qualify as image-schematic structures, the final decision might be subjectively biased due to the low number of judges. Due to that limited number of experts, it was also not possible to provide an inter-rater agreement. However, an evaluation of the quality of the schema identification process was conducted by means of the final cross-lingual comparison, which made for the re-evaluation of each individual schema candidate in each language. One way to improve on these issues is to have a larger sample of analysts that perform the image-schematic mapping. This should primarily be a method to obtain a gold standard as at the same time a stronger level of automation for the actual method is needed.

A clear preference for the SOURCE_PATH_GOAL together with SOURCE_PATH and PATH_GOAL schemas could be observed in all languages. Mandler and Cánovas (2014) claims that PATH_GOAL is more important and more prevalent in the (pre-linguistic) usage of schemas by adults and children, an argument supported by the findings of Lakusta and Landau (2005). They presumed that children do not require SOURCEs to conceptualise a PATH_GOAL, which is why it is often omitted in cross-lingual analyses of image schemas. This experiment could not provide strong evidence for or against this claim as both SOURCE_PATH and PATH_GOAL were the most frequently identified image schemas.

The definition adopted here is that image schemas are not just Gestalts but conceptual structures (Mandler and Cánovas, 2014). The omission and/or addition of a SOURCE or GOAL changes the perspective of the schema (Lakusta and Landau, 2005). It is important to differentiate whether the description explicitly states that an agent transfers an OBJECT or that an OBJECT is being transferred to a beneficiary (Lakusta and Landau, 2005). Along the same line of argumentation, it is here claimed that the directionality of the path as well as the number of paths and objects

involved in a SOURCE_PATH_GOAL schema influence the perspective of the conceptualisation. These two influential variables on the basic underlying schema as well
as the four new image-schematic structures that were identified can be considered
specifications of the overall MOVEMENT_ALONG_PATH schema.

Some of the terms were defined as combinations of image schemas. While only
PATH-following was looked at, it could be noticed that many concepts would have
been better described as combinations of a member of the PATH-following family and additional image schemas or image-schematic structures such as SCALING
or CONTAINMENT, so-called image-schematic integrations (Mandler and Cánovas,
2014). Such integrations as well as conceptual blends (Kuhn, 2007) (see Chapter 6)
repeatedly surfaced in the analysis as did different forces that might be exerted in
a schema. This supports the ideas in Chapter 5 which image schemas are combined
to form conceptualisations and in Chapter 7 in which showed that humans often
annotate objects with more than one image-schematic conceptualisation.

The analysis revealed differences across the four languages which could partially
be explained by grammatical decisions of the terminologists/experts, partially also
by inconsistencies across languages. While the sample in this experiment is too
small for any generalised conclusions, the results hint at a high consistency of image
schemas occurring across languages. The exact nature of movement along a path can
definitely be analysed in more detail by, for instance, investigating whether financial
descriptions consider the manner of movement, e.g. as done by Papafragou et al.
(2006) for a more general corpus.

Prepositions and verbs returned the most promising results in most bottom-up
approaches (e.g. Bennett and Cialone (2014); Johanson and Papafragou (2014);
Lakusta and Landau (2005)), which could not be confirmed in this experiment. Synonym sets of nouns returned the most image-schematic candidates here. However,
this might be attributed to the selection of prepositions and verbs rather than the
domain and not represent a contradiction of previous findings.

8.5 Chapter Conclusion

In this chapter, an experiment on automatic image schema extraction was presented.
It relied on syntactic pattern matching following the work by Bennett and Cialone
(2014) where static representations for the CONTAINMENT schema were identified
in natural language. In this experiment, the purpose instead focused on empirically
evaluating the PATH-following family that was introduced in Chapter 3 as well as
determining if it is possible to extend it by identifying novel members of this family.

The presented method illustrates how some essential aspects of complicated
terms and concepts can be described by using image schemas as a means for simplification. The analysis contributed two dimensions and four specifications to the
most central SOURCE_PATH_GOAL image-schematic structure. While in this study
PATH-following was the only image schema considered, in future work more image schemas could be integrated to better explain the concepts. In terms of data

sets considered, a comparison of image-schematic structures extracted from terminologies with texts provided by financial experts could provide further insights. In addition, a comparison of the results to other domains of discourse could further strengthen the claim of a domain- and language-independent existence of image-schematic structures. This extension of the approach could also be applied to the mode of communication since gestures are frequently used to underpin linguistic descriptions of movement (e.g. Mittelberg (2019)).

This approach not only contributes to image schema research by showing that the developmentally most relevant building blocks of our cognitive inventory are carried into abstract adult communication but also strengthens the idea that image schemas are linguistically and cognitively universal since they exist across languages. The practical use of this approach not only lies in the relation of image schemas and natural language but since the basis is provided by a formalised theory of PATH-following it also explores the relation between lexical and model-theoretical semantics as it bridges computational linguistics research and ontology construction. In this sense, it is believed that this image-schematic method provides an interesting approach to learning spatial ontologies from multilingual text to be explored further in future experiments. Since manual ontology engineering is cumbersome and error prone, automated approaches are required.

It can be argued that the combination of linguistic and formal analysis of image-schematic structures across languages can allow for their more specialised use in automated approaches and computational systems. Thus, future work will focus on the automation of image-schematic extractions from multilingual textual evidence based on formalised theories. This also includes exploring interconnections of image schemas in the form of integrations as well as conceptual blending.[6]

References

B. Bennett and C. Cialone. Corpus Guided Sense Cluster Analysis: a methodology for ontology development (with examples from the spatial domain). In P. Garbacz and O. Kutz, editors, *8th International Conference on Formal Ontology in Information Systems (FOIS)*, volume 267 of *Frontiers in Artificial Intelligence and Applications*, pages 213–226. IOS Press, 2014.

D. Gromann and M. M. Hedblom. Breaking Down Finance: A method for concept simplification by identifying movement structures from the image schema Path-following. In *Proceedings of the 2nd Joint Ontology Workshops (JOWO)*, volume 1660, Annecy, France, 2016. CEUR-WS online proceedings.

D. Gromann and M. M. Hedblom. Kinesthetic mind reader: A method to identify image schemas in natural language. In *Advances in Cognitive Systems*, volume 5, pages 1–14, 2017a.

---

[6] This work has been extended and further developed in (Gromann and Hedblom, 2017a,b).

D. Gromann and M. M. Hedblom. Body-Mind-Language: Multilingual Knowledge Extraction Based on Embodied Cognition. In *Proceedings of the 5nd International Workshop on Artificial Intelligence and Cognition (AIC-2017)*, Larnaca, Cyprus, November 2017b.

F. Guerin. Learning like a baby: A survey of AI approaches. *The Knowledge Engineering Review*, 00(0):1–22, 2008.

B. Hampe and J. E. Grady. *From perception to meaning: Image schemas in cognitive linguistics*, volume 29 of *Cognitive Linguistics Research*. Walter de Gruyter, Berlin, 2005.

M. Johanson and A. Papafragou. What does children's spatial language reveal about spatial concepts? Evidence from the use of containment expressions. *Cognitive Science*, 38(5):881–910, 2014.

T. Kollar, S. Tellex, D. Roy, and N. Roy. Grounding verbs of motion in natural language commands to robots. In *Experimental Robotics*, pages 31–47. Springer, 2014.

J. Krishnamurthy and T. Kollar. Jointly learning to parse and perceive: Connecting natural language to the physical world. *Transactions of the Association for Computational Linguistics*, 1:193–206, 2013.

W. Kuhn. An Image-Schematic Account of Spatial Categories. In S. Winter, M. Duckham, L. Kulik, and B. Kuipers, editors, *Spatial Information Theory*, volume 4736 of *Lecture Notes in Computer Science*, pages 152–168. Springer, 2007.

G. Lakoff and M. Johnson. *Metaphors We Live By*. University of Chicago Press, 1980.

L. Lakusta and B. Landau. Starting at the end: The importance of goals in spatial language. *Cognition*, 96(1):1–33, 2005.

J. M. Mandler and C. P. Cánovas. On defining image schemas. *Language and Cognition*, 6(4):510–532, May 2014.

D. K. Misra, J. Sung, K. Lee, and A. Saxena. Tell me Dave: Context-sensitive grounding of natural language to manipulation instructions. *The International Journal of Robotics Research*, 35(1-3):281–300, 2016.

I. Mittelberg. Enacted schematicity: Image schemas and force dynamics operating in gestural (inter-) action. In *Proceedings of TriCoLore*, volume 2347 of *CEUR-WS*, Bolzano, Italy, 2019.

A. Papafragou, C. Massey, and L. Gleitman. When English proposes what Greek presupposes: The cross-linguistic encoding of motion events. *Cognition*, 98(3): B75–B87, 2006.

S. A. Tellex, T. F. Kollar, S. R. Dickerson, M. R. Walter, A. Banerjee, S. Teller, and N. Roy. Understanding natural language commands for robotic navigation and mobile manipulation. In *Proceedings of the Twenty-Fifth AAAI Conference on Artificial Intelligence*, pages 1507–1514, San Francisco, California, 2011.

Appendix A
Previously Published Material

Some of the research presented in this volume quotes verbatim (in parts or in full) hypotheses, research and results from the publications below.

References

T. R. Besold, M. M. Hedblom, and O. Kutz. A narrative in three acts: Using combinations of image schemas to model events. *Biologically Inspired Cognitive Architectures*, 19:10–20, 2017.

D. Gromann and M. M. Hedblom. Breaking Down Finance: A method for concept simplification by identifying movement structures from the image schema Path-following. In *Proceedings of the 2nd Joint Ontology Workshops (JOWO)*, volume 1660, Annecy, France, 2016. CEUR-WS online proceedings.

M. M. Hedblom. Beneath the Paint: A Visual Journey through Conceptual Metaphor Violation. In *Proceedings of the 3rd Joint Ontology Workshops (JOWO)*, CEUR-WS, Bolzano, Italy, 2017.

M. M. Hedblom. *Image Schemas and Concept Invention: Cognitive, Logical, and Linguistic Investigations*. PhD thesis, Otto-von-Guericke University of Madgeburg, 2018.

M. M. Hedblom and O. Kutz. Shape up, Baby!: Perception, Image Schemas, and Shapes in Concept Formation. In O. Kutz, S. Borgo, and M. Bhatt, editors, *Proceedings of the 2nd Joint Ontology Workshops (JOWO)*, volume 1616 of *CEUR-WS*, pages 59–65, Larnaca, Cyprus, 2016.

M. M. Hedblom, O. Kutz, and F. Neuhaus. On the cognitive and logical role of image schemas in computational conceptual blending. In *Proceedings of the 2nd International Workshop on Artificial Intelligence and Cognition (AIC-2014), Torino, Italy, November 26th–27th*, volume 1315 of *CEUR-WS*, 2014.

M. M. Hedblom, O. Kutz, and F. Neuhaus. Image Schemas as Families of Theories. In T. R. Besold, K.-U. Kühnberger, M. Schorlemmer, and A. Smaill, editors, *Proceedings of the Workshop "Computational Creativity, Concept Invention, and*

© Springer Nature Switzerland AG 2020

M. M. Hedblom, *Image Schemas and Concept Invention*, Cognitive Technologies, https://doi.org/10.1007/978-3-030-47329-7

General Intelligence (C3GI), volume 2 of *Publications of the Institute of Cognitive Science*, pages 19–33. Institute of Cognitive Science, 2015.

M. M. Hedblom, O. Kutz, T. Mossakowski, and F. Neuhaus. Between contact and support: Introducing a logic for image schemas and directed movement. In F. Esposito, R. Basili, S. Ferilli, and F. A. Lisi, editors, *AI*IA 2017: Advances in Artificial Intelligence*, pages 256–268, 2017.

M. M. Hedblom, D. Gromann, and O. Kutz. In, Out and Through: Formalising some dynamic aspects of the image schema Containment. In *SAC '18: Proceedings of the 33rd Annual ACM Symposium on Applied Computing*, pages 918–925, Pau, France, 2018.

M. M. Hedblom, O. Kutz, R. Peñaloza, and G. Guizzardi. What's Cracking: How image schema combinations can model conceptualisations of events. In *Proceedings of TriCoLore*, volume 2347 of *CEUR-WS*, Bolzano, Italy, 2019a.

M. M. Hedblom, O. Kutz, R. Peñaloza, and G. Guizzardi. Image Schema Combinations and Complex Events. *KI - Künstliche Intelligenz*, 33:279–291, 2019b.

M. M. Hedblom, O. Kutz, and F. Neuhaus. Choosing the Right Path: Image Schema Theory as a Foundation for Concept Invention. *Journal of Artificial General Intelligence*, 6(1):22–54, 2015.

M. M. Hedblom, O. Kutz, and F. Neuhaus. Image schemas in computational conceptual blending. *Cognitive Systems Research*, 39:42–57, 2016.

O. Kutz, F. Neuhaus, M. M. Hedblom, T. Mossakowski, and M. Codescu. Ontology Patterns with DOWL: The Case of Blending. In M. Lenzerini and R. Peñaloza, editors, *Proceedings of the 29th International Workshop on Description Logics, (DL2016)*, Cape Town, South Africa, 2016.

O. Kutz, N. Troquard, S. Borgo, M. M. Hedblom, and D. Porello. The Mouse and the Ball: Towards a cognitively-based and ontologically-grounded logic of agency. In *Proceedings of COCO at SAC 2017*, Pau, France, 2017.

O. K. Maria M. Hedblom, Rafael Peñaloza and G. Guizzardi. Under the Super-Suit: What Superheroes Can Reveal About Inherited properties in Conceptual Blending. In *Proceedings of ICCC*, Salamanca, Spain, 2018.

Printed in the United States
by Baker & Taylor Publisher Services